PRISON MINISTRY

PRISON MINISTRY

Understanding Prison Culture
Inside and Out

LENNIE SPITALE

BROADMAN &HOLMAN PUBLISHERS   Nashville, Tennessee

0–8054–2483–0

Published by Broadman & Holman Publishers, Nashville,
Tennessee

Category: EVANGELISM/PRISON MINISTRY

Unless otherwise noted, Scripture quotations are from the
Holy Bible, New International Version, copyright © 1973, 1978,
1984 by International Bible Society.

5 6 7 8 9 10 07 06 05

Contents

Preface

IMAGINE A LAND where children are forbidden, where playgrounds are never built, and where the laughter of little voices is never carried upon the air. Picture, if you will, a horizon of blue sky and cold, gray cement in all directions, punctuated only by an occasional treetop that can never be touched or climbed. Conceive, if you can, a country whose citizens never bear children, yet the census continues to record wild population growth. Consider a society that has banished the use of such diverse items as fresh fruit, chewing gum, and ballpoint pens with clear casings.

No taxicabs will ever be hailed from these streets; vehicles are not permitted. Here there are no bus stops, train stations, or parking garages. There are no automobiles, airplanes, or bicycles. All traffic is pedestrian, but running is prohibited by law. The city has one road leading in; there are none leading out. There are no shopping malls, grocery stores, or fast-food restaurants. Banks are unheard of, as are credit unions, employment agencies, or ATMs. Cash is extinct; plastic is forbidden. All the apparel worn by the inhabitants of this alien landscape is identical. Colors are predetermined by the system; style is irrelevant. All mail, in or out, is subject to search, seizure, and censure. Big Brother is a reality; your every step and position, every hour of the day, is known and monitored. And though the dark Orwellian night has fallen; the lights are on. Always. Somewhere.

Welcome to the Fourth Dimension, a parallel universe vaguely mirroring your own. Step out of your own universe for a moment if you will; your tour guide awaits you. The doors are open, but they will soon shut with a singular clang as you leave your own time zone. The culture here is as different as that of any foreign country, but most of the inhabitants speak your language.

Welcome to the world of the incarcerated; their hospitality will surprise you.

The goal of this book is to present the reader with an "inside-out" view of prison life. That is, to view the prison culture more from the eyes of the inmate than from those of the external observer. It is an attempt to gain the perspective of the one *within* the box rather than from those without who, while perhaps often exposed to the culture, do not *feel* it in the same way as those who cannot go home at night.

The ultimate aim of this book is to help the reader understand the culture (from within the culture) so that those who hope to minister within its confines may be better equipped to operate, not only with compassion, but also with wisdom.

This is not a book of statistics, which, by their very nature, soon become obsolete. Nor is it entirely a reference work. It is a traveler's guide to a foreign country. It is meant to be of help to anyone who is interested in knowing more about what this unique territory is like and, more specifically, what the inhabitants are like. Anyone having an interest in understanding this culture would, in my humble opinion, gain some benefit from reading it. It is especially written, however, for those dear souls who are either traveling there already as volunteers or for those who are seriously considering doing so.

I believe that every church library should have this book available for the benefit of those who may consider their local prison or jail as a potential mission field. Just as we train our foreign missionaries in the culture and language of the countries to which they are being sent, why shouldn't we make the same preliminary training available to those who hope to penetrate *this* culture? My goal is that we might travel to this place "innocent as doves and wise as serpents," finding the best way to let a people who sit in darkness discover a great light—the love of God and the forgiveness of sins found only in Jesus Christ.

By now, you are probably wondering what gives *me* the right to speak from the inmate's point of view. As a young man, I was locked up on several occasions and eventually served a prison sentence for an armed robbery that was later reduced to assault and robbery. I had a tremendous problem with anger and restlessness, coupled with an equally hostile attitude toward any form of authority. This included parents, schoolteachers, employers, military officials, police, and authority figures of any kind. The total time of my incarcerations was only three and one-half years. I was a short-timer by many people's standards, but as anyone who has ever done time will tell you, even *one* day is too long.

On becoming a Christian in 1975, I experienced the overhaul of my life that only Jesus Christ can bring. He immediately cured the restlessness by bringing me into peace with him. Over a fairly short period of time, he also brought my anger under the control of the Holy Spirit. In February 1977, I began to lead a Bible study in a local jail and less than two years later was called into full-time prison ministry. I have never looked back; I know that God raised me up for this very work.

Although a large portion of my exposure to Christian prison ministry has been back on the tiers with the men in their own living areas and at the doors of their cells, that alone would not have given me the *feeling*. Doing time is a *feeling*. It feels like something, just as living in any other reality feels like something. Once or twice a year I still experience dreams in the night of going back to prison—dreams so vivid that I awaken with the *feeling* of returning to prison. I experience afresh the turmoil of emotions connected with the event: the hopelessness, the fear, the separation from my loved ones, and the awful, indomitable enemy of time that stretches out before me like a thick, steel chain that can never be broken.

I have become convinced that God himself allows these dreams so I might not forget the feeling of incarceration. He has called me to this work. I believe that the dreams, with their attending emotions, are a part of his design to keep me in touch with the unspoken anguish of a jailed consciousness. They bring back the reality of remembering how it felt to be leaving my loved ones until every long day that the calendar demanded had been paid in full. Even as I write this, I can still remember that awful feeling of helplessness and hopelessness.

Inmates are not different from anyone else; they simply live in a different culture. We have all sinned, and no person is the sum total of the sins he or she has committed. Unfortunately, that is precisely what many people on the outside have done with those in prison. Since they know nothing else about them, they have reduced the lives of inmates to the sum of a few paragraphs in the papers or a few sound bites on the evening news. On occasion I have met and ministered to the notorious faces behind the national headlines. They are little people who were charged with big crimes and are now inextricably caught up and forever associated with those crimes. And so it is with the thousands who seldom make much more than a few paragraphs in the local papers. But none of us is the sum total of the sins we have committed; there is more to us than that.

I am not saying that there should not be punishment for a crime or even that the natural consequences of such an action should not fall upon those who commit them. But I trust that I am speaking to those people who truly desire to understand the people who live behind those walls—for the purpose of ministering to them. Such people should understand that the only real difference between them and the people in prison is about eight feet of bricks and cement. Little else.

A closer examination of any field of study always reveals a multiplicity of layers that one formerly never knew existed. So it is with any attempt to understand the onion of prison culture.

There has long been a need, I believe, for a basic handbook that describes what the prison culture is like, a sort of reference guide for those dear-hearted Christians who desire to share the love of Christ behind those walls.

Prison *is* another culture. It has its own code of ethics, its own mores and social values. Prisoners have their own language. Words like "PC," "Pop," "Max," "kid," "lugged," and a host of other terms are all a part of everyday life behind the walls. New ones seem to be added to the list every week; it is impossible to keep up with all of them. Volunteers need to learn the basic, time-tested terms, however, or they will remain in the dark.

But prison is more than just a whole new vocabulary; it is an experience filled with different codes of behavior and unwritten laws that define what is acceptable and what is not. It is a mindset, a backdrop that swallows up the inhabitants by degrees and conforms them to the twists and weaves of its cold, gray fabric. The change is subtle, prolonged for some, stark and frightening for others. To remain as before is not an option.

This is not to say that individuality and uniqueness are obliterated—far from it. But it *is* to say that a life lived behind the walls *forces* adaptation to a world previously unknown. Each mind, alone in its confrontation with this culture, must find its own way to be safe—must find its own way to survive. Prison life is a prevailing and paradoxical encounter with loneliness—while living in the midst of a shoe box crammed with other people.

And while prison is a place of overt rules and regulations from the Department of Correction's point of view, a violation of the inmate's *un*written codes (whether consciously committed or not) can result in heavy consequences for the person who attempts to live out his or her life within this new and frightening venue.

Although volunteers are generally given a lot of slack by the residents in terms of forgiving the accidental violation of these codes, volunteers have now become a part of the culture themselves. A better understanding of the world they are entering will be of benefit to them. However, the opposite is also true: *not* to understand the culture can result in an immediate need for damage control. Sometimes the unintended slip can affect the ministry for many months to come, if not sabotage it altogether.

Before I go any further, let me say that when I speak of prison being another culture, I am not saying that the gospel cannot penetrate it (even though a person may be unfamiliar with the environment itself). The power of the Holy Spirit displayed in the life of a Christian bringing the truth of the gospel in the genuine love of Christ can penetrate even the darkest and hardest places. What I *am* saying is that a better understanding of the people and the places where such people live can make Christians who attempt to enter that sphere better equipped to allow the Holy Spirit to use them in that context.

The apostle Paul became "all things to all men" in order that he might win some. When he was in Athens (see Acts 17), he drew from his observations of the Athenian culture to find a point of mutual contact with which he could relate the gospel to the Athenians from their own worldview. Jesus himself was constantly drawing illustrations and parables from the culture around him.

In our desire to communicate with others, we often unconsciously do the same thing. For example, my wife says that she can always tell when the person with whom I'm speaking on the phone has English as a second language. My own vocabulary shifts gears to a level that I instinctively feel is on the other person's basic comprehension level, even though I am seldom conscious of doing this.

But whether on the phone or in person, the preaching of Christ—in a manner as relevant as we can make it to the hearer—is the goal. Hudson Taylor, early missionary to China, raised eyebrows at his mission's organization back home when he began to dress like the Chinese and even sport a *pigtail*. Although the home mission frowned on the practice, his popularity with the Chinese began to soar. Why did he do this? Because his goal was not to preach to the missionary organization but to win the Chinese people for Christ.

I am not advocating that volunteers go into prisons and act like the prisoners or even try to talk like the prisoners; this isn't necessary. What we must do is to be ourselves, speak the truth in compassion, and love them with the love of Christ. I *am* advocating that volunteers should attempt to understand better the culture they have entered so they can be better equipped to relate the gospel *within* that culture. I would also say that the more ignorant a volunteer is of the culture, the higher the risk that a serious social mistake can be made. This can occur not only with the inmates but with the officers as well; and *some* social mistakes are irreparable.

Having viewed both sides of the prison coin, I now praise God for this dual experience. He has enabled me to serve him in the California prison systems, the Florida prison system, and, since

1982, the prisons and jails of the six New England states. I mention this only to suggest that a person who has experienced nearly twenty-five years of direct, full-time prison ministry in all kinds of prison settings—state and federal, male and female, juvenile and adult—tends to learn *something*. The thoughts expressed in this book are a summary of the personal conclusions drawn from my years of experience. You may not agree with all I say, but it is my hope that it will, at least, be useful to you.

My further hope is that as we minister to those who are serving time behind bars, we will become aware that these are real people with real dreams, that they have real people they long to be with and a string of real days that separates them from their loved ones. My reason for writing is that you may be better equipped to move compassionately, yet wisely, among them as you bring the hope of a Savior to them. Only Jesus can provide the water they thirst for, even if they don't know what that water is.

Our Lord Jesus offered this water to the woman at the well in a compassionate but discerning way (see John 4:10). He understood her cultural setting. He approached her from within her Samaritan worldview, not His Judean setting. And although she had a difficult time understanding what he was offering her (challenging a cultural perspective always is), she knew she was thirsty. I actually met this woman once. Her name is Patti. I will tell you her story later.

I am occasionally asked by prospective volunteers how I think they will relate to those behind prison walls. Their fear is that they will not be able to relate to inmates. They conclude that my own prison experience is the basis for my comfortable relationship with the inmates, but while it is a great asset to me, it is not the principle reason. I have met many volunteers and chaplains over the years who have had little in common (either in demeanor or life experiences) with the prisoners and their world but have nevertheless proven themselves to be effective instruments for the gospel in that environment. I have come to the conclusion that there are only four requirements for effective prison ministry:

1. Be yourself.
2. Speak the truth with compassion.
3. Love inmates and correctional officers with the love of Christ.
4. Live under the influence of the Holy Spirit and the Word of God.

If you are careful to remember these things, you will not fail.

Acknowledgments

FIRST OF ALL, I give praise and thanksgiving to the Lord Jesus
Christ for his grace and mercy in my life, without which this story
would never have been.

I also want to thank the following people for the parts they
each played in the process.

To Les Stobbe, for the encouragement that his experience and
wisdom brought to me.

To Robin Erickson and Isabelle Breeding for their editorial
review of the first few chapters.

To Leonard G. Goss, Kim Overcash, and the staff of
Broadman & Holman, whose personal kindness and professionalism ministered to me.

To Don Moberger, whose faith in the project never wavered.

But I would especially like to thank my wife Wendy, who
reviewed the entire manuscript and whose love has been a never-
failing source of encouragement to me.

Part I
Feelings

1

The Big Hurt

AN EERIE STILLNESS pervaded the old cell block of New Hampshire State Prison the evening my friend Paul[1] and I were led to our cells on that first night of our sentence. We had just arrived from the county jail[2] where we had spent the last two months awaiting trial. But this was it. "The Big House." The end of the line. The catwalks were made of wood, and the sounds of our footsteps echoed throughout the cell block as we were led past the lighted cells of the other inmates. Paul, my codefendant, was on a level below me. I couldn't see him, but I could hear his footsteps matching mine as he was also led along by his correctional officer. I was aware that all the inmates on that side of the four-level cell block could hear us as well. Men without faces were listening to the steps of "the new fish."

Entering a state prison as an inmate for the first time isn't something one easily forgets, especially at twenty-two years of age. It felt vastly different from the experience of sitting in the county jail. This was partly due to the fact that in the county lockup I still had the hope that *something* could change my future since I hadn't been to trial yet; and partly because, even though the jail was crowded, it didn't feel so *big*. Our footsteps on the catwalks were echoing throughout four stories of cells that looked down upon "the flats," an old brick floor that stretched the length of this nineteenth-century dungeon.

We had been delivered, along with a few other hapless souls, straight from the county jail by police van, and we arrived at the prison after dark. As we were brought in, I didn't fully appreciate that I wouldn't be on the outside again for a long time. If I had, I might have taken a better look around to savor the feel of the

3

"outside air." But it wouldn't have mattered. What I didn't understand then was that outside air doesn't really *feel* like outside air until you are free.

Before our procession down the catwalk, our street clothes had been taken away and exchanged for denim shirts and jeans. We were then showered and deloused. Our cells were small, six-by-nine-foot cubicles, made of century-and-a-half-old bricks covered by countless layers of paint. Sometimes it felt like the ghosts of hundreds of previous occupants were still around, the spirits of men who had once experienced the same pain I was now feeling. The thought always made me feel a little better somehow. Others had been here. Others had suffered. And now they were gone. Someday maybe I too would be a ghost.

The ominous and somewhat rare silence of that first evening, the immensity of the place, and the impossible notion of a release date that seemed so far away—all added to the heaviness I was feeling. It wasn't exactly fear that I was feeling. It seemed a much more formidable enemy than that. I had been through nightmarish incarcerations in the past. A disastrous three and one-half years in the Navy had resulted in seven court martials and six trips to brigs that were run by the Marine Corps. Having endured those military incarcerations between the ages of eighteen and twenty-one had caused me to become extremely self-reliant—and somewhat cocky. But as the shock of entering New Hampshire's state prison began to wear off after the first few hours, I began to experience a different form of pain—a pain that I had never felt before. It was a sense of being trapped.

Prison is about freedom—the lack of it.

As I wrote those words, I thought that perhaps I should have chosen terms that describe the opposite of freedom, such as "bondage" or even "slavery." But somehow these words do not fit. The man or woman in prison doesn't actually think of himself or herself as a slave. And though they have often been bound as they were transported in cuffs and chains, few would concede that they are *in* bondage. They seldom use the word *slavery,* except in their poetry. No, the issue is freedom. They are not free.

I can remember thinking to myself that this was the ultimate insult. I fancied myself as a free spirit. To capture such a creature—to clip its wings and *cage* it—was the ultimate slap in the face. My parents' home couldn't confine me; I had run away from it. The Navy couldn't hold me; I had gone AWOL—Absent Without Leave—six times. The pressing conformity of society couldn't mold me; I had quit dozens of jobs and taken to the open road by hitchhiking across the country on numerous occasions. I had even written a somewhat autobiographical song containing these words:

> "If the wind is blowin'
> that's where I'm goin'."

So to be caged, to be trapped like an animal, was an agony that is hard to describe. I would look at the clouds and wish I could fly. I envied the birds that chose, of their own volition, to swoop down and settle upon the prison yard, and then, also of their own volition, to fly away whenever they felt like it. I'm sure I speak for millions of inmates who have wished that very same thing.

It's at this point that the observer who wishes to understand the prison culture must begin. It is at the core of this discussion concerning the lack of freedom where the inmate's pain is most encompassed. It may include the awareness of lost years that can never be recovered, or it may find its roots in the desperate longing to be with that "certain someone." But it's the reality that they are no longer free to fulfill their dreams that drives the nail so deeply into the coffin. It is suddenly stopping in the middle of the prison yard on a sunny afternoon and imagining that you just sniffed the memory of a day at the beach in the smell of the summer air. It is hearing endless prison banter and the constant clanking of steel bars when you know you could be with that special someone who is still young and still out there—*at this very moment!* "What is she doing right now?" the heart cries.

Callous outsiders have observed that some prisons seem more like "kiddie camps." They have "this luxury" or "that amenity" and "why are we catering to prisoners, anyway?" They resent the fact that some prisons have television sets and ball fields or that some inmates are even allowed conjugal visits. Such observations and comments are heard with regularity, even in some Christian circles. And if such people do admit to the hardships of incarceration, they are apt to add something like, "Well, if they didn't want to go to prison, they should've lived a different lifestyle." Or when hearing of the reality of Christian inmates, some will ask, almost with incredulity, "But do you think they've *really* changed?"

Questions and comments like these, especially by Christians, are sad. They reveal a doctrinal viewpoint that, in terms of sinfulness, appears to place the commentators in a less guilty place. They also reveal a lack of faith in the transforming nature of the gospel. Why is it any less a miracle to wake the dead *anywhere*—whether in a prison or a palace?

It has been my observation that people who seem to respond compassionately to this emotional pain of separation are those who have experienced lengthy separations from loved ones themselves. This separation might come through a military assignment or an extended hospitalization, and, of course, those who have gone through the incarceration process themselves. For the potential volunteer in the prison setting, it is essential that even though you may have never experienced this particular pain yourself, you must be aware of it. You must acknowledge that it is real. You must recall the old prison saying (seldom admitted to, but often thought): "Everyone cries at night." You must hear inmates with your heart when they try to explain to you about their wife or husband or loved ones. You must try to imagine how deep are the waters in this well of lonely frustration.

As most people who are caught for a crime they have committed experience, life on the outside is usually interrupted suddenly. It doesn't matter that you have been sharing your life with people whom you love. It doesn't matter that you were in the middle of a mutual routine. Suddenly, you are cut off from them. And, as far as the pain itself goes, it doesn't even matter that you have brought it upon yourself or that the lifestyle you were leading made such a trip almost inevitable; the pain is still there—not only for yourself but also for those you have left behind. If it is a girlfriend, the pain of sudden, complete separation comes crashing in on you. If it is a wife who has been good to you, it is even worse. If there are young children, it is worse still.

The greatest pain of incarceration is the forcible separation from those you hold most dear.

In a Bible study that I hold in a county jail for men awaiting trial, a man in his thirties recently said, "If it weren't for my kids, I could face all this. But the thought of being away from them is the hardest of all." The man sitting next to him agreed and said that if it weren't for that, "it would be easy."

I have heard both sides of this story over and over again. Mothers phone me because their son or daughter has entered the prison system. Sons and daughters weep over what they have brought upon their families. I know a dear Christian woman serving a life sentence for murder who experienced the horror of learning that her youngest son had just been picked up for murder. How her heart was crushed by the pain of being without him but knowing that he too was beginning this nightmarish journey. Her pain ultimately went beyond all comprehension when she discovered that the person he had killed in an argument was his older brother.

The hardship of prison life is in not being able to go to the ones you love *when* you want to go to them. It does not matter how great or how few the amenities may be. (Those who are not acquainted with the culture focus on such things.) But those who have lost their freedom know just how excruciating is the prick of this particular thorn. The real pain lies hidden deep within the bush—no matter how many roses may adorn it.

I once read that 80 percent of those who are married when they enter prison are divorced within the first year. But what may surprise some is that this is not always initiated by the mate on the outside. Fears rising in the heart of the newly incarcerated inmate, especially among the men, often lead them to such a course of action. One of these fears is insecurity.

This holds true for those who are not married as well. If it's a girlfriend, thoughts of *"What is she doing now?"* are raging through his head. *"How long will she hang in there? Who are her friends? Who is she with? Is she falling for someone else?"* She may be having no such thoughts, but he is face-to-face with the reality of his time. He can't go to her. He can't change the calendar. He knows that time machines do not exist, so rather than face what he feels is the inevitable rejection, *he* decides to end the relationship. At least this is done on his own terms, and the pain of losing her won't take him by surprise. For those others who fear it but can't end it, the occasional visits often disintegrate into stormy disagreements brought on by his increasing suspicions, fears, and insecurities. This too, is a subtle form of controlled rejection. At least he's aware of *when* the end is occurring—as he reluctantly and inevitably takes part in bringing it about.

For other inmates, though, the last thing they are prepared to face is the loss of the relationship they care most deeply about. It is especially painful for those who were constantly in each other's company right up until the time of the arrest. The following excerpt is from a letter I received from a young man who was awaiting trial in a county jail in Maine:

> I've lost my mind, my freedom and my girlfriend
> because she met someone else and decided not to wait,
> which she said she always would. I love her to death.
> She couldn't even wait to find out what will happen to
> me. The false promises and leaving me for another per-
> son is what hurts the most. She told me she still loves me
> and would write and visit but it was a lie. I haven't
> heard from her . . . .

The letter was six pages long, an endless torrent of turmoil, pain, and fear. He had been jailed before and was dealing with the dark reality that he was facing another long sentence. The time when an inmate awaits trial is a greater period of fear and uncertainty than the actual prison sentence. It is hard for the mind to settle down because it doesn't know what it is settling down *to*. In some cases the future can hold the possibility of merely a few months in jail or several years. How does one make plans? How does one dare to hope? How long must he tell her she has to wait?

In this case, the young woman made the decision for her boyfriend. And though it was painfully early, it will actually help him adjust more quickly. At least she showed him the mercy of letting him know what he was dealing with up front—by immediately abandoning the grace of faithfulness. Although it makes his current nightmare even more unbearable, he is now forced to begin to adjust. The prisoners who don't either self-destruct or fall apart. This particular man was in danger of the latter. His letter spoke more than once about losing his sanity.

What does an inmate do with the strong emotional attachments that have been suddenly interrupted? How does one cope? In cases where visits and letters are infrequent, the end often comes sooner. Some prisoners choose to shut themselves down emotionally. "I don't care about her anyway" is the prevailing thought that eventually becomes a self-fulfilling prophecy. It was so in my case. I thought I was deeply attached to a girl I was seeing when I went to prison. Insecure and unable to handle what I felt was an impending rejection, I closed myself down emotionally. If I convinced myself that I didn't care, then it wouldn't hurt as much. I was so successful at this that by the time I was released I didn't have even the slightest inclination to look her up. But the problem with taking this route is that the inmate trains himself never to attach to anyone else on a deep level. I realized years later that I had been disciplining myself in this art long before I went to prison.

Incarceration intensified this coping mechanism of mine. I had been ripped away from the very people who gave me a sense of self-esteem, balance, and identity. So I reached into the closet to grab that trusty, old armor of emotional coldness and was forced to wear it day in and day out. I had to, to survive emotionally. The relationship I was in when I went to prison had to be dealt with immediately. Although the battle was for my mind, it was the heart that was shedding blood. How was I going to deal with the questions that were raging in my heart? What is she doing now? Who is she with? Is she going to forget me? Will she stay in contact? In my heart of hearts, I already knew the answer.

Those types of questions are driven by insecurity. I knew that the basis of our relationship was not very solid. So I chose another road and convinced my heart that it didn't care. One would think this could be a rather lengthy process, but not when emotional survival depends upon it. I was dreaming of other girls in only a couple of months.

Another "fix" is to fall in love again through fantasizing or resurrecting old flames. Many prisoners actually bring these romances to life through letters, phone calls, or new relationships, whether appropriate or not.[3] Some try to numb themselves through drugs or medication. Some do lose their minds. Volunteers need to be aware of the dull ache that many inmates carry around with them—due to their longing to be with that special someone who lives in the world beyond the walls. The ache is more prevalent at certain times than others, but it is usually not too far away. It is a part of the fabric of prison life. Be compassionate. Try to imagine how you would feel, or perhaps how you did feel when you lost someone unexpectedly. Breaking up *is* hard to do.

But when it is a wife who is left behind, sometimes inmates actually end the relationship for less selfish reasons. I have known many prisoners who encouraged their wives to divorce them because they didn't want the consequences of their own sin to ruin the lives of those they loved the most. For every married person that enters prison, there are two people doing time. Both are forcibly separated from the one they love. Many men can't justify stealing years of a potentially normal and happy life from the one they feel was an innocent bystander in an action or lifestyle *they* chose to take. They would rather release them.

While this is a gallant and understandable gesture, the Christian volunteer must encourage the hurting prisoner, as sensitively as possible, to remain with his wife if she is willing. Explain to him that if it is true love, she agreed that it would be "for better or worse." The volunteer must encourage him to see the present not as stolen time but as an adjustment that requires new and innovative ways for them to continue to build their relationship.

A former prisoner and his wife once pointed out to me that when a spouse goes to prison—say for three years—they are not three years apart when he or she comes out but *six* years. She has spent three years going in her direction and he, going three years in his. While this is true in some respects, there are still healthy practices they can adopt to build togetherness while they are apart. For example, studying and reading the same passages of the Bible at the same time of day is a positive activity they can learn to implement together. The idea is to build shared experiences as much as they can.

The lonely pain of forced separation is perhaps the greatest single hurt that most inmates share in common. If the Christian volunteer is aware of this, it will make him or her more sensitive to it. A rule of thumb I generally follow is that I'm cautious about sharing *recent* family events with inmates who have families. I'm referring to such activities as the birthday party we just had for one of our children or some other joyous family activity. To do so runs the risk of highlighting the pain of missed birthdays, soccer games or band practice, anniversaries, vacation times, or favorite places. My fear is that it will remind them painfully of what they don't have. Trading such stories at a later time, when it is safely in the past for both of you, may be more appropriate. It's not that most inmates I know would object to a recent family story; it's just an inherent sensitivity I feel for them.

A contrary opinion, however, was recently expressed to me in a letter I received from an inmate in Massachusetts. He wrote, "I thrive on those things because it helps keep the real world alive for me so that I don't forget it. . . . Painful? Yes. But a good kind of pain, a healthy kind of pain, because it keeps me from ever getting too comfortable in here. I don't want to be completely comfortable in here because then I would change in ways that I don't want to change."

This inmate makes an excellent point. He is fighting to maintain the standards of normalcy that are common to life on the outside and is trying to resist the subtle takeover of institutionalization. That he is aware of the fact is, in itself, a sign of health. But I still recommend sensitivity in the things we share and the ways in which we share them. Timing is important. How *much* we share also depends upon the emotional health of the person with whom we are interacting, as well as the health of our relationship.

"Remember those in prison," says Hebrews 13:3, "as if you were their fellow prisoners, and those who are mistreated as if you yourselves were suffering."

2

Time Won't Let Me

I HAVE KNOWN MEN who escaped from prison. (Only one that I know of is still at large.) Some were able to escape over the walls, some even out of maximum security. Another even made it to the roof of Florida State Prison one night but broke his leg when he jumped from the building. He wasn't able to climb the double twenty-foot fences that still separated him from the outside world.

But for most inmates, it's not the walls or the fences that separate them from freedom. Nor is it the towers with armed officers in the turrets or the multiple layers of tiers with locked cells. It is not in the steel doors or the electronic surveillance cameras, or in the cement or the fences or the endless rows of razor wire. Nor will it be found in the teeth of the security dogs or in the keys of their keepers. All these are only symbols of a much more indomitable foe. Its name is *time*.

It is the hands of a clock that keep them shackled, not the hands of the guards that escort them. The calendar is a chain of twelve links sealed with a lock that no master smith has ever picked. The jailers are the endless years—those faithful, blind servants that do the bidding of the prisoner's ultimate enemy. Time is their master. The reigning adverb in this culture is "when" not "how."

It is hard to describe the frustration that this foe creates. Unlike a human enemy, you cannot defeat it, cajole it, bribe it, or flatter it. It does not relent. It does not change its mind. Therefore it becomes, in itself, currency. It has inestimable value. It is the stuff of plea bargains and the force that bends the arms of loyalty, turning former accomplices against one another in court. It is the golden carrot of good-time[1] and the fire-breathing threat of parole officers. It is the black widow of the inmate's world. They will woo her for her favors and at the same time fear the sting that can so quickly turn against them.

Paul Simon wrote and sang, "The closer my destination the more I keep slip-sliding away." Those words adequately describe the dilemma of the man or woman in prison. Except for those who have received a life sentence without parole, most inmates will eventually be released to the streets.[2] A date exists that will finally arrive, bringing with it the eligibility to leave the prison. The problem lies in the dual reality that every movement toward that date is also time that is "slip-sliding away" from life on the outside. Every day is another marker that prevents inmates from growing along with the rest of society in a normal, adaptive way. The closer they get to their destination, the more they are losing ground with the everyday pace of society. They are aware of changes on the outside, but these developments are viewed with a sense of detachment. There is no need to concern themselves with things that are not a part of their immediate reality. No, that anxiety will only begin to grow as they get closer to release.

But life is slip-sliding away in other areas as well. They are getting older. They are missing out on events in which their loved ones are participating. Many have not received visits or letters from their families for years. Just this week I received word from a man who learned that his daughter had graduated from high school because he saw her name in a local newspaper. At least it was *some* news about how she was doing, and he was grateful to the Lord for having learned of it.

For "short"[3] inmates, time is little more than a temporary victor, but for others it is nothing less than an undertaker—a graveyard worker who will eventually bury them. In fact, for most people in prison, the feeling *is* one of being buried alive—neither dead nor free.

The length of an inmate's sentence also plays a large part in the adaptation process. One who is thinking of a release date two or three years into the future will make decisions and appraisals quite differently than one who must slowly face up to the reality that release is not an option. (Or at least not one that can be seriously entertained any time soon.) The former thinks in terms of pacing himself while the latter tends to think in terms of living day by day. This difference results in different thought processes, different decisions, and in many cases, different ethics. That which is untenable to a short-timer becomes possible, and even probable, to a lifer. And vice versa.

Time itself is viewed differently. While the lifer is aware that time is passing, it ceases to become as much of a slave driver to him as it is to the short-timer. That which seems within reach is closer to the conscious mind than that which seems so distant and unreal. However, everyone who has been in the situation of being close to the end of a sentence, no matter how long, has experienced the unique travail of "getting short"—that agonizing time when the days seem like years and the minutes seem like days. It is a time of growing apprehension and, for many, even fear. The curious cohabitation of grand desires and gnawing apprehensions grow together like the wheat and the tares as the big day slowly approaches.

Prison is about time. Nowhere have I experienced "time's thievish progress to eternity"[4] as much as in those periods when I myself was incarcerated. The prisoner is at war with time. He can fight it, he can attempt to fool it, he can wrestle, play, pray, and waste it all together, but he cannot defeat it. The best the average man or woman can hope for is to make a peace, of sorts, with it. The industrious ones will use it to their advantage, such as in the pursuit of education or certain job skills, but even they are aware that a river is flowing whose waters can never be reversed. And it carries the flotsam and jetsam of their lives with it. Loved ones such as parents, children, wives, husbands, girl-friends, and boyfriends alike—are all swept along in time's irre-versible current. They are painfully aware that these are moments that can never be recovered. How *much* they are aware of it varies with the length of time they are serving.

I have never forgotten the story told to me by an inmate named Steve, who was serving a considerable amount of time in Florida State Prison. He recalled that after a period of many years, he was finally to receive a visit from his mother, who lived in another part of the country. His cellmate watched him as he spruced himself up and bounced happily off to the visiting room for the long-anticipated rendezvous with his mom. When he returned, his friend was surprised to see him break down in tears, repeating over and over again, "She's old! She's old! My mother is an old woman!" His cellmate tried to appease him by saying, "What did you expect? It's been years since you've seen her!"

"But I didn't expect her to look so old. *My* mother is not old like that!"

For Steve, as it turned out, his mother was not the older woman in the visiting room, but the one who smiled sweetly up at him from the worn photograph he had cherished all those years. Steve had fallen prey to the spiked drink of time and memories. Although he knew that he had done years in prison, he had become intoxicated into thinking that those dear ones who lived "out there" were still the way he remembered them. He wasn't present to experience the slow, subtle changes that age had painted on the faces of its subjects day by day. *His* mom was the woman in the photograph. She had looked that way when he left, and she had remained that way throughout the years—each time he had looked at her. She *couldn't* be that old woman in the visiting room! But Steve realized how slowly and inevitably time was stealing his life from him as it wended its way on its "thievish progress to eternity." The volunteer must always remember that, for the inmate, the enemy is not a physical foe; it is time.

How then is the prisoner to cope? The responses are as varied as the inmates themselves. I have known some men who seem able to *sleep* their time away. I call them the "Rip Van Winkles" of the prison system. Although most prisons require job assignments, some men refuse to work, incurring instead a trip to segregation where, for punishment, they are locked up most of the day, every day. I have known some who can actually sleep up to nineteen hours in a twenty-four hour period.

In state facilities that permit individual TV sets in the cells, I have known others who are overdosing on the familiar pills known as ABC, CBS, and NBC. One man I met at MCI Walpole was literally a soap opera addict. He knew every character on every show and was in a position not to miss a single episode. Some have surrendered to the enemy. They have accepted the terms of the environment as *their* environment. And while this may be a good thing as far as adaptation goes, it is the first step to institutionalization.

Many inmates, however, take as much advantage of the time as they can. Thousands have earned their GEDs,[5] and countless others have received Pell grants to take college courses by correspondence. Recent shifts in welfare politics, however, have made such grants difficult to obtain, and in many cases they are no longer available.

Countless others have enrolled in Bible correspondence courses. Many groups offer these within a wide range of doctrinal diversity and curriculum difficulty. One good example would be those that the Emmaus Bible School offers.[6] They have over fifty separate courses that an inmate may proceed through, and I have known a few men who have taken all of them. Many smaller resources exist, such as the Bible study booklets prepared for prisoners by Gospel Express.[7]

Others get involved in hobby crafts or trades such as welding, culinary arts, computer programming, carpentry, auto mechanics, and a variety of others. Being a prison, of course, invites abuses. Occasionally, these mishaps result in the termination of the program. For example, at one Massachusetts prison not too long ago, an inmate drove a car he was repairing in the auto shop through two fences in an attempt to escape. At another facility, the computer training program was terminated when it was discovered that a few of the inmates were running an outside gambling ring from inside the prison. My personal feeling on this is why punish the whole for the actions of a few? If providing a trade is the goal, why cut off one's nose to spite their interfaces, so to speak?

Many inmates are voracious readers and will read anything they can get their hands on. This has worked to the gospel's advantage over the years. It is a wonderful reality that of the over two million inmates incarcerated in this country, most have access to a

Bible if they want one. Untold millions of New Testaments and complete Bibles have been distributed over just the last few years alone.

In one prison I go to, for example, there is a tier known as the "New Line," or classification unit. Classification, or "Orientation" as it is sometimes called, is the process that takes place when men and women first come into the prison system. They are usually housed on a temporary tier until it is decided where best to place them within the prison population. Such things as reviewing personnel files, sentence obligations, meetings with psychologists, counselors, and other prison staff will often occur during this period. Bracelets or ID cards for identification purposes are issued with photos, as well as clothing and other necessary items. A booklet containing institutional rules is usually given to the inmate with the strong "recommendation" that it be read and understood. In short, all the preliminary stuff necessary for a stay at "the hotel" is taken care of during this orientation period.

As in many prisons, the inmate is usually stripped of all the items that had accompanied him to prison, leaving him in a cell with absolutely nothing but his mattress—and the likely presence of some other hapless stranger. There is nothing to do. No radio, no television, and absolutely nothing to read.

Enter the smiley-faced Christian with his arms full of reading material! I have come to refer to the classification tier I mentioned previously as the "Bermuda Triangle for Bibles." It is a literal, black hole through which tons of Christian material have disappeared over the years. The men are usually there for only a week, so every seven days a new crop of stir-crazy individuals is there to greet me. And they will read! They will take whatever material you have, just to have something to do. But what has always interested me the most is that the book they request above all others is the Bible. Even before I get to their cells, they are calling out for a Bible—and most are genuinely grateful to receive it. We take the opportunity to meet them and to let them know the times of the Christian programs and services. It has also proved to be a very fertile place for the gospel. That particular tier has heard the salvation prayers of many, many inmates over the years.

But whatever the circumstances, or no matter the fashion in which inmates choose to spend their days, time remains a force to be reckoned with and an enemy to be endured. The daily skirmishes are recorded by a series of Xs on a calendar. Everything falls under the heading of "doing" time. The very phrase itself evokes the language of having to serve time or to pay homage to it in some way. Every endless game of spades, checkers, or chess only serves to feed the beast. Every joke, boast, or curse falls on its deaf ears. Every threat, argument, and occasional explosion of violence reverberates in its apathetic corridors. How do men and women survive in a kingdom ruled by such a callous lord?

The short answer is that there are no options. The only choice one has *is* to endure—or to quit the fight all together. Sadly, there have been many inmates throughout the years who have opted for the latter. Unable to cope with the fear and the loneliness, they choose death through suicide rather than fight such an apathetic and indomitable foe. The enemy is simply too much for them.

Many times I have come to the cell of a man who has that kind of fear in his eyes—that deep, despairing look that says the enemy is about to win. The Christian volunteer must never underestimate what a crucial role he or she plays in the lives of these dear men and women in such moments. In many cases, it is literally the difference between life and death. The kind word, the listening ear—and most of all, the thread of *hope*—are offered through the physical presence of the volunteer. We know, of course, that it is Christ himself expressing his love through us, but at that moment the imprisoned soul may know only that *someone* cares.

And when the offer of God's love and forgiveness is accepted, it is only then that the Goliath of time is toppled. The Christian message gloriously transcends time and space.

I can't tell you how many inmates throughout the years have wound up praising God for sending them to prison—and meaning it from the bottom of their hearts. They realize that God has saved them from their self-destructive courses and slowed them down long enough to think about, and comprehend, ultimate reality. It is grace that has enabled them to take a long, hard look at themselves and realize—perhaps for the first time—that they were literally destroying themselves and, in many cases, the lives of those around them. God has given them a chance that many of them realize their friends never took. They are keenly aware that some of their closest associations are dead from drug overdoses, AIDS, or drug deals gone sour, and these people were doing the very same things they were doing.

When I was a volunteer at CMC Norco Corona in California, a prison for offenders for drug-related crimes, the inmates used to greet their returning friends with the phrase: "Man, you weren't arrested, you were *rescued!*" They would say this because some of their buddies who used to weigh two hundred pounds or more would come in weighing about 110 pounds, their bodies devastated by the abuse of drugs. In fact, I still repeat that phrase with many inmates today. "You weren't arrested, you were rescued—and *God* did the rescuing."

Prisons, for all their sadness, fear, and frustration under time's dark reign, are a wonderful place to hear the footsteps of him who *conquered* death and time. The Lord Jesus loves prisoners; there can be no doubt about this wonderful fact. He has opened the doors for thousands of volunteers, many of them ex-offenders like myself, to enter prison every day for the sole purpose of preaching the gospel. And even more telling than that is the great evidence of those thousands of inmates who are so faithfully serving him while they *remain* in prison.

I find that the majority of prisoners have been humbled to one degree or another and tend to be honest about their spiritual condition. I am not saying that they are all humble but that they have been humbled. They are honest about their need and their own inability to make their lives work. No wonder the Lord finds such fruitful vines growing in this vineyard! Many on the outside are still wrapped in the prideful cloaks of their outward appearances, possessions, and social positions in life. But inmates have had all that stripped away from them. And it has turned out to be a marvelous grace.

"But he gives us more grace. That is why Scripture says: 'God opposes the proud but gives grace to the humble'" (James 4:6).

"Therefore, I tell you, her many sins have been forgiven—for she loved much. But he who has been forgiven little loves little" (Luke 7:47).

"On hearing this, Jesus said to them, 'It is not the healthy who need a doctor, but the sick. . . . I have not come to call the righteous, but sinners'" (Matt. 9:12–13).

It is the job of the Christian volunteer to point to eternal truths, to lift the inmate's eyes to the hills from whence their help really comes, and to help them gain an eternal perspective. We are to teach them not to fear the one who can merely kill the body (mere mortals) but to fear him who can throw body *and* soul into hell. And to let them know that this one who holds the future in his hands desires that they should share their futures *with* him.

It is not our job to cause inmates to put their hopes in their release dates. If that were the case, what would our ministry to lifers be? It is not our job to predict that God will prepare them for a great work on the outside some day (though for some that may well be the case) but to let them know that *no* day is ever wasted in his sight and that he has a purpose for them right where they are. Nor is it our job to say that God will give them the peace they need to make it only to their release dates, but that God has true and lasting peace available to every one of his children right *now*, no matter what their circumstances.[8]

There is another day coming. Another time coming. One that, if they are Christians, can never be feared because its joys can never end. It is *that* kingdom which Scripture encourages us to keep our eyes upon. We are privileged, as volunteers, to be a part of directing those in prison to the way of comfort, courage, and peace in their present condition—and a *true* perspective on time that the world can never give them.

3

Born to Be Wild

SOME YEARS AGO, upon the frantic request of his mother, I began to assist a young man who was beginning to get into trouble. He was only seventeen, and his "troubles" consisted of minor skirmishes with the police over such things as receiving stolen property (a bicycle), damage to public property (a fire alarm), vagrancy, and disturbing the peace. None of these charges was very serious, but he was performing them in concert with the wrong group of kids. Most of these associates were older than he was and often took advantage of him, getting him to steal things for them and turning him on to marijuana.

When I became involved, I began to take him out for an occasional breakfast and arranged for him and his mother to begin attending a local church. Stopping by their house and discussing the Bible with them also became a part of my routine. I wouldn't say they were avid students, but they welcomed the visits and verbalized an interest in spiritual things.

Two years later he was arrested for possession of drugs and given a six-month sentence at the county jail. He was very frightened when I first visited him but later seemed to adjust well enough to do his short amount of time. Not long after his release he became involved with an older woman, married her, and was soon divorced. He continued to hang with the wrong people, and occasionally I would hear that he had been beaten up or cited for drunkenness. By his late twenties, he was in a relationship with a woman who had been institutionalized for psychotic behavior. His mother continued to support him (as well as his girlfriend), but there was little evidence of any real spiritual growth in any of their lives.

22

I had involved other Christians in the mix, and there were others who had attempted to help them along the way. For example, two young men from a local singles group teamed up to take the son on outings and involve him in other church-related events. One of them continued to stay in touch with him even after he had gotten married. Women from the church would pick up the mother for worship services. Eventually, though, the pattern of no change resulted in each of the relationships drying up.

Throughout this time, however, both he and his mother expressed the *verbalization* of an acceptance of Christianity. Looking back, I don't think they were entirely insincere in this, but their "acceptance" seemed superficial and motivated by self-interest. (They were always needing something.) The fruit of the Christ-life—that passion and hunger that typifies sincere believers—was never truly displayed. His last phone call was a request for dental assistance. Many of his teeth had become rotted or broken off at the gum line and were now giving him serious trouble. I called a Christian friend who was an oral surgeon, but they never connected. That was a few years ago, and I haven't heard from him since.

Beyond all the superficiality, however, persisted another reality—something I would call an unredeemed, *cultural* thing. When he was a young man, his favorite TV show was *Cops*. He watched every episode. The interesting thing was that it had never been the police with whom he related; it had always been the "bad boys." He identified with them. He attached a certain glamour to their rebellion and their badness. He wanted to be like them. The "bad guy" mystique had become a part of his psyche. He esteemed them, looked up to them, and somehow felt that if he were like them, others would look up to him as well.

Unfortunately, he was a simple lad. He had neither the brains nor the cold, calculated meanness to be like his heroes. His skirmishes with the law always amounted to penny-ante stuff, and his brushes with his older "heroes" usually ended with his getting used, ripped off, or beaten up. In a sense, he was a double loser—never able to be a real bad guy and scoffed at by those who were.

I have met many others like him who *were* tougher. And what they often shared in common during their teenage years was *Cops* or some other show that glamorized the bad guy. The existence of so-called copycat crimes, I believe, is often linked to this sort of identification. There is an "outlaw mentality" out there. A whole subculture that takes pride in "badness" and whose heroes are bad guys. Unless we examine this reality a bit before we proceed, we will miss an essential element of the culture we are trying to penetrate.

When I was seventeen years old, my favorite show was *The Untouchables*. This was a program that was set against the prohibition days as a backdrop and portrayed the often-violent struggle between federal agents and mob-linked bootleggers. I recall that I never related to the "good guy," Eliot Ness, but always to the gangsters. Guys like Frank Nitti and Al Capone— *they* were my heroes.

In real life, I soon began to attract their mirror images—other teens who also esteemed the gangster culture. These peers gave me the emotional strokes I needed as I began to manifest the culture's values. I was constantly in fights or threatening confrontations; I backed down to no one. I even challenged one of my teachers in high school to "step outside." My first arrest was for carrying a switchblade and threatening a store clerk with it. I was elected the vice-president of a forty-member gang on the south side of Chicago and had gained a reputation as a tough guy.

I got my "strokes" from such behavior; I was receiving from my peers the esteem I felt I needed. I couldn't get it at home where my father and I were often at odds, but I could get it on the street where, to my friends at least, I was something.

I'm not saying that a TV show is the cause of juvenile delinquency,[1] or even that drugs or alcohol are the cause. They are fuel, to be sure, but the motor was already tuned that way. The root causes are often driven by a need for significance, at least among the men. To *be* somebody—when deep down they feel like nobody. Being a criminal is a power trip. The criminal feels in control. He gets to rape and plunder, loot and kill, when *he* wants. He feels empowered; others are at his mercy. He feels important. He has *identity*.

Let's return to my young acquaintance for a moment. A few Christians have entered his life. They help his mother. They help *him*. They take him out to breakfast and spend time with him—and he does respond. There are "strokes" there. But when they are gone, who is he? He has already chosen a culture, and his street friends—no matter how rotten they are to him—are a part of that culture. However low on the totem pole he may be, he still has identity. He knows his role. He knows how he fits. And as long as Christ never truly becomes Lord in his life, his inner man changes little.

I have seen this same dynamic played out in the lives of so many others I have known over the years. There was the tough young man who went to an adult prison at seventeen and eventually became one of the most genuine threats to anyone in the institution. A no-bluff, no-nonsense, true, tough guy. He made a decision for Christ at one point and truly began to change. But some people, both guards and inmates alike, began to taunt him and challenge him, misreading his new gentleness for weakness. Big mistake on their part. He was too new to the teachings of Christ to rise above the years of his conditioning. He struck back and eventually maxed out[2] his sentence in the maximum security unit, but not before he had sent several inmates to the hospital.

When he was released, we were there to meet him and assisted him and his new wife and daughter as much as possible, but eventually the mentality of the tough guy reclaimed him. He dropped out of sight for a while but was later picked up and charged with two more violent assaults.

Another man I know has done over thirty years in prison. He was released to a Christian program and was doing well. He liked his job and was beginning to grow in his knowledge of the Bible. When he reached the point in the program where he could have visits, his new wife (a former girlfriend from his biker days), came to see him. Not long after that he disappeared from the program, went on a long drinking binge with his lady, and violated his parole.

A young woman that my wife Wendy and I know received a lot of attention and help from Christian volunteers while she was incarcerated as well as when she was released. But her weakness had always been men. Men who, for the most part, operated on the darker side of life. Her past had been primarily one of prostitution and drugs. She told us that before she became a Christian in prison she had never labored at an honest day's work in her life. She was extremely street-smart and tough.

After meeting the Lord during one of her incarcerations, she slowly began to change. Her street language diminished, the cocky strut in her walk disappeared, and her attitude became increasingly gentle. She was released knowing what her weakness was and yet soon became involved in a live-in relationship with another man—an ex-con she had met at the halfway house.[3] Her parole was rescinded, and she was returned to the prison for a "dirty urine."[4] She has since been rereleased, spent a year at a drug rehabilitation center, and at last report was doing well. She met someone new and has been married for three years. Both she and her husband were regularly attending a church.

What is the point of all these stories?

Over the years, I have heard many psychologists and sociologists dissecting the behavior of prisoners. While many of their conclusions have validity, some of their diagnoses appear to underestimate the entrenched influence that the "bad boy" culture continues to generate in the lives of the people they are studying. Many times their treatment consists solely in addressing the symptoms of their particular crimes. In DOC[5] and rehab[6] circles, these remedies take the form of a "program" of some sort. There are programs directed toward sexual offenders and violent offenders, programs for people who struggle with anger or substance abuse. In some circles, "working the program" is actually the catch phrase that is applied to someone who is attempting to comply with the guidelines of their particular group's discipline.

Many good programs exist, including AA and NA. Their time-tested results reflect the biblical principles upon which they were founded. Troubled individuals can also be sent to "this" residential center or to "that" counselor, and so on. But the directors of these agencies will usually admit that if the person they are attempting to help does not himself want to change, then no program will help him.

I know of several good Christian programs designed to help the ex-offender or the struggling addict, and they all have a stringent and difficult interview process. The reason for this is mainly an attempt to determine, as much as is possible, whether the person being interviewed really *wants* to change. The reason so many experienced program directors are still fooled from time to time is because the person they are interviewing really *believes* he or she wants to change. Sincerity is convincing. The problems arise because the person's desire to change, though sincere, is still enfolded within the context of his or her old worldview.

If this dynamic can be troubling for personnel who operate experienced programs, what are the implications for the average volunteer? It at least means you must go in with your eyes wide open. You must ask the Holy Spirit for help in determining, as much as possible, where the person is in terms of how he or she views reality. Learn to develop questions that assist you in your attempts to better understand inmates. It is difficult to lead them out if you don't know where they are. Because they are *in* the culture, their perception of what they need may be totally different from the sound recommendations that seem obvious to you. The strong influence of their prevailing worldview means you must remain realistic in terms of your expectations.

I have known some men and women who, while they were in prison, were among the spiritually strongest people I have ever met. And I have also watched some of these same people flake out shortly after they were released. The lesson is plain: You can often remove the individual from the culture, but removing the culture from *them* is a totally different thing. It's a part of their worldview and an integrated part of their value system. From a theological perspective, it's where their flesh still believes it gets its strokes.

It is difficult to underestimate the sense of well-being these "strokes" provide, however warped the foundation may be. I took pride in being a misfit. I was an outlaw, and I had an outlaw mentality. My perspective of life was viewed through a lens of rebellion. It was a part of who I was. Changing my geography did not change my value system. A spirit of anger that had been forged in childhood dominated me. I was restless, violent, and discontent. I *reveled* in being an outlaw.

I was also not a Christian. The greatest agent of change the world will ever know is a personal encounter with the Lord Jesus Christ. Some of these people I have mentioned never made a serious commitment to him. Others, I believe, tried. You as a volunteer need to be convinced that if the inner person has not been changed, you are working with the same old person. You may help to rearrange the furniture in the rooms of their lives, but they are still living inside the same old house.

For example, going to prison convinced me that I didn't want to keep doing this. I minimized my trips to prison by making some necessary changes. I was rearranging some of the furniture of my life, but it was merely moving sofas and chairs around the same old room. My basic thinking remained unchanged. When Jesus Christ came, he tore down the whole house and built a new one from the ground up. "Therefore, if anyone is in Christ, he is a new creation; the old has gone, the new has come!" (2 Cor. 5:17).

As for those who did make an honest commitment to Christ, and later failed, I still believe their last chapter has yet to be written. I also believe that these new sheep were never truly enfolded into the new culture that Christ brings. If they became Christians in prison, they experienced Christianity within *that* culture. It is a genuine Christianity to be sure (and in some ways more dynamic than most will experience when released), but they have yet to experience this new culture on the streets.

What's more, as soon as these young believers step outside, they will be welcomed by the society that formerly embraced them. It is *that* culture which seems most familiar. They know how they fit. They have friends within this culture. And what's more important, significance and self-esteem can still be found within it. The temptation to return to this old society can become especially strong if they continue to feel awkward and uncomfortable within their new, "outside Christian" experience. Often their initial impression of Christians in churches on the outside is that they all seem to have their acts together. It tends to make them feel very much out of place.

To further make things difficult, they discover that among their old peer group, having been to prison is akin to having been given a medal upon returning home from a war. It is tantamount to a badge of honor in the "bad boy" culture. You were not only "bad" when you went in; now you are *really* bad. It's as though you've been to war while all your friends evaded the draft. You now come back as a decorated hero.

All this may sound ridiculous to some who have never been a part of that mind-set, but I know that's how the culture thinks. I was a part of it. The volunteer at least needs to be aware of the powerful forces at work upon those who grew up singing (and truly identifying with) "Born to Be Wild" and not to underestimate the siren song of the outlaw. It is where they got their strokes and their sense of self-esteem in the first place, and it has long made up a part of who they are.

The only remedy for this is a true encounter with the Lord Jesus Christ, who alone can succeed in rebuilding their lives (see Gal. 2:20; Col. 3:4). Then it is God who becomes the one they most want to please. But in their fledgling state, they need all the support they can get. It is we who must demonstrate the love, acceptance, and approval of the Lord Jesus Christ in physical and tangible ways. When they are finally able to trade in their former source of significance for the reality that Christ died for them, and to discover their true value in the fact that God loves them to *that* degree, they will be well on their way to the healing psychology of divine truth.

Once they have the chance truly to taste and see that the *Lord* is good, such people often turn out to be among Christ's most loyal and dedicated soldiers—and an asset to any church that is blessed enough to receive them. But the church *must* take the initiative to reach out to these dear souls and incorporate them into the life of the body of Christ.

Help them make that transition by being conscious of where they have been and being thoughtful about finding ways to integrate them into their new Christian culture. The Holy Spirit *will* accomplish his beautiful work of sanctification. He is, after all, continuing to transform each of us from our "former way of life."[7] We *all* had a former worldview and, by God's grace, have all had teachers along the way who taught us how to walk in this "newness of life." As a volunteer, you are in that very same role. To understand better where inmates have been allows you to become a sharper tool in the hands of the Holy Spirit and enables you to guide them to where he wants them to be.

4

One Against the World

MANY PEOPLE WITHIN THE CRIMINAL CULTURE have a worldview that could be described in terms of jungle warfare. They tend to perceive themselves as lone combatants engaged in a guerrilla-type conflict, pitted against incredible odds. The enemy is "the system," a dark Goliath that seeks to swallow up their lives and overpower them at every turn. For these self-styled resistance fighters, getting over on the enemy is the name of the game. Hit and run. Attack and evade. They can even perceive that the stand they are taking against this monolithic foe is not only valiant—it is noble.

How can this be, one may ask? How does someone engaged in criminal activity come to perceive reality in this way? What twisted pathways must be journeyed before the lines between good and evil become so blurred and distorted that they actually become inverted?[1] The theological answer lies in the deceptive nature of the flesh, which always seeks to place self at the center of the universe. But sin has also seized the opportunity that societal forces have provided as well.

In the American psyche, there is an almost romantic notion for the concept of the "rugged individualist." We love stories about people who beat the odds or who win in spite of overwhelming obstacles. We root for the underdog and remember the Alamo. Ingrained in our collective consciousness is how we birthed a nation by throwing off the fetters of the mighty—and superior—British Empire. Our movies and our legends abound with heroes and heroines who overcame great odds. This American romance with the underdog extends to all arenas of life and includes its villains as well as its heroes. Even gangsters have become glamorized

31

as Hollywood romanticizes the lives of people like Pretty Boy Floyd and Scarface Al Capone.

I can still remember my father's disgust at the near glorification of Bonnie and Clyde. "They were vicious and cold-blooded murderers," was his angry comment. He couldn't understand the country's fascination with contemporaries of his who, in his own generation's estimation, were little more than cruel and cold sociopaths.

Yet what may be a vicarious fascination for the majority of folks on the outside is a lived-out reality for many young people in prison today. Often, long before they hit prison, their lives have clashed with a variety of authority figures. It usually begins at home where the young person finds himself at odds with one or both of his parents. It will then extend to other authorities such as schoolteachers, stepparents, or foster parents. Brushes with the legal system begin to appear, court appearances are made, and occasional lockups ensue. All these encounters have one thing in common: the lone individual has come into conflict with those who have the power.

This common denominator creates the mentality that a person is at war—a great one-sided war. The individual is pitted against "the system." The powers that be (whether they are fathers or police, schoolteachers, or correctional staff) are the enemy. The unempowered person is convinced that those in power "don't understand." He or she is forced to go it alone.

When I was engaged in stealing, I never stole from an individual. I always stole from businesses. These establishments, I believed, could "afford it." They were nameless, faceless. They probably treated their employees unfairly anyway; they deserved to be robbed. I saw myself as a modern Robin Hood, robbing from the rich (them) to give to the poor (me). Every break-in became an adventure—an adrenaline rush fueled by the potential danger. On a few occasions, I found myself in situations that could have ended my life, but still there was an excitement to it all. It was me against the system. As long as I wasn't caught, I was winning. I was a commando entering enemy territory under dark of night, carrying off a daring raid and escaping once again.

The same mentality prevailed when I joined the Navy. (A great mistake given my immaturity and my problem with anger and authority!) I was court-martialed seven times in three and one-half years, six times for going AWOL and once for assaulting an officer with a frying pan. I had joined the service only because one disastrous semester at a Chicago-area college convinced me that continuing education was the furthest thing from my mind. I also reasoned that joining the military would lessen the blow when my father beheld the dismal row of "F's" descending neatly down the report card. I announced—as I passed him that semester's grades—that college was not for me. I would join the service instead!

Ironically, it did serve to soften the blow. He was probably thinking, *That's just what this kid needs, a good dose of the service!* I promptly enlisted as soon as I turned eighteen. (I chose the Navy because my father was a career man in the Air Force, and I wanted no possibility of running into him while I was on assignment.)

What I didn't realize at the time was that if I thought a stint in the military was to be my deliverance, it was already too late. The young man who signed the contract to join the service was already full of anger—and his anger was directed at authority. The enlistment turned out to be a major disaster. With several trips to the brig to my credit, I made three escape attempts. One was successful; two were not. At one point, I pulled a Bonnie and Clyde of sorts. On one of my AWOLs, I returned to Chicago, took my girlfriend and her parent's car, and we drove all over the country. I would burglarize to keep us going financially, but after three months we turned ourselves in.

This escapade with my girlfriend is important to note. It also fits the pattern of many within the outlaw culture. If their battle against the world can be fought with their sweetheart at their side, the life of the misunderstood rebel is given an even greater measure of significance. Now it is the two of them against the world.

Today I feel sorry for parents who are trying to break up an unhealthy relationship in which they see their son or daughter involved. They most likely will find themselves in the impossible situation of being "the establishment." Everything they do or say is received as being broadcast through the tyrannical bullhorn of *them*. The frantic parents have themselves become *the system*. They don't "understand." The more they try to intervene with the young couple, the more it drives the lovers together. "Your parents hate me," says the outlaw. "But I love you," says the sweetheart. They are united. They are in love. No one "understands how much" they love each other. The system only wants to tear them apart. Now they are both outlaws. They give support and solace to each other in the romantic notion that their love will win out over these impossible odds. The underdogs will be victorious. Their struggle becomes the grand struggle against oppression and tyranny. It is, after all, the American way.

Then the young man finds himself in prison. And what is prison but a big collection of loners, individualists, and rebels? A virtual Sherwood Forest with walls, teeming with the misguided Robin Hoods of our society.

The brotherhood of criminals is a romantic myth. When you put outlaws together in a single institution, they do what they have to do to get by. Survival requires it. Prison is, of course, the ultimate confrontation with authority, and they do share that reality in common. Inmates are totally under the thumb of "the man," so their mutual oppression is the common link. (When the collective oppression becomes too severe, there can even be enough unity to riot.[2]) But the common bond of a shared experience is very different than saying that they feel a universal brotherhood with one another.

Although the fanciful notion of a universal brotherhood among criminals is not reality, neither is it true that the average newcomer to the prison experience will attempt to isolate himself from the other inmates. Most, in fact, will eventually gravitate toward a specific "group" in which they find social identity and safety. Over time, each resident will usually have two or three close friends that he or she knows well and may even trust. The problem is that each person lives side by side with hundreds of others, sometimes thousands. He may have many acquaintances—many "friends" on the socially interactive scale—but in the end, who among them is really his friend? He is fully aware that behind some of these smiles are possible enemies or hearts that could quickly switch allegiances for any number of reasons.

In spite of these tenuous relationships, prison enhances the loner mentality. Now it not only *looks* like the world is winning; deep down inside it *feels* like the world is winning. Now it really *is* the loner against the world. Ultimately, the prison experience forces men and women to hunker down deeper into the foxhole of their lives to find the strength to survive. They have to find refuge and resources within themselves. Cut off from any emotional support they may have had on the streets, they find themselves slipping more and more into the ultimate realization that they truly are alone. As for the support of those former emotional attachments, they must choose either not to think about it or try to lose themselves in a private world of fantasy, dreams, and poetry.

This human ability to dig deep down inside oneself for survival, to call on resources that were never before needed but now are desperately so, is a part of the human drive to survive. In certain settings it makes heroes. POWs who survive their ordeals come home with inspiring tales of human endurance and will power that was exercised under the cruelest and most hopeless of situations. We applaud the lost mountain climber who survives his ordeal or the flood victim who is rescued because she hung on under impossible circumstances.

As attractive as this "hero quality" might be, there is a darker, more sinister side to this power of the flesh to survive. Under the wrong conditions, it succeeds in hardening the heart even further. For example, the DOC[3] has tried certain programs that are based on the idea that fear is a great motivator. Although its initial intent may have been constructive, such programs inevitably force the participants to depend entirely upon themselves for survival. What has become known as "shock incarceration" is widely used throughout most of the states. These "shock programs" (or "boot camps," as they are sometimes called), are usually one of a judge's options in dealing with first-time offenders.

If the charge is serious enough to warrant a prison sentence, and if the person facing the bench has never been incarcerated in a state institution before, some judges have the option of sentencing them to a shock program.

These sentences are usually shorter than the average amount of prison time given for the crime committed, but the judge can offer it to a young offender as an alternative (and hopefully a deterrent), to going to the state prison. The idea is that the young defendant will view the shorter sentence with more relish and will also see it as a way to avoid going "upstate." They are also informed that the shock program will be no picnic. It will be run much like a military boot camp, and their lives will probably be a living nightmare for three months or so.[4] Although some states tout wonderful statistics regarding these programs, I believe the jury is still out on most of them. Biblically, I think they all contain a fatal flaw. "Fear of man will prove to be a snare" (Prov. 29:25a).

When I was serving military time in various brigs around the country or aboard ship, I was unaware that I was experiencing earlier versions of the "shock program." Given the choice, I would rather do a year in a state institution than six months in a brig. The Marines do not intend that the experience be a pleasant one for those who wind up there, and in this they succeed. But the experience also succeeds in arousing the hero quality's darker side, that two-headed steed found in the power of the flesh. It forced me to dig deep down inside myself for strength. Survival became the name of the game. "They weren't going to break me," I resolved to myself. I would never let the system bend me to its will. The power of the flesh to survive, then, is at one time a wonderful resource in difficult circumstances but at other times, a terrible thing to reinforce.

On military bases, boot camps provide a sense of team as well as the discipline necessary to lay the foundation for good soldiers. But that's where it belongs—on military parade grounds—not in the criminal justice system unless, of course, it is admitted that the primary goal is to punish. But I think it encroaches upon the realm of naiveté to call it a deterrent. Prison boot camps *are* training soldiers—the kind that already feel they are at war. What we *are* succeeding in doing is making them tougher. We are unwittingly reinforcing the outlaw mentality and feeding the psyche of the *loner*.

What happens to those young men who have "graduated" from the shock program if they commit another crime and are then sent to the state prison?[5] My own observation has been that they tend to adjust to prison life much more easily than those who are entering the institution for the first time—not merely in terms of experience (shock *was* an incarceration, although brief) but in terms of attitude. They are cockier and less threatened by their new environment. And I know what they are thinking. They have made the satisfying discovery that compared to the treatment they received at the shock program, prison is a piece of cake! Maybe a little longer time to do but, hey, so what!

Their experience in the fear-based program of shock incarceration has actually prepared them to be a tougher inmate than the average newcomer might normally have been. Unwittingly, the states have set up boot camps that are producing a tougher breed of convict, at a younger age, than they would have otherwise been dealing with—all at the taxpayer's expense.

Some secular programs bring teenagers (who are beginning to get into trouble) into the prisons on a scripted tour to meet officers and inmates. At one particular jail I am involved in, I often arrive at the time such a group is being guided through the facility. I watch as the specially selected convicts they encounter tell them how bad prison is and perhaps even menacingly suggest what will happen to them should they ever be sentenced there. I listen as the officer goes through his spiel. "See those water pipes above you?" he says as he points upward with the suspenseful sweep of an experienced teller of ghost stories, "One guy hung himself from those pipes as soon as he arrived here. See over there? That's 'the Hole.'" And on it goes.

I watch the kids. They are polite for the most part, but some look decidedly bored. If gum were allowed, the girls appear as though they would be popping bubbles any moment. The guys cast half-smiles at one another that seem to say, "Wow, this is scary!" Of course, the guards and the inmates notice this as well, which only makes them beef up their threatening statements. The horror stories increase, the threats become more jaded, and the teens adjust with the appropriate responses, trying their best to cooperate.

My point is not to discredit these programs. At least well-meaning people are trying to do *something*. And to intimate that these programs have few successes would be false. These tactics do work on some young people—the wiser ones who can figure out that prison is still no place to spend your life. But the topic of this chapter is specifically dealing with the mentality of a sub-culture whose mind-set is the self-reliant loner. The prison experience reinforces that the only one who will be looking out for Number One *is* Number One. It strengthens the self's ability to "make it." Its backdrop is a continuous mural that seems to say, "It really *is* me against the world." And if this is their predominant worldview, then it is important to be aware of it from the standpoint of those who are attempting to enter that world to provide assistance.

From a spiritual standpoint the challenge becomes obvious. How to help those who have trained themselves—and in some cases *been* trained—to dig down deep in order to survive by the sheer strength of their human wills? How do we help them come to the realization that they can turn their lives and their dependence over to an unseen God? And further, that they *must*?

If this were a challenge that could be accomplished through mere human efforts, I would have little hope. The Lone Ranger/Robin Hood mentality is too deeply ingrained in many of those we hope to reach. These self-styled warriors project a shield that proclaims: "I need nothing and no one." They have battled against great odds their whole lives, and it has now become a part of who they are. They will fight—and still believe they will ultimately win. This self-reliance may partly explain why some of them view "the Christian thing" as a crutch. "It's for weaklings," they say.

But if one can recognize that his or her leg is broken, then there is no shame in reaching for a crutch. Christians, thankfully, are *not* involved in a merely human effort. The volunteer can trust that God continues to be in the business of healing broken lives. They can be assured that the Holy Spirit is still at work, bringing lost rebels to the end of themselves. The prodigal son "came to his senses" in a pigpen (Luke 15:17). The demon-possessed man came to his "right mind" in a graveyard (Luke 8:35). Prison is a great place for the Lord Jesus Christ to help captive men and women realize that they have no power to direct their lives. It is better to enter a house of mourning, Ecclesiastes tells us, than a house of feasting (Eccles. 7:2). Sometimes it is better for our spiritual condition to go to a prison than a party.

Spirit-led volunteers will be alert to what the Spirit is doing. They are more apt to be in tune with the workings of grace in a person's life and to recognize the fingerprints of God. They can identify the handiwork of a sovereign Father, even when the one with whom they are speaking does not.

Help inmates see that it is possible they have come to this place in order to realize their need for God and that there is a source of strength that comes from beyond themselves. Pray for God to soften those old defenses and for the individual to receive the grace of trust. Apart from that grace, Robin Hood still thinks he can defeat the Sheriff of Nottingham (or even Friar Tuck, for that matter). But the stubborn, pursuing love of God will not be denied. The Christian volunteer is an arrow of that love, sent to let these wounded sheep know that it isn't necessary to go it alone in this world.

Remind them that you stand in front of their cell as a visible evidence of God's love.

5

All Alone Am I

THE LONELINESS THAT PERMEATES the air of those cement canyons we call prisons is not a loneliness that is visible to the naked eye. But it is there nonetheless. Every man and woman attempts to keep it hidden, buried behind a hundred facades. It is too painful. You can't let it out. You can never take the chance of having that pain tossed out on the floor like dirty laundry for everyone else to see. Never! Better to die a thousand deaths than to have that sanctuary invaded. Even a callous shakedown[1] that rips at all your private correspondence and tosses letters and pictures out on the tier can only catch traces of it, but they can never find it. It's hidden too well. The loneliness is yours alone. You can't share it. It's an inner sanctum too holy ever to let the pagan feet of the undefiled trespass it. But everyone experiences it.

Loneliness is a cold wind that blows in the corridors of an inmate's life. Sometimes it seems to howl, and at other times it just whispers, but it never entirely goes away. It makes the heart feel like a hollow dungeon, occupied by a single prisoner. Even the keepers do not venture down there. Its walls echo with only the beating of the occupant's heart.

The dull ache that loneliness creates is often the major driver behind the distractions and the substitutions, such as letter-writing and poetry, TV shows and books, art and hobbies. Distractions may lift one out of the dungeon, but it is only a temporary respite at best. The hollowness of the stone cellar is never too far away. The scratchings and carvings of former tenants inscribed on the walls of their cells are like the old, rusty chains that hang from the walls of the Bastille—reminders that other poor souls have shared the same fate.

Strangely, there is some comfort in those chains. Intense loneliness will seek even ghosts for company. I can recall feeling a
sort of kindred spirit with the former, faceless tenants of my cell,
even though they had long since disappeared. But this feeling
usually dissolved into an even greater sense of loneliness as I
came to grips with the fact that they were gone and I was still
there. It didn't even matter that most of them had long since
died. "Gone," in prison, means *free*.

And because everyone is dealing with his or her own feelings,
protecting his or her own sanctuaries, another specter soon rises
out of the dust like Samuel before Saul. It is the stark reality that
nobody really cares. Not really. How can they? The name of the
game is survival. Everyone has to look out for Number One. You
are—in spite of the hundreds of souls around you—desperately
alone.

This particular pain is almost tangible at times. It can arrive
slowly, crushing the heart in a vise and squeezing it like a grape.
It feels like the soul is bleeding, that something has departed and
what remains is slowly dying. At other times it is like a sudden
blast, forcing the tormented soul to hug the body and rub the
arms as though the temperature had plummeted to zero. Most of
the time it is a dull ache that never quite goes away. The nights
are the worst. At least during the day you can be busy. Perhaps
something will happen today to ease the pain. "Maybe it will go
away," hopes the heart, but then a sweeping sense of hopelessness reminds the inmates that there is no one. Nothing else. No
one but them.

That's why a letter is more than a letter to someone who is
serving time. It is something real, from someone else beyond
yourself. It means that *you* must be real. After all, that *is* your
name on the envelope, isn't it? I recall an essay that a friend
wrote while serving a term of six or seven years. He entitled it,
"The Waiting Is the Hardest Part." The whole work, several
pages in length, consisted of one day's experience in waiting for
the mail to arrive.

He vividly described the sound of the mail officer's footsteps
on the wooden catwalk as he went cell to cell dropping off those

paper lifelines. He could tell how far away the carrier was and whether or not some men had received a letter or whether they had been passed by. He described the mounting anticipation as he heard the steps approaching his own cell. In the next few seconds he would know whether he would be filled with a gust of exhilaration or plummeted to the painful depths of disappointment. Either way he would have to wait for the next day, and then the process would begin all over again. Every afternoon it would either be the highlight of the day or its biggest letdown. The waiting, as he had entitled his piece, was the hardest part.

Even as I write that paragraph, I am glad for him that his ordeal is over. He has been out of prison for over ten years now, and is married. I ran into him at a Burger King one day, and he had two little girls with him, his daughters. He had a good job and was doing well. But his essay still haunts me because I know it is the experience, in one form or other, of so many others who are still in prison. Letter-writing does play an important part in helping to deal with the loneliness, and concerned Christians can play an important role here. However, I would strongly encourage anyone who is contemplating this service first to contact an established prison ministry for letter-writing guidelines.

Loneliness is not the sole property of inmates. Its shroud is felt by so many on the outside as well. Even many Christians experience it. You can find them in any church. The busyness of our lives is often a curse that keeps us from reaching out to the lonely, but it should not be so. You can see the traces of this solitary pain in the face of the single mother or the guy who never seems to fit in. They are all around us. Sometimes they *are* us.

This shared experience should make us even more sensitive to those in prison. Most of us have experienced loneliness at one time or other. Remembering how we felt might enable us to empathize with their reality. Few will talk much with you about the loneliness, but that's OK. The goal isn't to highlight it; it's to apply the Balm of Gilead to it. We just need to remember that the pain is there. And in spite of the reluctance of inmates to speak directly to the issue, it finds its expression in other ways.

So often, as I have stood at the doors of their cells, the quiet conversation will turn to someone whom they care deeply about on the streets. It can be a parent or a spouse, a sweetheart or a child, but suddenly, the tears will start flowing. Their normally alert defense system has been breached. Not necessarily because I was probing in those particular areas but perhaps because of their perception of my role. They consider the sincere Christian volunteer someone who is "safe." He or she represents God, they reason, and God's people must care. I don't think they are consciously thinking these thoughts at the time, but still, your presence tends to draw these deeper feelings out of them.

I believe that, at such times, it is the presence of Christ's Spirit within you that is doing the ministering. There *is* a compassion being felt. There *is* a desire to bring comfort and healing. You *are* listening, and you do want to know about them—and they sense it. When such times occur, the volunteer can sense that he or she is being used as a vessel of Christ's compassion and a messenger of his grace. It is all his doing, after all. It is *his* grace, *his* compassion, *his* desire to bring healing and comfort. We can take no credit for that, but we can rejoice in the privilege that he has chosen us to be used in this way. And as the conversation continues, the volunteer can often observe that comfort being received by the dear soul in front of him. There is a gratefulness in the tears, a smile that finally breaks through like a sliver of sunlight on a cloudy day. And you know that God has lifted their hearts and that the shadows of loneliness have been dispelled, at least for the present moment. Whether you're writing or visiting, you have become a part of that process. By bringing Christ to them, you are bringing the *answer* to their loneliness. *He* will never leave them or forsake them (Heb. 13:5).

Even if your particular situation in prison ministry doesn't allow for private communication because you are always in a group setting, your presence can still have a great impact. Just being conscious of this hidden pain will make you more effective. It will also keep you from sounding too abstract or distant as well as too judgmental. Your words will become seasoned with grace, and God will more easily bring his comfort through you.

Nor do you have to speak directly to the issue of loneliness in your presentations. Point, rather, to the all-sufficiency of Jesus Christ for *all* situations. The Holy Spirit will direct their hearts to the right application.

As Jesus is lifted up, they will know where their help comes from. Provide them with practical suggestions about how to find their comfort in him. Turn them to the Word, which has given them everything they need for life and godliness (2 Pet. 1:3–4). Give illustrations from your own life. These are always helpful. Prisoners, as most people, love stories. In a group setting you also have the added advantage of perhaps having the testimonies of other inmates available to you.

Loneliness is a part of the fabric of prison life. But if you can combine the awareness of that pain with the compassion of Christ, you will find yourself an effective instrument in the Lord's hands.

6

The Emotion of Anger
and the Role of the Father

"WHY DIDN'T YOU TELL ME this was going on?" the red-faced officer shouted at me as he barged into the cell where the two men were fighting. He immediately broke up the fracas and had both men sent to Punitive[1] to await further action. As a volunteer, I had been standing only a few yards away when the commotion broke out. I was talking with another inmate at his cell door. It had happened abruptly. One minute there was the usual hubbub on the tier and the next there was the unmistakable sounds of crashing, thrashing, and bumping coming from a cell a few doors away. I immediately turned and looked at the guard who was sitting at a desk a few yards farther on. (Unless you are standing directly in front of an inmate's door, you cannot see what is happening inside any given cell. So neither he nor I could see the situation, but we both knew it needed intervention.)

My only responsibility (I felt) was to make sure the officer knew something was wrong, especially since the door of the cell had to be opened from a control panel. Our mutual eye contact verified that we were both hearing the same threatening sounds. His angry remark to me as he burst into the cell was generated by his own adrenaline. As I later thought over the incident, there was really nothing else I could have done. I had known the officer for many years, and we later smoothed things out.

The fight between inmates, however, was not atypical. Tempers flare in prison—it's just a way of life. Confrontations often occur, even between good friends. When my codefendant and I were awaiting trial in the county jail, we had been assigned the same

45

cell. As best friends, we had hung out together virtually every day on the streets. We committed the same crime together, were arrested together, and were even given the same sentence. But I can still recall one particular time that we both got so mad at each other over a card game that it nearly escalated into a physical fight. It didn't—but it was proof that our nerves were on edge and that tensions were high.

A couple of seasons ago in a local jail where I hold a Bible study there was a riot in an entire dayroom over the outcome of the NCAA basketball championships. The room had to be locked down, and the riot squad, complete with mace and shields, had to be called in.

The only time I have ever been personally assaulted in prison was when, at Florida State Prison, I tried to break up a fight in the choir. Charles Spurgeon is credited with saying that "when the devil fell out of heaven, he landed in the choir." If this is true in some of our churches, I certainly found it to be true on that particular day in prison! I was in charge of the midweek rehearsal when two men suddenly began hitting each other. When I went over to break it up, one of them missed his opponent and struck me squarely on the cheek instead. Down I went between the folding chairs, and there I decided to stay. Proverbs 26:17 immediately came to my mind: "Like one who seizes a dog by the ears is a passer-by who meddles in a quarrel not his own."

The men never even knew they had hit me. Big James, the chaplain's clerk, came over and broke up the fight by separating the two combatants. James never tolerates any disrespect for "the Lord's house," and no one was ever foolish enough to disrespect Big James, no matter *how* angry they were.

I could give example after example of angry confrontations, fights, and assaults with a variety of prison-style weapons. Sadly, some of these examples had tragic consequences. If there is a normative emotion behind the walls, it is anger.

The vast majority of people in prison struggle with problems of anger. It includes both men and women and covers the scope of most crimes. The late Gerry Hindemuth was chaplain of the Bridgewater State Hospital for the criminally insane in

Massachusetts for over three decades. He also ministered regularly among the state's most dangerous sexual offenders. I once heard him make the statement that in over thirty years of ministry, he "never met a sexual offender who wasn't angry."

Although anger is a serious issue for those sitting behind the walls of our prisons and jails, it is by no means restricted to them. It is a viable candidate for the predominant emotion of our own culture as well. Sometimes it seems like the whole world is struggling with anger in one form or another. If you're at home, they call it "domestic violence." If you are on the highways, they call it "road rage." If you internalize it, they call it depression. No one escapes rejection; everyone is exposed to it in some form—and to some degree—many times throughout their lives. That some are able to handle it more constructively is a cause to be thankful rather than a cause to be boastful.

Dr. Henry Brandt, well-known Christian counselor and speaker, says that whenever a potential client comes to see him, the first question he usually asks is: "OK, who are you mad at?" Invariably, he has concluded that no matter what his patients thought the issue was, the emotion of anger was usually at the root of their problem.

Dr. C. R. Solomon of GFI Ministries in Denver, Colorado, identifies rejection as the source of most anger problems. He believes that rejection causes anger, which in turn creates more rejection. He says that the underlying principle is: "You reject me and I'll reject you!" My wife and I sat under his teachings when we were with Campus Crusade for Christ. I have to admit that when it comes to my own personal experience, in prison ministry in particular, his observations have definitely proven to be true. Nor does it take too long, in most conversations with inmates, to discover the source of their anger. The pages of their lives are often marked with rejection and abuse in one form or another.

After more than a quarter century in prison ministry, I have concluded that the lion's share of the blame for most of this rejection lies squarely at the feet of the fathers. I admit that I have never done a professional or clinical study on this, but I offer the statement simply as the result of my own personal, empirical observation. No matter what else may have befallen most inmates in the course of their lives, the initial pattern of their anger can usually be traced back to some problem in their relationship with their fathers. I believe this is true of female inmates as well.

Although many are aware of this connection, I meet many people in prison who do not realize their fathers may be the source of their rejection and subsequent pattern of anger. C. R. Solomon does a good job in enumerating the many types of overt and covert rejection in his book, *The Ins and Out of Rejection.* The "absentee father" is just one of his many examples. This particular individual may be a good dad in many other aspects of fatherhood, but his time away from home can send the message to a toddler that dad is gone because he doesn't want to be at home—where the child lives.

The "workaholic parent" can be an absentee parent. Ironically, many Christians fall into this category as well. Not only are they busy at their regular jobs, but "church" activities also threaten to make orphans of their children. Such youngsters can grow up subconsciously resenting the church for taking their parents' time away from them. Ministers and full-time church workers are especially vulnerable to this problem.

Another example of covert rejection is the parent who engages the child in criminal activities. Among women this can include incest, prostitution, or other forms of sexual abuse.[2] Many inmates whom I have talked with can remember being dragged from bar to bar while their parents engaged in some form of criminal activity. Many a woman in prison can tell the story of how their drug-addicted parent sold them for sex as children. The stories are as tragic as they are innumerable. When I was on the board of Straight Ahead Ministries (SAM),[3] part of my responsibilities included interviewing potential candidates for the residential home in Westboro, Massachusetts, where the kids could be sent upon their release from the juvenile centers. Another staff person and I did most of the interviews.

On one occasion, Carol Utter[4] and I met with a young lady of sixteen who was incarcerated in a youth facility in

Massachusetts. As she matter-of-factly told her story to us, I was dumbfounded by what I was hearing. She had been raped from the ages of four to six by a family member. When DSS[5] found out about it, she was removed from the home and placed in foster care. In this particular home, she was raped until the age of twelve by an older foster boy. Then she ran away with an older man in his thirties. Captured and placed in another home, she again ran away with the same fellow and had since been apprehended again and placed in DYS.[6] It was at this point of her incarceration that we interviewed her for possible placement in a SAM home for girls.

The girl was attractive, polite, and almost shy in her interactions. When Carol went over the rules of the house that future residents were expected to keep, she had no problem with any of them until the "no sex" rule was mentioned. The look that came over her face was not one of defiance but of absolute unbelief. "Why?" she asked, raising her eyebrows in surprise.

You might as well have told her that not eating candy bars on Thursdays was one of the rules. It just didn't make any sense to her. She had been taught, from the earliest ages imaginable, that fornication was a normal part of life. It began to dawn on me that, with such a past, how could she think any differently? She was accepted into the home but didn't last. She ran away within a couple of weeks, and we never heard what happened to her. We could only guess that her future was going to be a continuation of her disastrous past. She was already being treated for a sexually transmitted disease while in DYS.

The results can be equally devastating for young boys who have been encouraged into sinful activity by a parent. I had a friend in Florida State Prison who had been condemned to die in the electric chair, but he later had his sentence commuted to life. Originally from New York City, he was always telling me about how wonderful his dad was. One day, he related the story about how his father taught him the art of robbing concession stands in Central Park when he was a boy. He was actually proud of his dad for teaching him this skill of armed robbery!

He went on to a life of crime and was eventually arrested for murder. He didn't realize that his underlying anger was actually directed at the man he admired most—and from whom he sought admiration in return. But this type of rejection is subtle because it sends the veiled message, "I don't care what happens to you. Even if you go to jail." It remains hidden because the rejected person doesn't see it. I never told him what I suspected, and as far as I know, his dad never came to visit him.

The "sin of the fathers" (see Exod. 20:5; 34:7; Num. 14:18; Deut. 5:9) is still taking a toll upon the children, at least in terms of life's consequences. One doesn't have to dig too far into the history of most men in prison to discover that something was wrong in the relationship with their father. I used to think that if it was the fathers who messed up the male inmates, then it must have been the mothers who messed up the women. I have since discovered that this is not true. In most cases, the father is still the culprit. Something was amiss in that crucial relationship.

I can still remember my first attempt at running away from home. I had departed for the woods near our house and had spent the entire day hiding in the security of the trees. By supper time, bored and hungry, I slipped back to the house and positioned myself under the living room window. Convinced that my parents would surely be missing me by now, I wanted to hear how distressed they were by my absence. But from the sounds of the unconcerned chatter coming through the open window, it was clear that they hadn't even noticed I was gone. Hungrier than I was defeated, I trudged inside for supper. I never let them know that their eight-year-old boy had "nearly" run away.

But eight-year-olds grow up. I eventually did run away nine years later at the age of seventeen. This excursion was also short-lived. My friend Gary and I were picked up for vagrancy three days later in Elkhart, Indiana, and spent the weekend at the local jail. A year later I joined the navy and "ran away" legally.

My father was an angry man. He was frequently verbally abusive, yelling obscenities or demeaning phrases at the top of his lungs. His explosive temper often resulted in corporal punishment with the leather belt that he would strip from his waist or, on occasion, with the use of his fists. The long and short of it was that *I* got mad. Although this relationship fueled a desire within me to leave home, I found myself in the same paradoxical situation that many others have found themselves in. While I wanted to get away from him, I desperately needed his approval at the same time.

But I was never able to please my father. The measuring stick of acceptance seemed to be always just beyond my reach. The belt, the anger, and the constant disapproval of who and what I was seemed to be the major weave in the fabric of my days at home. I hated it. Ironically, the one sphere in which I could occasionally please him was in the area of toughness. My father esteemed this trait. He had taught his three boys never to back down from a fight, no matter what the odds. For a kid with a rapidly developing anger problem, I began to find many opportunities *outside* the house to express it.

There were times when fights were a weekly part of my life, and I would seldom lose. This wasn't because I was particularly skilled but because I was unconquerably angry. The emotion I could never fully release at home found unbridled expression outside of it. I could easily be set off by an idle comment, a questionable look, or a perceived challenge of any sort. If these confrontations escalated into a physical fight, my rage would not permit me to quit until the other fellow was totally beaten.

On arriving home after one of the few fights I ever lost, I can remember sitting at the dinner table with a classic purple ring around one of my eyes. I still recall the rare beam of approval being reflected back from my father's eyes as I ate supper. He was proud of me! That I lost the fight didn't matter to him, as long as I hadn't backed down. Yet all along a young man was being trained in the way he should go.

I was to have many more fights after leaving the home of my parents, but the thought of losing one never occurred to me. I would become so angry that physically destroying my opponent was the only possible outcome, no matter how big or small they were. Size matters only to someone who is thinking rationally, but rage is like an emotional forest fire that burns out of control.

It doesn't think before acting. "Like a city whose walls are broken down is a man who lacks self-control" (Prov. 25:28).

What began as an issue of acceptance with my father grew into an ingrained hostility toward all authority. For all the fireworks of the rebellious years following my exit from home, I was totally unconscious of the fact that there was any connection between the initial anger I felt toward my father and the anger that I was transferring to every authority that entered my life from then on. And I can see that same obliviousness in the lives of so many of the young—and not so young—inmates I meet today. They don't make the connection.

In retrospect, I continued a pattern of "running away" long after I left home. Even in my decision to join the service, I think there was still an element of hoping to win my father's approval before I left. Although it was definitely a diversionary tactic to soften the blow for the dismal report card, I'm also sure my decision contained still another attempt at winning a military man's blessing. But my conscious purpose at the time was predominantly one of escape. I was finally to be out of the house! But I had underestimated my own emotional immaturity and the depths to which my hostility toward authority had grown.

I did not fare any better in civilian life. By the time I was thirty years old, I had held—and lost—over thirty different jobs. I would work one or two months, occasionally longer, but would soon come into conflict with my employer or supervisor. My temper would flare up over some perceived injustice, and I would rant and rave, curse and threaten, and then abruptly quit in a huff. If I could somehow sabotage the work before I departed or storm out at some crucial time for the company, all the better. I regularly stole items from my employers, not so much because I wanted or needed them but because it was another way of getting back. I was only fired twice in those thirty-plus jobs, once for coming to work intoxicated and the other for beating up a fellow employee. All the other times I quit. I was blind to the fact that this was just another way of running away from authority.

I repeated the pattern of restlessness geographically, moving again and again. From one apartment to another. One state to another. One coast to another. At the time, I didn't see it as a pattern. To me, I was relentlessly looking for happiness. I knew it had to be out there somewhere. If it wasn't where my body was currently living (which it never was), it must be around the next bend or in the next situation. I wasn't able to comprehend that the problem was internal. I was carrying the beast around with me.

It was the same in my relationships. I bounced from one girl to another. As soon as I would win a girl's heart, I quickly lost interest and began to seek another's love. I didn't do this on a conscious level; I always thought I was being sincere. The real problem was that I had a Grand Canyon-sized need in my heart and didn't know I couldn't fill it. I needed constant affirmation and the feeling of winning someone's love was food for the beast. But the beast was always hungry. "But the wicked are like the tossing sea, which cannot rest, whose waves cast up mire and mud. 'There is no peace,' says my God, 'for the wicked'" (Isa. 57:20–21).

A pastor showed me that verse after listening to my testimony not long after I had become a Christian. I never forgot it. It described me to a T. That's exactly who I was. Restless, wicked, without hope, churning up nothing but muck and mire in my life and forcing everyone whom I came into contact with to swim in it as well.

It's important to me that the reader clearly understands that I do not blame my father for any of the consequences of my life or even for the poor dynamic we shared for most of my growing-up years. He was also a product of his own upbringing; and without Christ there is no illumination, no ability or *power* to break the cycle of rejection and anger. The sin of our first father, Adam, just keeps being passed down from one generation to another. "Therefore, just as sin entered the world through one man, and death through sin, and in this way death came to all men, because all sinned" (Rom. 5:12).

Only in the family line of the "Second Man" is there a change in the product. We need to be reborn into another family. "So it is written: 'The first man Adam became a living being; the last Adam, a life-giving spirit. The spiritual did not come first, but the natural, and after that the spiritual. The first man was of the dust of the earth, the second man from heaven. As was the earthly man, so are those who are of the earth; and as is the man from heaven, so also are those who are of heaven. And just as we have borne the likeness of the earthly man, so shall we bear the likeness of the man from heaven'" (1 Cor. 15:45–49).

I can honestly say that from the time the Lord Jesus Christ came into my life in that spring of 1975, I have never experienced another day of restlessness. The old dictator of anger that so dominated and ruled my life has been dethroned. He echoes in the hallways of my flesh from time to time, but he no longer rules. The law of the spirit of life in Christ Jesus has set me free from the law of sin and death (see Rom. 8:2). And best of all, I've come home. My real Dad had been waiting for his prodigal son the whole time, never ceasing to stand and watch at the road that his boy had run away on. I believe he found my earthly dad on it, too.

My father died four years after my heavenly Father rescued me. And God extended much grace to us during that time. A lot of healing between my father and me occurred during those four years. I knew he had come to regret a lot of what had transpired between us. In spite of all that had happened, I realized I loved my father. I was able to forgive him, and I know that, in his own way, he extended that forgiveness to me as well. I also felt, in that last year of his life, that he understood the gospel and, again in his own way, had reconciled with Christ. I was even blessed with the grace of being able to give a salvation message at his funeral. Later, at the graveside, his only brother came up to me and thanked me for my words. With tears in his eyes, he said, "For the first time, I really understand." He also died shortly after.

What had become especially meaningful for me was that as my wife and I began to raise our support to go into full-time prison ministry, my father was excited about it. In fact, he and my mother began to contribute toward our monthly support. The Lord had brought everything together in such a way that I now had that which had eluded me all my life—my earthly father's approval. In this, I was greatly blessed. Not many people in prison have ever found closure with their fathers. And yet they need the same thing. You will not be in prison ministry very long before you realize that most of the men have unresolved issues of hurt, rejection, and anger that often have their roots in their early relationship with their fathers.

Although many men and women in prison experienced physical, verbal, and emotional abuse at the hands of their fathers, a large number of them never even knew their dads. Some fathers abandoned the home so early that the children hardly remember them. Others, while present in the home, were absent emotionally, for a variety of reasons. Children of an alcoholic parent have their own set of scars. Stepfathers and foster fathers can be a source of other alienating traits and experiences.

Why is it that I cannot ever remember getting a request for a Father's Day card when I've been on the tiers? I've given out bunches of Mother's Day cards over the years, but I do not recall ever passing out a single Father's Day card. I am not saying that all inmates have had serious problems with their fathers, but I believe that most of them suffer some form of "father deficiency" in their lives. Some, like the friend I mentioned in Florida State Prison, aren't even aware of the influence their fathers still exert. He couldn't connect his dad's early example of knocking off concession stands with the fact that he wound up on death row. Others, like Frank (a man I met in Walpole's infamous "Ten Block"), are fully aware. He waited patiently for hours on the roof of his family's garage until his dad came home from work one evening. Then he carefully pulled the trigger of his father's rifle and shot him dead in the driveway.

I'm convinced that the only lasting remedy for this type of anger is a total transformation through the power of the Holy Spirit. Although I believe it is possible that non-Christians can eventually bring their anger under control, I have personally seen little evidence of it. Only by becoming a totally new person can the *source* of the anger be thoroughly rooted out. Only in Jesus Christ is the kind of *forgiveness* that is required for permanent and lasting release able to take place. I have long since forgiven my dad. And I was able to tell him before he died that I was sorry for all the damage *I* had caused in our relationship. I was not an easy kid—not by any stretch of the imagination. Jesus accomplished the miracle by putting to death the old person who was a slave to that anger. The old me died at the cross, and God made something totally new when he revealed his Son to my heart. It's no wonder that 2 Corinthians 5:17 remains a universally favorite verse among prison inmates. "Therefore, if anyone is in Christ, he is a new creation; the old has gone, the new has come!"

Christians have a message to tell in the *manner* in which they tell the message. There is a peace about them. When an inmate asks me how I was able to bring my anger under control, I know he is asking the question for himself as well. My response is always the same: Jesus Christ broke the hold for me.

I also let them know that it wasn't an overnight process; I had been dominated by that emotion for most of my life. But God has taken off the shackles by paying the debt that sin and death demanded (see Rom. 8:1–4), and I was *really* set free, not just in theory. Nor was it the result of my own self-will. Unlike the "Little Train That Could," I was not huffing and puffing up the hill under my own steam saying, "I think I can. I think I can." No! Jesus really broke the power—just as the power in his death and resurrection is able to break *any* bondage to the sins of our old lives. It's a matter of taking him at his word and learning how to walk "in newness of life."

When I first began to do prison ministry in the late 1970s, I was more like a big brother to most of the inmates I encountered. I was about the same age, or just a few years older. Now, in my mid-fifties, I have come to realize something that is extremely important for this phase of ministry. I have entered what I call the "father stage." I have become acutely aware that for those with whom I have developed some degree of relationship, there is often a subconscious transfer of identity going on in their perception of me. It is not that they think of me as their father but, rather, that the manner in which I relate to them carries subconscious overtones of that relationship in their minds.

I have witnessed how a simple word of encouragement or affirmation from me can have a noticeable impact on them. They will usually beam from ear to ear when they hear a word of "well done" from me for something they have said or accomplished. When that happens, I believe I'm striking dormant chords that a father was meant to strike a long time ago. Music that, for whatever reason, was never played.

So I have become more intentional in my words of encouragement. By the same token, I have noticed that my words of advice, caution, or even correction also tend to be heeded in a more serious way. I have taken this new responsibility to heart and try to be aware of when its dynamics are in play. It's my personal conviction that if volunteers in this "father stage" fully realized what a crucial role they can play in the lives of these young men and women, they could be more effectively used of God to bring a hope and identity—as well as a godly self-esteem—into the lives of those who so desperately need it.

In the delicate role of men in women's prisons, this nurturing esteem can hold true for women inmates as well. But it is critical that the male volunteer in a woman's prison be in touch with his own feelings and motivations. He must be a mature believer who has his heart warmed and examined daily by the Holy Spirit. Such an individual can bring a lot of healing into the life of a young woman whose life has been scarred by unhealthy memories of her father. Ideally, it would be best if such a volunteer were accompanied by his wife in this setting. I'm always grateful when my own wife, Wendy, can accompany me. Most veteran volunteers will agree that it is healthy for those among whom they minister to see examples of Christian marriages. Most inmates have had few healthy models to work from.

Over the years I have known three women who wanted me to give them away at their wedding. One, in particular, still calls me "Dad" and introduces me to others as her father. And to her, I really believe that is who I have become. Released now, she and her husband still stay in touch with Wendy and me. We count these relationships as special gifts from the Lord and one of the many blessings of this particular ministry.

If you are in this "father stage," it isn't anything you can verbalize to inmates, as such, because most aren't even aware that a subtle transfer is being made. I only mention it because, if you have gained that trusted place in their lives, your words may carry more import than you realize. The tongue has the power of life and death says Proverbs 18:21. A word of acceptance and encouragement, or approval and pride, can go to the deepest places of a young man or woman's heart and result in blessing and healing. They can bring hope, significance, and a sense of identity. It means more than I think we will ever know this side of heaven. Just a simple "I believe in you!" can change a person's life forever. "A word aptly spoken is like apples of gold in settings of silver" (Prov. 25:11). "The tongue that brings healing is a tree of life" (Prov. 15:4a).

And when this stage is over, I look forward to the "grandfather stage." When I was a young volunteer at Chino West in California, I can recall how an old man in his seventies used to come in and talk to the guys. "Old John" was the name the inmates had affectionately given him. He had an old, faded tattoo on his forearm that had been applied when he had done time in Sing-Sing back in the forties. The guys used to flock to him. He would just go around the yard, discipling those he could, and preaching the gospel to others. I understand now that he was a father to many of them and for others, a grandfather as well. I do not know how much more time the Lord will give me in this ministry, but I do know that there will never be a stage when I become irrelevant to them. To everything there is a season.

Volunteers are precious in the sight of God. They are physical expressions of his compassion. In a world where so many fathers have abdicated their roles, these "expressions" are sorely needed. Ultimately, we represent Jesus. We bring our heavenly Father's words of hope and forgiveness, the Son's compassion, and the encouragement and comfort of the Holy Spirit. Our task is to enter the lives of inmates with wisdom and compassion and always to be pointing toward the cross. It was at the cross that Jesus died. And for all those who believe in him, it is at the cross that *their* death occurred as well. A death to the old person. And with it, all the slavery to anger's dominance, yea to sin's dominance, has forever ended. Anything that falls short of that message just plain falls short.

It wasn't until I met God through Jesus Christ that I realized that all my early rebellion was not against my earthly father at all. When I threw off my earthly father's authority, I was really rebelling against my heavenly Father. And the rebellion wasn't environmental; it was genetic. We are born rebels. I thank God eternally for the undeserved grace he has given me. It is a freedom that can infect, engage, and touch the next generation of angry young men and women. Jesus alone has that kind of power! In his *Confessions*, Augustine said, "Thou hast made us for Thyself, O God, and our hearts are restless until they find their rest in Thee."

Sleeping with the Enemy

PRISON LIFE requires that some sort of adjustment be made to living with fear. The place seems scary and unpredictable, especially for newcomers. And as our previous chapter just depicted, many of those who live in prison have anger problems. When one considers that a significant percentage of these residents has already demonstrated—just by virtue of being sentenced to this place—that they can hurt people, the possibility of danger seems even higher. Individuals from all walks of life are thrown into this same small fishbowl and are expected to swim around together without so much as a formal introduction. Add to this mixture the volatile combination that (1) they are not happy about being here, and (2) there is no way out, and there exists the makings of an explosive concoction in a very small bottle.

This shroud of fear affects everyone to one degree or another—from inmates, to staff, to volunteers. I am not saying that the threat is a continually conscious thought; it isn't. Adaptation has occurred, and a routine has been settled into, but this adjustment has incorporated dealing with fear. Those who do not adjust find themselves unable to swim out of an ever-increasing maelstrom of paranoia.[1] Officers, for example, report to work each day in an environment of guarded hostility. Inmates must live within it. Volunteers, for their part, are aware that both the inmates and the officers are constantly watching them.

Safety, relatively speaking, is found in these few things:

1. *Numbers.* The basic premise here is that there is strength in numbers. One needs friends. Most inmates will

gravitate toward a group of some kind shortly after they enter the prison.

2. *Routine.* Officers and inmates alike know that there is less tension when everyone understands his or her roles and what is expected. Although inmates complain about tight security measures, most will secretly admit to you that the more secure a prison is, the more secure *they* feel.[2] An inmate also feels a growing measure of confidence when he has been there long enough to know what his own routine is. He is familiar with his cellmates, has a regular job assignment, and has settled into his own place on the social ladder. Life may be boring, but it is relatively secure. This is the normal experience of the average inmate who is doing a fair bit of time.

3. *Power.* This can be broken into five categories: (1) Physical strength (you are big enough). (2) Political strength (you have influence based on some activity or proficiency). (3) Economic strength (you can buy things). (4) Popularity strength (you are well liked or respected, or both). (5) Reputational strength (you are feared because of some past, demonstrable behavior).

Let us examine these a little more closely:

Physical strength means that few people will actually want to challenge you in a confrontation.

Political strength can include such activities as being a jailhouse lawyer with the ability to file legal briefs for other prisoners, or the talent to draw pictures of girlfriends, or of having an "in" with other powerful inmates. It can also include illegal ventures such as having a hand in running gambling or drug activities.

Economic strength means that you have a good flow of money, either in your inmate account or in some other jailhouse currency such as cigarettes or drugs. This keeps you well supplied in canteen items and other amenities that a poorer inmate may not be able to enjoy, placing you in a position to barter these items in exchange for other types of favors.

Popularity strength is one of the most solid commodities. It means that you are well liked for who you are. Your personality keeps friends at a maximum and enemies at a minimum. It can also mean that there is something about you that other inmates respect.

Reputational strength carries a lot of weight in the prison environment. You have already earned your stripes, so to speak, and the respect (or fear in some cases) from other inmates is high. Ironically, disliked inmates can also fall into this category if their behavior has proven so volatile or threatening that others stay away from them. Even crazy inmates are usually left alone because you can't reason with them. They leave no room for bluffing.

All of these things can help to minimize the ever-lurking presence of fear, but the reality is that spontaneous danger can erupt at any moment. The older, wiser prisoner can usually spot the early warning signs of a potentially volatile situation and try to avoid it. Unfortunately, there are other times when trouble just comes to you, and there is little you can do about it and nowhere to run. Someone may take a disliking to you for reasons that have little to do with your ability to correct, or you may get caught in some sort of political crossfire. These, and similar situations, are the kinds of things that even the older inmates know are a part of the culture they live in. That is why I believe that at least the awareness of the old enemy—fear—is never buried too deeply in the consciousness of most inmates. The prison environment is a powder keg occupied by matches that can spark unexpectedly.

The best advice I can give to anyone entering prison, especially for the first time, is to keep a low profile. In other words, stay out of the way. The less acquainted with your name that an officer is, the better. Obey the rules; do not make a fuss. If you are not a problem for them, in most cases they will not be a problem for you.[3] As far as dealing with the other inmates goes, the same rule applies here: do not draw attention to yourself for any reason. Find a few good friends—who are not getting into trouble— and stick with them. Be polite and friendly with the others, but do not get drawn into negative or trouble-making circles. If you are a Christian, by all means make the Christian community your group of choice.

One of the more subtle motivations that fear creates in this particular setting is the obvious need to fit in. If one is accepted, then less antagonism is likely to come one's way. Sometimes, however, this means giving at least tacit approval to situations that one may or may not agree with. For example, a group of inmates in one's living area may decide to do something illegal, like making some jailhouse mash.[4] At this point, *all* the inmates in the unit have become complicit in the action, whether they are directly involved or not. The inmate code requires that they not report it because getting tagged as a rat[5] would be an even worse fate. If the brew is discovered by security, all the inmates in that living quarter are guilty by complicity.

Another example might be an unpopular inmate being singled out for verbal abuse or practical jokes by other inmates. A weak bystander may not agree with the attack (and may even sympathize with the poor victim), but if he says anything about it, the abuse could easily shift toward him. This person finds himself in the uncomfortable position of having to keep silent in order not to draw attention to himself.

The monotonous routine of prison life can also sweep the unwary heart into the prevailing winds of negativity. The shift in attitude is so subtle that inmates are often barely aware that they have become caught up in it. Then suddenly, when a negative incident does occur, they can find themselves participating in the action so easily that, upon later reflection, they are surprised and disappointed in themselves for having done so. Given the environment, it is not surprising that the general atmosphere is one of negativity. Complaints are common, and there is a virtual kaleidoscope of issues to grumble about. Everyday conversations can run the gamut from being boring and mundane, to negative and confrontative.

Different people choose different ways of coping with fear. Some, for example, opt to attack, believing that a good offense is the best defense. One young man that my coworker, Al LaMorey, and I know was seventeen when he came into the adult prison. He was to wind up serving thirteen years. He was a tough kid when he arrived, but now he was in with the big boys. What would he do? He decided early on that he was not going to lie down for anyone, so he became assaultive and aggressive instead. He went on the offensive and was in one fight after another. He would attack anyone, guard or inmate alike; it didn't matter. He made several trips to the hole and served nearly his entire sentence in maximum security. Soon people began to leave him alone, young as he was.

He had learned his role so well that *he* had become the aggressor. Not content to defend himself, he had now become the threat. As he grew older his reputation grew, and few inmates were foolish enough to challenge it.

Others who may not have the wherewithal to be tough may have the ability to use their brains. I have a good friend who is in his sixties and is serving a life sentence. He is an extremely talented writer, well-educated and world-traveled. His acumen and journalistic ability came to the attention of a large newspaper in the state, and his editorial column soon became a regular feature with a wide following. He became something of a nettle for the administration, because he was an astute set of eyes *inside* the prison for a wide audience of readers *outside*. Possessing a keen sense of fairness, however, he wrote about incidents of injustice or hypocrisy wherever he found it. His targets included officials of the DOC, as well as improprieties he discovered among some of his fellow inmates. Although he was occasionally threatened for this, he managed to stay above the storm.

Another inmate I know escaped from prison by forging his parole papers so expertly that he was actually escorted out of the prison by its own officials! This proved to be such an embarrassment to the DOC that when he was finally apprehended, three years later, they kept him confined to a maximum-security cell for several years. What was he doing when they caught him? He had become the editor of a newspaper in Colorado.

Several other alternatives exist for prisoners who wish to minimize the fear factor. Another path one may choose to take is to come under the protection of a tough inmate in return for favors of some kind. This may include keeping the influential prisoner in a regular supply of canteen goodies or, as is often the case, the granting of sexual favors. Outsiders have often been bewildered by this choice. What they fail to comprehend is that sometimes it is not a choice. Threats can be made against weak or unconnected inmates that are essentially offers "that can't be refused," as the well-known quote from *The Godfather* goes. Sometimes these vulnerable people rationalize that it is better to come under the protection of one inmate than to have to deal with many, and so they will agree to the relationship.

Some choose to sign themselves into protective custody. This is known as "taking a PC." However, having made this choice, they can usually never return to the regular population.[6] Protective custody, as its name suggests, is a special unit within the prison designed to protect those inmates who would be in danger in the regular population. It can include informers, juvenile inmates, ex-policemen, court officials, inmates who can't pay their debts, or anyone who, for one reason or other, cannot function safely in the general population. The majority of its inhabitants, however, are usually sexual offenders.

The fear dynamic affects volunteers as well. Usually, when someone visits the prison for the first time, there is a sense of apprehension. This is normal and reasonable. In fact, I would be somewhat suspicious of anyone who *wasn't* initially apprehensive. But this uneasiness usually disappears after the first visit or so. The volunteer then experiences what the ministry is like and discovers that the prisoners were not at all what he expected. After this initial exposure, the volunteer realizes that he *can* do this ministry and his confidence level greatly increases. The image that Hollywood feeds us about the average inmate seldom portrays what prisoners are really like; but unfortunately, this media image is usually all the volunteer has to go on.

Occasionally, inexperienced volunteers can buy into this media portrayal. I once participated in a large evangelistic crusade that came into Florida State Prison while I was serving there as a chaplain under Campus Crusade for Christ. The outreach was being hosted by a well-known southern ministry, and a volunteer rally was held at a large church the evening before the crusade was taken into the prison. One of the leaders addressing the group of some seventy men explained that they would be blitzing the various tiers of the prison with the gospel. He then began to outline some basic expectations and procedures. At one point in his speech, he told the volunteers never to shake hands with an inmate. I stood there dumfounded as he went on to say that this was because some prisoners hide razor blades in their hands!

In all my years of prison ministry, I have never experienced anything even remotely close to that possibility. The shaking of a prisoner's hand is one of the most natural and friendship-oriented actions available to us, and I wholeheartedly endorse it. I don't know which surprised me more—the fact that he said it or that he said it as a *leader* of the ministry. However it came to be, it was spoken through an obvious lack of experience and by someone who probably shouldn't be going into prison at all. He had fallen prey to the media's portrayal of prison life.

But there are more subtle ways in which I see volunteers succumbing to fear's influence. Occasionally I will observe them spending a lot of their time with the "Joe Cools" of the prison, the heavy hitters that are respected by the population at large. In itself, this is not bad; one should minister to all prisoners, including the tough guys. The problem evolves when volunteers begin to spend most of their time with such people and minimize their ministry to the less popular elements of the society, such as those in PC. They could be doing this for two reasons. They may have a subtle prejudice toward those in PC themselves, or they may be afraid of what the tougher inmates would think if they were seen ministering to sexual offenders. The first reason is indefensible as a Christian, and the second is an example of giving way to the fear dynamic.

Another temptation for volunteers is to spend most of their time in the chapel, ministering only to those who attend worship services. They may feel that this is less threatening than being "out there" with the unknown and secular segment of the population. In most cases, volunteers are not allowed to be in other parts of the prison anyway; they are usually restricted to the chapel or some other area designated for religious use. If this is the case, it is a moot point.[7] But I am addressing here those volunteers who do have the option. To be spending most of their time in the chapel, when they *could* be out in the yard or in the cell blocks, suggests another subtle surrender to the demon of fear.

A similar concession to this dragon is observed when a volunteer begins to spend most of his time with the same few people. He feels comfortable with them, and it is natural to want to plug into them. But sometimes the motivation is *because* those relationships are comfortable, and it makes the volunteer's ministry in the jail less intimidating because he is always dealing with known factors. The Lord's servant should examine himself to see if this behavior is simply good discipleship or if it emanates from the fear of moving out into new territory.

Most inmates learn to cope with the fear factor in some way. While aware that trouble can erupt at any time, they have developed an almost "standby alert" status for it. Their body language sometimes reveals this "condition yellow." You can notice it in such things as where they choose to position themselves when they are talking to you. Most will automatically select a place that has the optimum viewing advantage, or where there is nothing behind their backs but a wall. You can observe it in their eyes, which are often darting back and forth throughout your conversation. They unconsciously take in everything that is going on around them, registering every new figure that appears on the scene. Their minds are constantly calculating, sizing, estimating, and assessing, but it has become almost second nature to them. In the concrete jungle, it is mandatory that they know what is going on at all times.

You can imagine how refreshing it is, then, when they can speak to someone who has no other intent but to befriend them in the name of Jesus Christ. They may not understand the spiritual dynamic, and some may think you're a little funny that way. But make no mistake about it—they recognize sincerity when they see it. And it is genuinely appreciated. You are not a threat to them; and this is especially meaningful in a place where the terrain itself is threatening. Most Christian volunteers who come into the prison on a regular schedule are a sight for sore eyes to the average inmate who has gotten to know them. You have a calming effect on the environment just by being there.

Most of all, you represent a sense of peace that Jesus alone can bring them. You have no hidden agenda; you genuinely care for their well-being. And, if the inmate happens to be a brother or sister in Christ, you experience that particular joy of sweet fellowship that is unique to Christians everywhere. You bring with you the reminder that *all* things are under God's control and that everything works together for the good of those who love Him (see Rom. 8:28). You are equipped to turn their focus toward the solid rock and comfort of the Scriptures, from which pour forth a steady stream of encouragement and hope to those who so desperately need it.

The Bible has much to say about gaining and keeping the right perspective regarding fear—in light of who God is. As a volunteer, learn where these passages are. Make note of them, and be ready to set forth their principles in practical and relevant ways for those who live within the prison environment. Always be prepared to proclaim that there is an anchor for the soul, which the world can never provide—the triumphant message of God's unconquerable love and presence.

"What, then, shall we say in response to this? If God is for us, who can be against us?" (Rom. 8:31).

Part II
Perspectives

8

It's a Small World after All

TWO YEARS AFTER MY RELEASE from prison I was permitted to switch my parole from New Hampshire to California, and thus entered what I call my "hippie stage." It was the late sixties.

Finding a small studio apartment in San Francisco, I first took a couple of jobs as a factory employee and then as a cab driver. Since I still had an inherent problem with authority, becoming a "hackie" appealed to me because I basically worked for myself. (A cabdriver has no boss looking directly over his shoulder.)

This period in my life suited me well because, apart from a girl-friend, I socialized little, drove the cab at night, and stayed basically to myself. Having to navigate the rocky reefs of parole and attempting to start over, I felt I needed time to reflect and withdraw. So I seldom left the city. I didn't have a car and didn't feel the need for one. Even though my job was driving a taxi all night, I had to rely on buses or trolleys for my own transportation when I returned my cab to the garage at the end of the shift.

What I discovered about living in a major metropolis was the subtle realization that one never has to leave the city. Ever. All basic requirements for life are available within the confines of a few city blocks. A person can shop, live, work, and spend his leisure time all within a fairly small area. To the city dweller, it seldom occurs to him or her that one's days are being lived out within a very small area (comparatively speaking). Although the city itself is large, a person can live his entire life within its confines and never experience a fraction of all that goes on within it.

Many times when driving my cab, I dropped people off at rock concerts at the Fillmore West or for special shows downtown that

71

I myself had never attended. Years can pass, even a lifetime, and a city dweller may never venture out beyond the city limits. Because the totality of life's needs can be met within this culture, the edge of awareness that life is unfolding *outside* the city tends to become dulled. San Francisco covers a large area but not in comparison to all the beautiful, grape-growing counties surrounding it. New York City is considered a sprawling lion of a world within itself, but it seems caged when viewed next to the endless green beauty that stretches all the way to Canada.

Were it not for the fact that I had parents who lived fifty miles north of San Francisco, in the garden community of Santa Rosa, I could easily have been engulfed by this small-world perspective. The occasional family get-together required me to take a bus across the Golden Gate Bridge into the verdant countryside north of San Francisco. I remember always being mildly surprised at the rolling hills and the spacious views that would meet my eyes as the bus emerged from the tunnel above Sausalito. Only then would it occur to me that I hadn't seen such things for a long time. There was a whole world going on out there that I would somehow *forget* about as I lived my mouse-in-a-maze type of existence in the city. The scenic views would expose me—no, jar me—back to the reality that there was more to life than what I was experiencing.

So it is with the prison culture. The inmate's world has shrunk.

Life, and its most basic needs, is carried out entirely within the confines of a very small area. It is amazing how quickly its inhabitants can unconsciously adapt to the thought that this world is all there is. Their meals, their job assignments, their interests and hobbies, their social structure, their *lives*—all this is lived out in the same small space, with basically the same people, day after day, year after year. The prison volunteer must realize that he or she has entered a culture of deprivation. Because of this deprivation, the lives of the residents will, to a certain degree, be out of balance. Thoreau wrote that most people "live lives of quiet desperation." In the case of prisoners, I would add that they also live lives of quiet *frustration*.

It is difficult for outsiders to relate to this because they go through their daily activities unaware that anything is missing. What they lack can be purchased, charged, saved for, acquired, or pursued in some other way, but not so for the inmate. The mundane experiences that we, in the free world, take for granted become the stuff of dreams for those behind the walls. For example, as visitors drive toward the prison for a rendezvous with their incarcerated loved ones, they are traveling through a gamut of experiences in which the imprisoned individual can no longer participate. If it is summer, the drivers may have their windows rolled down or, if it is too hot, the air-conditioning can regulate the temperature of their cruising cubicle. They are probably not even conscious of the sensation of *riding*.

But consider for a moment the reality of a society that contains no form of travel beyond that of walking. To sit in a vehicle and to experience speed is not possible for the imprisoned soul. To see scenery flashing by in all its multihued variety, to feel the vibration of wheels upon a road, to pass the faces of complete strangers on the sidewalks of different towns—all of these experiences are absent from the inmate's life. To touch trees, ride a bike, fill a gas tank, go to the mall, or stop for an ice-cream cone are all impossible in this context. The sudden urge for a chocolate milk shake or a bag of french fries from McDonald's must remain an elusive dream.

Never to see children prancing down a street, let alone hear them laugh, is surely beyond the boundaries of common experience. Never to interact with people of the opposite sex, apart from a clinical or punitive discourse, must surely twist and challenge the soul. How does one walk the tightrope of that which is natural and normal, apart from that balance? How can one be sure that he is progressing naturally, in terms of interaction with the opposite sex, if that journey cannot be measured? Outsiders see children and other adults in all sorts of contexts and in many different places. These encounters provide the normal balance of interaction for comfortable, progressive development. What if one never has that interaction? Do the men and women on TV portray the standard? Is watching life as a spectator conducive to the development of normative social adjustment? Does a screen with colors and images dancing behind the glass do anything to satisfy the need for personal interaction?[1]

If you want to talk to a friend, you can simply pick up the phone. Not so for inmates. They can pick up the phone perhaps, but only at certain restricted times in which they are allowed to do so, and then only if someone on the other end accepts the collect call. There are no dimes in their pockets, and, in fact, they have not felt a single American coin or dollar bill in their hands since they arrived in prison. They have no cash money and no street clothing. This is a militarylike domain; there is neither civilian clothing nor furloughs to town. One is always confined to barracks, and the scenery of the camp never changes.

I recall actually dreaming once about a cold, quart bottle of Budweiser while I was in prison. Not just imagining it or fantasizing it, but seeing it in my dreams. I can still see the frosty droplets of water condensing on the sides of the amber glass and the clear, transparent pathways they forged as the beads trickled down the sides. I awoke craving a beer. I no longer drink, and haven't for years, but I did then. And what I lacked, I dreamed about.

This small-world syndrome has many ramifications. One is that molehills tend to become mountains. Little things in this little world can become big things with big consequences. Because the average inmate lacks the "bigger picture" perspective that comes from the free person's ability to travel, he or she, like the city dweller, loses the perspective that life is varied. And big. Things the outsider takes for granted—such as changes of scenery, the feel of green grass under the feet, coworkers who are both male and female, the sight of children playing, a shake and fries, and a myriad of other experiences—are missing in this culture of deprivation. But for those few things that *are* within sight, the impact of their reality is magnified.

For example, taking another inmate's seat in the chow hall can be construed as a personal insult.[2] Don't forget that one finds his or her cultural niche in this society based almost entirely upon one's perceived image. What seems a minor disappointment to someone eating at a restaurant on the outside, such as being denied one's favorite seat by the window, can—in the shrink-wrapped world of prison—be taken as a personal challenge to one's reputation. And because this life is lived out in a fishbowl where nearly all interpersonal relationships are constantly observed by others, the slight becomes a challenge of medieval proportions. The confiscated seat becomes a glove-slap in the face, so to speak, by a challenger.

Small grudges can also escalate into feuds. What can begin as a problem between two inmates can affect pre-war alliances that precipitate world wars. Homosexual relationships can easily lead to jealousy, hatred, and murder.[3] An unpaid loan can escalate into violence. The refusal to bend to a strong-arm tactic[4] can force someone to take a PC.[5] We will describe these things in more detail in the next chapter.

The small-world syndrome can also affect the quality of visits. Most incarcerated individuals love receiving a visit but, ironically, can wind up sabotaging these sacred moments themselves. A visit, for all its meaning and joy, is similar to my bus trips north to Santa Rosa. It breaks in upon their sleepy consciousness like a strong wind and reminds them that there is a whole world out there beyond the walls—a world that they no longer share with their loved ones. They have been genuinely awaiting this visit, anticipating it like children on Christmas morning. It's been marked on their calendars for weeks, perhaps even months. They've spruced themselves up and waited for what seemed like hours for their name to be called to go down to the visiting room. And even though all this special preparation was not a part of their daily routine, it was still being experienced within the scope of their world. All a normal part of life behind the concrete walls.

Then comes that joyous moment of bouncing into the visiting room, spotting the loved one, and beginning a precious interaction. Inmates hear themselves speaking words that leap beyond the culture like green rolling hills beyond the city limits. It makes them realize afresh how much there is to life that they are not experiencing; but unlike the city dweller, there are no buses leaving for freedom. They experience the bittersweet emotions of joy and sorrow at the same time.

When the visitor starts to sprinkle the conversation with events that are happening outside the "city," storm clouds can begin to gather on the horizon for the inmate. The inmates need this conversation to provide life's "bigger picture," but some find themselves growing more and more agitated. If they are able to put their finger on what is troubling them, they might discover they are wrestling with feelings of resentment, jealousy, and anger—resentment that the visitor has a life they so desperately want and jealous and angry that they can't share it. I do not want to imply that this is true of all visiting-room experiences; it is not. But I believe it occurs frequently enough to serve as an example of the small-world syndrome.

How then does this dynamic affect the volunteer? In two ways. First, we have to be sensitive and thoughtful about the things we say and how we say them. As mentioned in chapter 1, I usually encourage volunteers not to bounce in, fresh from their day at the beach, and begin to tell the inmates what an excellent time they had. Not everyone will agree with me about this. Their argument would be in defense of providing a healthy counterbalance against the small-world syndrome. I wouldn't argue that point or deny that it is needed. What I *am* arguing against, however, is the insensitive way in which this information can be conveyed.

Don't ever forget that they can't go to the beach. They can't take their kids to a ball game or sing "Happy Birthday" around a candled cake with friends and family. As much as they are happy for you that you had such an excellent day with your family (and would seldom reveal their hurt to you), they are reminded again by the exuberance of your fresh experience and that the experience is a jewel beyond their possession.

Even the clothes we wear can reflect a lack of sensitivity in this area. I once took a group of volunteers into a major woman's institution for an Easter service. The women inmates had taken special pains to make themselves as fashionable and attractive as possible. There was makeup in evidence, special hairdos, and a joy in their faces that matched the realities of this joyous, Christ-centered day. Their prison clothes were clean, pressed, and especially neat. Most of the volunteers were also dressed appropriately for such a day.

Unfortunately, a couple of the volunteers seemed a bit over-dressed. The inmate women certainly shone, but you can only do so much with state-issued sweatshirts and jeans, all dyed in the same institutional color. I couldn't help but wonder if any of the inmates felt conscious of their sweatshirts when they stood beside these volunteers.

Again, I am not saying that there is anything wrong with a volunteer looking extra nice on Easter. And actually, for some inmates, dressing sharp is an esteemed value. It's just that I'm asking that consideration be given to those who can no longer have what they used to have. I believe that it is possible to find an appropriate middle ground between dressing sharply and dressing with sensitivity. One volunteer confessed to me later that she had felt self-conscious wearing her perfume when she realized that the women inside the prison weren't allowed to have any. She decided never to wear any again out of deference to them, reflecting, I believe, her Savior's compassion.

The second thing would be to find sensitive ways in which to counteract the small-world syndrome. I believe there *are* ways to convey "outside events" such as ball games and trips to the beach, but it would probably be better to speak of them some time *after* the fact, and in the context of a mutual and natural conversation. For example, an inmate could be describing how she helped her son or daughter play a particular musical instrument. At this point it would be natural for the volunteer to share a similar experience. The conversation would be appropriate and the shared experience, for both the inmate and the volunteer, would have taken place in the past.

The volunteer can also provide good reading material or show movies. For example, if you knew a certain inmate was interested in boating, you could ask the chaplain if it would be permissible to bring in a couple of magazines on boating.[6] There are many excellent Christian movies that can be shown on video. Films like

Joni and *The Hiding Place* are especially popular among inmates. Some Christian bookstores will even rent videos at minimal cost for specific use in prison ministry. These stories succeed in expanding their world, at least for a time.

For inmates who have highbrow interests, the culture of deprivation can include the lack of intellectual stimulation. This is a particular hardship for those who were accustomed to a wide variety of interests, social experiences, and academic pursuits. The average prison-yard conversation can often leave such people frustrated. Their particular world expands through knowledge and the use of their minds. The volunteer who is acquainted with such inmates can be sensitive to this need and, whenever possible, find creative ways to fulfill it.

I knew one man, for example, who enjoyed playing Scrabble and completing difficult acrostics. When he was on the outside, one of his habits was to complete the daily acrostic in the *New York Times*. One day I brought him a book containing a collection of acrostics from that newspaper. It turned out to be one of the most significant milestones in our relationship. He is serving a life sentence, and the connection we made through those few puzzles kicked off a friendship that remains to this day.

With prayer, a little creativity, and compassionate sensitivity, the volunteer can do much to provide healthy "bus trips" out of the shrunken world of the prisoner's city.

9

Nowhere to Run

PRISON IS NOT FOR THE MODEST. The right to privacy is all but surrendered. And although there are many private and modest people in prison, the environment has stripped them of most opportunities to practice it, at least in the manner to which their natures are accustomed. A single cell[1] is the equivalent to beachfront property on the outside—a luxury that few can afford in these days of overcrowding. Prison populations have doubled, tripled, and, in some cases, soared far beyond reasonable projections.[2] I have personally encountered as many as four men occupying a cell originally designed for one inmate. In other places, it has been necessary to fill the hallways and corridors with temporary bedding.

States are carving enormous chunks out of their budgets for the building of new facilities and the maintenance or renovation of existing prisons. It is now commonplace to build "pods" designed to house scores of men in one large room. Dormitories remain fashionable and, in some states, modular housing units are purchased or leased from private suppliers. Some states are now spending more on corrections than they are on education.

A natural by-product of overcrowding is the further diminishment of privacy. While this facet is of little concern to the states or the taxpayers, it does affect the prisoners. And what affects the prisoners affects their culture. What does it mean to live in a fishbowl society? What does it feel like? What does it look like? For starters, it means that there is nowhere to run and nowhere to hide. Not only do the other inmates know everything about you, but Big Brother is constantly watching you as well.

The residents themselves quickly adjust to this privacy deprivation, at least on a conscious level. After all, you are stuck with what you are stuck with. A rabbit has little say over the condition of his cage and spends little time, I suspect, thinking about it. Nevertheless, the environment does affect behavior.

For instance, the rare jewel of privacy affects the way inmates relate to the correctional staff. In the name of what has been termed "progressive," female officers serve in male institutions, and male officers serve in female institutions. That abuses and pregnancies, rapes and humiliations have been going on for years should surprise no one. Anyone denying it should read the child's story "The Emperor's New Clothes."[3] I have personally seen the stainless steel tables in the dungeonlike cellar of a New England woman's facility where abortions were once carried out with regularity. In another nearby institution a woman inmate waited until she was released to bring charges against an officer who sexually assaulted her. He was temporarily relieved of duty (with pay) while they investigated the charges. Eventually he was found guilty and is now serving a ten-year sentence.

Most male and female prisoners do not appreciate having COs[4] of the opposite sex do body searches on them or observing them while they are taking showers or dressed in their underwear. If anything is hidden, it is certainly not their displeasure. One might think that men and women would relish the prospect of seeing the opposite sex around, be they officers or not. But in these particular circumstances, any predilection for the practice is outweighed, once again, by the privacy factor.

I received a letter just this week from a man in Massachusetts who told me he had refused a visit with his wife because a female officer insisted on giving him a body search prior to his entering the visiting room. The inmate said he was willing to be searched by a male officer, but the request was denied, and so the visit did not take place. Upon transfer to another prison, this same man refused to be strip-searched by another female officer. His refusal, in this case, resulted in an immediate trip to the hole.

Dignity is a lady who does not surrender easily; she must be ripped from the grasp. I recall the answer an inmate at the Maine

State Prison in Thomaston once gave to the question, "Which animal do you feel most like?" We had posed the question as an icebreaker between a group of inmates and volunteers participating in a Prison Fellowship seminar. He quietly expressed, "I feel like a trapped mink." I had never heard this particular reply before, so I asked him why he felt that way. It turned out that he had recently seen a documentary on mink-farming. Although most of the animals had been bred in captivity, apparently some had been captured in the wild. He had noticed a striking difference in the eyes of the animals that had been captured. "Something had died in them once they were caught," he said. "A light was gone from their eyes, and it was so noticeable you could see it. That's how *I* feel."

Incarceration causes subtle changes on human beings and, like the mink, can often be noticed in the eyes. If you have ever spoken to the average person behind the walls, you will notice that his or her eyes are always moving. As I mentioned previously, inmates are cognizant of every thing that is going on around them. It is even more noticeable if you are out in an open space, like the yard.[5] Maybe they have enemies. If so, they must know when those inmates are nearby. They must also know where the guards are and what they are up to.

This, of course, is true of the guards as well; it is imperative that they know what the inmates are up to. Most security officers will admit that no matter which precautionary measures they install, the residents are usually two steps ahead of them. Most procedures and rules that have been put into place over the years have tended to be reactionary rather than proactive, direct results of the weaknesses or loopholes that inmates have discovered and probed. "They have much more time to think about these things than we do," many officers have admitted to me.

The fishbowl society requires knowing who and what is going on around you at all times. Guilt is often assigned by association in prison. If an altercation occurs in any given area, everyone within proximity is usually lugged[6] to a punitive cell until Security figures out who knows what. (And also who is willing to talk about who knows what.) Guilt by association also includes whoever the inmate is seen talking *with*. Just as the eyes of the person you are speaking with are observing everything around him or her, so too the eyes of all the *other* fish in the bowl are observing you as well.

For example, if an inmate is seen talking to a religious volunteer, is he getting religion? If she is speaking with an officer, is she ratting?[7] If he is speaking to a homosexual, is he one? And on it goes. Guilt by association. He or she will probably hear about it later. Suspicion abounds.

As the months go by, however, inmates become familiar with the overall character of other inmates, especially if the observation has continued over a lengthy period of time. As the months pass, guilt is bestowed less by association than it is by the testimony of a life that has "proved" where he or she is coming from. A "stand-up con"[8] can pretty much speak to whomever he wants.

So how, then, should this dynamic affect the behavior of the volunteer? The primary thing to remember is that everyone, including yourself, is being watched and scrutinized, whether consciously or unconsciously. Although it may not seem like you are being watched directly, you should be aware that everyone in your vicinity already knows you are there. And every time any movement occurs from one location to another, it is being reregistered, reanalyzed, and recalculated—by somebody. The volunteer needs to be aware of not only how an encounter with an inmate appears but how it makes the *inmate* appear as well. Are you in a compromising situation, by perception? Have you disappeared momentarily from view? What does that mean? What are you doing?

We need to be aware of what we are saying and fully expect that others are *hearing* what is being said. (This is sometimes a great advantage for the gospel. Not only is the person with whom you are speaking listening to what you have to say, but everyone else within earshot can also hear the conversation.) However, if your dialogue is less than Christ centered, be aware of your content. It might make perfect sense in the context of your conversation, but how does it sound to others? Could it be misconstrued? A grave misunderstanding could possibly jeopardize your volunteer status, but the greater risk is for the inmate with whom you are conversing. He or she will hear about it later if something unwise or indiscreet has been said or done. Never forget that you go home at the end of your visit; they have no place to run to and nowhere to hide.

The big challenge for Christian inmates is this: they must live out their Christianity in full view of the unbelievers every day, all the time. Every flaw is observed, and very often these frailties are seized upon as evidence of their apparent insincerity. To keep what this means in perspective, which Christian on the outside could withstand the scrutiny of observation by neighbors or coworkers twenty-four hours a day, seven days a week? Who would come out perfect? To those inmates unfamiliar with the principles of Christianity, becoming a Christian means that one changes immediately. There is little grace extended for time-oriented maturity.

They are quick to point out the failures of young Christians. "How come you're still smoking?" I hear them challenge. "I thought Christians weren't supposed to swear?" "I saw you with that *Playboy* book last night! Some Christian *you* are!" "What are you getting so angry about? You sure don't act like that down at the chapel! What a phony! If the volunteers could see you now!" And on it goes. Sanctification is not a process that unbelievers generally comprehend.

But again, time is a convincer. There are many strong Christians living out their lives with faithfulness and conviction in front of the other prisoners. The proof is when you hear the other residents giving testimony to the integrity of a particular Christian inmate. Then you know that this inmate's faith is deep and consistent.

In many prisons today the old model of a single cell for a single inmate is a thing of the past, with the exception of one area in particular—the maximum security unit. Ironically, the men who have their own cells are those who are causing the most problems for the administration. If someone breaks a prison rule of a fairly serious nature, they are usually lugged to an isolation unit or thrown in the Hole.[9] An outsider might think that this would tend to *promote* disobedience—since the punishment, a single cell, is almost a reward of sorts. But maximum-security time is hard time. There is little to do and recreation time ("rec time") spent out of their cells is almost nil. The days can drag and every inmate knows that activity makes the time fly faster. Very few of them want to spend their days in a SHU.[10]

But there *is* a breed of inmate who is willing to make the exchange. This is the man or woman who values privacy (and an escape from the "games" being played in population) more highly than the "freedoms" that the GP[11] provides. Unfortunately, many cell areas in maximum security are now doubled up as well. The exceptions would be for individuals with whom it would be dangerous to place *any* roommate. I know one man who warned the officers on duty that he wanted to be alone and would kill anyone they put into his cell as a roommate. Unfortunately, they did not believe him. As soon as his door was opened the following morning, he shoved the lifeless body of his cell mate out onto the tier. He has had his own cell to this day.

Another exception would be in the case of privilege. Some maximum units have what they call "honor tiers." These are used as an incentive for good behavior. The inmates on these tiers are generally used as the unit's workers, thus giving them more time out of their cells. These honor tiers are also used for compliant inmates who, for one reason or other, are doing so much time in maximum security that the officers feel they should at least have their own cells. Some *choose* to stay. At least (they feel) they have their privacy and are willing to surrender the advantages of population for it. Honor tiers tend to be quieter than the other tiers. The inmates want to hold on to their private cells so they tend to police themselves.

Another aspect of the fishbowl society is that there is simply nowhere to hide from an enemy. If you and I have a problem with someone on the streets, one sensible solution is simply to avoid them. This is not an option in prison. You must face your enemy every day. If you and I have a problem with one of our neighbors, for example, and the situation escalates, we have choices. The police can be called, or there are courts in which to file our complaints. Not so for the people in prison. To make any appeal to *their* authorities for relief is to become immediately branded as a rat, which will make their former troubles seem light in comparison. They must somehow work the situation out for themselves.

When I was in prison, one of the lifers took a disliking to me. Unfortunately, he was so dangerous that even my friends would not defend me if it meant incurring his wrath. He was in prison for murder and while awaiting trial had also killed a correctional officer. So I knew the threat was real, not imagined. If I had been a lifer myself, I would have had it out with him. At least a fight tends to set livable boundaries. But the problem for me was that I had four years of parole hanging over my head and only a year to go before I was eligible for it. I had everything to lose; he had nothing.

So I walked on eggshells whenever I was around him for the remainder of my time. I bore the insults and the taunts and was eventually released on schedule. He had threatened to mess me up before my release date, hoping that I would lose my good time and have to serve four extra years. But he had many more enemies than I had. He got into a fight with someone else a couple months before I left and didn't get out of the Hole till after I had been released. A few years later, I heard that another inmate had stabbed him to death.

A situation like this makes doing time even harder than it would normally be. I always feel badly for those I meet who are in these tight places. The Christian volunteer has a crucial role to play in these situations. For those of you who work one-on-one with inmates, you will occasionally hear about such troubles. You should realize, if they open up to you about the conflicts they are having with other inmates, that you might be one of their only relief valves. You might, in fact, be their *only* relief valve. Chaplains, who work with inmates day in and day out, will encounter these fearful confessions much more often than you will as a volunteer, but you should be prepared for them nevertheless. What should you do?

Very often the inmate will not want you telling the administration about it because others would know that any subsequent action by the authorities would reveal that the inmate told *somebody*. It is imperative that you remember your unique role here. Only spiritual warriors can fight spiritual battles. Pick up the weapons of your warfare (see 2 Cor. 10:3–5) and step onto the field of battle. Pray with them. Pray fervently so that the one who has come to you for assistance will clearly understand to Whom *you* appeal for help.

I have prayed often for men in these tight places. They are experiencing the affliction *(thlipsis)* Paul spoke of in 2 Corinthians 1:8—those narrow places where the pressures of our troubles often squeeze us, causing us to believe there is no way out. Listen to the sounds of the battle:

> We do not want you to be uninformed, brothers, about the hardships we suffered in the province of Asia. We were under great pressure, far beyond our ability to endure, so that we despaired even of life. Indeed, in our hearts we felt the sentence of death. But this happened that we might not rely on ourselves but on God, who raises the dead. He has delivered us from such a deadly peril, and he will deliver us. On him we have set our hope that he will continue to deliver us, as you help us by your prayers. Then many will give thanks on our behalf for the gracious favor granted us in answer to the prayers of many (2 Cor. 1:8–11).

As a result of these prayers, I have seen the hearts of mockers change, the swords of enemies turned upon each other, and foes removed from the field of battle. So join the fray on behalf of God's people. Only Christians have the weapons you have!

One final comment I want to make before we leave this chapter is a word about the church in prison. Inmates don't have the privilege of choosing which church they would like to attend, as we on the outside do. If a member of a church on the outside doesn't like a service, or a pastor, or some other member of the congregation, he can leave and go somewhere else. (And evidenced by the amount of church-hopping that seems to take place, it seems to be a freedom many a disgruntled member chooses to exercise.) But inmates don't have that choice. Their church *is* the church in that prison, like it or not. This means that they have the opportunity to display the unity of Christ in a way that is seldom achieved, even on the outside. What an irony that Jesus is accomplishing this unity in institutional chapels across the country, and he is doing it with prisoners—many of whom are baby Christians at that!

What volunteers should keep in mind is that their participation at any chapel service is also under observation. Special attention given to any inmate is noted, as is attention given to doctrinal issues that have tended to divide Christians. Don't forget that this is their only church. We don't want to find ourselves before the Lord as having been the reason for dividing his body. It becomes essential that we do not bad-mouth other Christian volunteers in any way, even if we have differing doctrinal issues. It is also important that we do not make our "pet" doctrines an issue for division. Focus on the essentials. There are many beautiful fish in this aquarium.

If we remain aware of this fishbowl dynamic, then we are likely to be careful about what we do or say and how others may interpret it. "Do not revile the king even in your thoughts, or curse the rich in your bedroom, because a bird of the air may carry your words, and a bird on the wing may report what you say" (Eccles. 10:20).

10

The Culture of Hardness

MANY BELIEVE that we are products of our environment. This reference is usually to one's childhood and early environmental influences, but in prison the statement can also be applied to the physical reality as well.

As mentioned in the previous chapter, many of the cultural differences between prison life and the world that exists just outside its walls are due to deprivation. Like protons and neutrons circling the nucleus of an atom, there are particles of our lives that constantly weave in and out, helping to maintain a healthy balance. The presence of children, women, a frosty beer, a shake and fries, and the feel of soft grass under one's feet—all these conspire to keep our gyros spinning happily on course. This chapter is devoted to a more subtle deprivation: the absence of softness.

Like many sensations that free people take for granted, softness is woefully lacking behind the walls of concrete and steel. Prison is a culture of hardness. Nearly everything one sees, hears, and touches can be described as hard. The senses are confronted with hardness at every turn. Its pervasive influence etches its characteristics into the lives of the inmates. It would be a relatively simple task to list those few items that are *not* hard. The velvety threads that are so richly and naturally woven into the fabric of everyday life on the outside are reduced to just a few solitary items behind prison walls: a mattress, a pillow, a blanket, the limpid food in the chow hall, clothing, music (some), the sound of a bird, a kind word, a memory, a tear.

But these things are quickly swallowed up in a relentless sea of harshness. This is a place where men and women are caught up in the culture of the cool and the callous. Spoken words are hard, even when meant to be friendly. Orders are given with the bark of authority. Conversations are shouted from cell to cell because visual contact is often impossible when people are locked up. The clank and clang of doors shutting and locks clicking, the gliding of metal doors on their metal tracks being controlled by some invisible hand behind a bullet-proof control room, and the tinny sound of a voice crackling through an inadequate intercom system—all these sounds are heard so often that one's ears no longer register them. Nearly everything the sense of sight beholds encompasses a petrified landscape of stainless steel sinks and toilets, riot gear and helmets, bars and razor wire. And like the stomach of some gigantic whale, a catacomb of cement has swallowed the inhabitants alive, hemming them in on every side; it has become their earth, their sky, their walls.

The cursing, the angry challenges, the bragging, the threats, the constant noise, the intermittent noise—even the silences— seem frigid and unfriendly. There is no grass, ever, under your feet. And in prison yards that do have lawns, the rules usually make it an infraction to walk on them. The prisoners are required to stay on the maze of concrete walkways.

Attitudes are tough, eyes are unrevealing, tattoos are defiant, muscles are flexed, gaits are cool, fists are clenched, scars are deep, and weakness is scorned.

Even the guards are affected. Some take it home with them. Spouses and children can sense the frustration. Marriages can end in divorce. Drinking problems abound. Even many female officers seem unable to resist the siren song of *hardness*. Sensing that they are in a hard man's world, they try to overcompensate. Some hide their femininity behind profanity and crudeness, often outmatching the foul mouths of even their male counterparts. Their demeanor is tough; their treatment of prisoners often brash and threatening. They feel forced into proving they can handle the culture.

Ironically, I have noticed that new volunteers occasionally feel that they, too, have to play into the prevailing atmosphere of the "bad" and the macho. I have heard seminary students, for example, use vulgarisms in their messages or make borderline jokes.

This is partly because they are afraid and partly because they assume it is a quick way to relate to their audience. On one occasion, I brought in some Christian musicians who were going to conduct a mini-concert for the men at a local jail. It was their first performance in a prison of any sort. The lead guitarist was also the lead singer, and he would dialogue with the men between songs. During the course of the evening some of his jokes included vulgar references to bodily functions and other tasteless comments.

After the evening was over, I had to correct him on his choice of words and let him know that it wasn't necessary to perform in such a manner, just for the sake of trying to relate to his audience. I explained that it was not only unnecessary, but that the Christian inmates in the audience would probably have been offended. The volunteer received the rebuke well and admitted that because he had felt uncomfortable, he had gone a little overboard in attempting to relate to the men.

But behind all the concrete and steel are real people, both inmates and officers. Real people with real needs and real feelings. Some who love art, fine music, meaningful conversation, and the warmth of a touch. In no way am I trying to paint a picture that sweeps all its participants under the cruel brush of a darkened stereotype. There are many people, officers and inmates alike, who are able to resist the tide of toughness. And even among those who seem unable to resist, they are often quite different people under the threatening veneer. It is the culture that supplies the canvas of this painting and provides the backdrop for all the colors within its borders.

Few inmates fight it. Few believe they want to fight it. Many believe they fit within it. Some do. Some *are* hard; some *are* genuinely tough. But it really doesn't matter; it's the name of the game, and everyone must play it. Or at least pay tolls to its government by not going beyond the bounds of the code. Even those brave souls who do not pretend to be tough, and are individualistic enough to plot their own courses, still operate within the respectable borders of the country's highways. It is, after all, foolish and dangerous to drive beyond the guardrails. To say that this environment of hardness has no effect upon those who live there would not be true. One notices it in the little things. For example, inmates love to joke and fool around. There is a lot of horseplay. This releases tension. They will often shove one another or punch one another in the arms, all in good-natured play. And while I don't want to get too psychological here, I have wondered at times how much of this shoving and punching is related to the basic human need for *touch*. People need to touch and be touched by another human being. But the caution signs in the adult male prison say that touching is beyond the guardrails. It is uncool. It hints at other things. Even the institutional rules prohibit the horseplay they indulge in. So they punch one another.

Weakness must not be admitted, whether physical or emotional. Nevertheless, we *are* weak. So what shall we do? We can't let anyone see it because weakness invites the wolves. Yet still, the need remains. Some inmates write letters or poems or stories— literary products that usually abound in the expressions of touch. Others rely on their visits. Most just hide their need. One of the oldest prison proverbs is: "Everyone cries at night." The next day they will pick up the mask of the tough guy and venture out again. The name of the game is how tough you are, how bad you are. Some prisons are worse than others. Some prisoners *are* deeply troubled. Their presence alone can change the dynamic of the atmosphere; it becomes almost electric. Everyone's ears are tuned to the same frequency. Unpredictability. Volatility.

Enter Christian volunteers, this paradox within the culture. They smile in unfeigned friendship. They seem genuinely happy to see you. They shake hands. They touch. In many chapels across the country they actually *hug!* They speak kind words, soft words, words of friendship, and personal vulnerability. They display weakness. They talk about Jesus. The message of *his* touch breaks the bonds of the culture. When truly received, his incarcerated children are also able to break the mold, escape the siren song, and discover their true selves. There is no freedom like the freedom Jesus Christ can bring. Hanging on the walls of many chapels across the country are colorful banners that declare: "If the Son sets you free, you will be free indeed" (John 8:36). Jesus sets us free from the need to defend ourselves. He releases us from the need to project an image that is other than what we are. The mask can come down without fear.

Tens of thousands have discovered Christ's gentle touch while serving time in prison. In my mind's eye, I can see their faces beaming from cells and tiers in every state of the union. I see it on the faces of the officers who know him as well. Men and women together, free to be themselves.

Jesus Christ loves prisoners; he moves freely about on every prison yard and every dimly lit tier. He knows that prisons are a great place to find him. Men and women at the end of their own resources, needing someone to touch them. And he does.

The Prisoner's Song©
by Lennie Spitale

Y'know I watched you movin' as you shuffled 'round the yard,
Your face was lined in bitterness, your eyes were cold and hard,
And if you had some wounds inside, well ain't no one else can tell,
Cause your role—it is the hard man—and you play it oh so well,
You play it oh so well.

But every night's a nightmare, you know every day's the same,
You wake up in the mornin' and you play the hard man's game.
You are a prisoner's prisoner, a con among the cons,
You got your money on tomorrow, but all your dreams are gone.
All your dreams are gone.
But you don't need no preachin', no one tellin' you what to do,
You've been to the valley and I know you've paid your dues.
You've been to the valley and I know you've paid your dues.

But late at night when you're locked up tight, and you lie there all alone,
The mask comes down and you're free to think about things all your own.
You gaze up to the window, past the towers and the lights,
And you dream about some loved one who seldom seems to write.
And you see a star that's twinklin' there, somethin' natural that appears,

And your mind inside is screamin', "Boy, What are you doing here?"
"What are you doing here?"

But you don't need no preachin', no self-righteous saints
To tell you what you is, my friend, or to tell you what you ain't.
Cause they ain't none no better to be talkin' down at you,
You've been to the valley and I know you've paid your dues.

But you still got a hole inside ain't no one else can fill,
And I got a Friend waitin' outside, I know He always will.
He'll bring you a peace like you've never known, He'll bind up all your scars,
You ain't gotta wear a mask for Him cause He knows right where you are.

Don't wait for a day that never comes, It's just another lie!
If there were somethin' you could've done, then why did Jesus die?
Just take the gift He offers you, run to His side and say,
"Lord, you know that I've been wrong. Come in my life today.
Come in my life to stay."

But you don't need no preachin', no one tellin' you what to do,
But He's been to the valley and I know He went for you.
I know He made that valley 'cause He's been there for me, too.
He's been to the valley and He paid up all our dues.

11

Life in a Cage

ONE OF THE JOB ASSIGNMENTS I had while serving time in New Hampshire was in the print shop. From time to time, small tours would be led through the institution, and the print shop was one of the stops along the way. The state was happy to display how progressive it was and the opportunities it provided by way of vocational training. The prison's officials were proud to reveal that nearly all of the state's letterheads and envelopes were being produced by prisoners, saving the taxpayers a great deal of money—as well as teaching inmates the printing trade. (Some of the men in federal institutions already know this trade quite well, which is part of the reason they are there in the first place.)

Inmates, for the most part, enjoy these tours themselves, as they usually include females in the group. The excursions usually come from local schools and colleges, or they may be part of some community program. But I remember all too well that it was us, the inmates, who were really the ones on display. I always made a point of staring back at every member of the tour (partly in defiance and partly to see the girls) because I resented being made to feel like an animal in a zoo. But the tragic comparison was uncomfortably close to home. In prison, men and women *are* living in cages.

I still recall approaching the cell of a man at MCI Cedar Junction[1] as I was making one-on-one visits down the tier of his particular cell block. I had never met him before, and as I came abreast of his cell, I found him pacing wildly back and forth. He then did something that I have not experienced before or since. He *snarled* at me. I had the good sense to keep on going, but the incident is still vivid in my mind.[2] The man so resembled a panther

94

pacing back and forth in its cage that I have never forgotten it. Even those volunteers who have never had the experience of being growled at cannot forget the overwhelming scene of looking up at a multitiered cell block with row upon row of little cages, each containing one or two *human beings*. It is a picture of great sadness and tragic irony.

"What," one may ask, "are *men* doing in cages?" This condition should be reserved only for wild animals on display. It becomes even more heartrending when one considers that there is likely to be more public outcry over *animals* in captivity than there is for men and women. Something is wrong. How can men and women made in the image of God be reduced to such a state—a condition that has been traditionally reserved for animals? The devil has come to steal not only our souls but our humanity as well. When you see men and women in cages, the doctrine of sin leaves an indelible impression upon your mind and leaves little room for doubting its existence.

I am not saying that crime should go unpunished; the perpetrators of certain criminal acts *need* to be isolated from the community at large. What would be surprising to many, however, is that most inmates would also agree with this. Some have even confessed to me that they should never again be allowed out on the streets, for fear of what they might do. But what I am appealing to, especially from those who call themselves Christians, is a sense of compassion and sadness. Compassion for these poor children of Adam and sadness that they can be reduced to such a state.

A few months ago I met a man who was chained to a chair. His arms and legs were strapped with wide bands of seat belt material; his hands and feet were shackled and cuffed to the chair, and the chair itself was shackled to the bars of the control station. He was a big man, and he was crying.

There he was, out in the middle of the control area between the tiers, for everyone passing by to see. Life in a zoo means sharing space with the other creatures as well, but his current pain went deeper than his humiliation. He was beyond caring what anyone else thought because his own thoughts were in such deep turmoil. He had probably been placed in these restraints to prevent him from hurting himself. (An inmate later told me that he had put his fist through the hard plastic sheet covering the window of his cell door.)

I had just finished doing a Bible study in one area and was heading for the tier on the opposite side to do some cell-to-cell visitation. When I saw him in that condition, my heart went out to him. I immediately went over and squatted down beside his chair. I introduced myself as a Christian volunteer and asked if there were anything I could do for him. Through his tears he choked out, "Yes, you can get me a pill so I can kill myself!"

His distress was so great that I had a difficult time getting anything else out of him. He would respond only with one- or two-word answers. He wasn't impolite in any way, but his emotional pain made it impossible for him to focus on anything else but his own private thoughts. I did manage to get his first name, and that he was originally from Haiti. Then I asked him if anyone had ever told him about Jesus, and he nodded. I asked him if I could pray for him and he lowered his head and nodded again. I put my arm around his shoulders and prayed for the mercy and comfort of Christ.

When I began to pray for his family, his sobbing increased. After the prayer, I tried to continue talking with him. I think I felt that if I could get him to talk, it would help him in some way. I was wrong. When I asked him if he was concerned about a particular person on the streets, his whole body became agitated and a long, low cry rose slowly up from his chest and culminated with a loud scream. He shook wildly in his chair with frustration and futility.

In the middle of the outburst, he threw his head back, and it came into contact with the steel bars behind him. When he realized he could hurt himself in this way, he threw it back again. I also realized it at the same time and quickly put my arms between his head and the bars. I tried to move his chair away, and that's when I discovered the chair was also chained to the bars. Several officers were there in a flash, and one held his head while another strapped a black helmet over it. Another officer told me they had also called for the psychiatrist.

There was nothing else I could do. A crowd of correctional staff was around him now, so I continued on to the tier I had originally been heading toward. When I returned, he was still in the chair. Only now he was completely quiet and slumped over, with his head on his chest. The helmet had a dark visor covering his face so I couldn't see him. The medical staff had probably given him something to sedate him.

What had stung me from the beginning was that this poor man, made in the image of God, could have been reduced to such a state. It pained me to see him that way. And I realized afresh what a dreadful thing sin is. What a monster of degradation it is upon the creatures whom God loves. How it must pain *him!*

The good news is that I met this inmate again about a month later. He had been shipped out to a psychiatric hospital for a thirty-day evaluation but had recently been returned to the prison. Through a discussion with another volunteer, I learned that he was back, and we went to visit him at his cell. After explaining to him for about forty-five minutes the wonderful news about the forgiveness for sins found in Jesus Christ, he suddenly waved his arms toward his chest and spontaneously cried out twice over, "Lord Jesus, come into my life!" Immediately he felt better. When I visited him a week later, he had underlined many passages in the Bible and said he had been reading it for about four hours a day. I never expected to see him again, let alone to be given the privilege of seeing him come to Christ! We continued to touch base with him until he was released.

Sin *is* terrible, and we *are* in a degraded condition—and it takes grace for us to realize this. When men and women get even an inkling of how great are the depths to which they have plunged, it makes the rescue all the greater. God sent his only Son, Jesus, to rescue us. He sent him into this low estate and caused him to bear the full brunt of sin's terribleness at the dark cross of Calvary, where he died in our place. Prison *is* a low estate, a dehumanizing experience; but if it causes us to cry out, "Lord Jesus, come into my life!" it is a marvelous grace.

The suggestion I would make to volunteers is to be sensitive about how you are *looking* at inmates. They are able to recognize the difference between genuine concern and fascinated curiosity in your eyes. I can still recall how some relatives came as a group to visit me a few days after I had been picked up for armed robbery. I was still in the county jail, and the visits were held by the gate at the end of the cell block. It struck me that their eyes and their comments had everything to do with my environment and very little to do with me. They barely looked at me. The sights and sounds they heard fascinated them, and our conversation seemed to be dominated by their curious observations and questions. I couldn't blame them. They had passed these old brick walls—as I had—many times from the outside only. Now was their chance to see it from the inside. But still, I can recall feeling even lonelier and less significant as a result of their visit.

As Christians, we are there for the people. As volunteers, you will have many occasions to observe the workings of the zoo, but do this privately and discreetly. Prisoners are not animals; they are people made in the image of God. The Son of man came to seek and to save that which was lost; that's why his Father sent him. And he is still doing it—that's why he sent you.

12

Unwritten Code of Ethics

ONE DAY I WENT UP ON THE TIER of an awaiting trial unit where I hold a weekly Bible study. Upon arrival, I discovered that four of my regular attendees were missing. They had been lugged to the Hole for an altercation that had involved a physical attack upon a "skinner."[1]

A couple of these guys had been coming to the Bible study for quite some time and were showing signs of spiritual growth. At first glance, one might be tempted to ask what happened. How could they be involved in beating someone up and violating such a clear command of Scripture? Their actions, however inexcusable from a spiritual standpoint, are quite consistent with the prison culture.

As in any culture, there is a code of conduct by which the citizens of that society operate. Prison is no exception—as the hapless individual who was assaulted soon discovered. (He was OK but was immediately shipped off to another institution for his own protection.) When it comes to understanding what this society's code of ethics is, however, most of it is unwritten. The new guy who suddenly finds himself thrust into life on the tiers must quickly learn what this "law of the jungle" requires. Mistakes made early on can set the tone for the remainder of one's entire sentence.

In some cases, such as the sexual offender mentioned above, the nature of the crime sets the tone even *before* the prisoner's arrival at the prison. Most inmates have access to radios, and in some cases TVs and newspapers. They are always reading, and they are always listening. They are especially attuned to newscasts that carry information about any crime, no matter how big or small. They know way ahead of time when someone will be coming to the prison and, in most cases, what he has done. When you add the fact that many of those who are incarcerated personally know many of the individuals on the streets who are committing crimes—and regularly hear about them by phone or visits—they often know, even before the police do, that so-and-so is "running crazy" and will soon be picked up and apprehended. It's only a matter of time.

In the case of an arriving sexual offender, the prison must make sure that he is placed on a tier where he will be protected. The incident mentioned above involved a jail tier where men are awaiting trial. Although the jails try their best to ensure the safety of such prisoners, the classification period is just beginning. Classification officers know that it's dangerous to place a sexual offender on a "population" tier. Why they didn't in this case, I don't know; but it's a prison taboo, nonetheless.

There are others. Secretly informing the prison's security department about the activities of other inmates is among the top no-no's an inmate must never engage in. Better known as "ratting," it probably ranks as the number one social taboo. Why anyone would place themselves in such a dangerous position baffles most observers, but let me suggest a couple of reasons some inmates succumb to it.

Occasionally, revenge is the motive. An inmate may simply want to get back at another by passing on information that implicates his enemy. Another reason may be to receive favors from the administration. Some of these "favors" are not favors at all; they are little more than an offer that can't be refused. A person can be "encouraged" by security officers to gather information about the activities of other inmates through a variety of methods. One, unfortunately, is just plain coercion.

This usually involves the threat of getting written up[2] on some convenient charge—which is fairly easy to do if an officer is so inclined. This threat becomes especially foreboding if the inmate is getting short.[3] A write-up could jeopardize one's chances at parole or even threaten his accumulation of good-time.[4]

But sometimes favors can actually mean favors. For inmates who are serving a lot of time, for example, the supply of funds from the outside can dry up as time goes by, leaving them with few resources to buy extra things from the canteen. A shrewd security officer can arrange for such goodies to be dropped by a man's cell in return for information. In some heavier situations, the information can actually be used to indict people who are still on the outside evading conviction. Though this may sound like Hollywood to some, it occurs with a fair amount of regularity.

When one thinks about it, where are these information-holders likely to be? Testimony against drug lords, organized crime, gangs, and other dangerous groups have often come from those already in custody. In these latter cases (which usually involve the federal system), the identity of inmates is actually changed, and they are transferred all over the country to various correctional institutions where even most of the prison officials don't know who they are. Many state prisons have contracts with the feds and have often taken in federal inmates under assumed names and bogus crime jackets.[5]

When a man we knew at a certain prison assaulted an officer with a pool cue and never received so much as a write-up, the suspicion of the other inmates was immediately aroused. Members of a motorcycle gang began to piece together that he was a federal informant. He was immediately transferred to places unknown. (He had become, however, very open to the gospel before he was shipped out.)

Being known as a rat can be deadly. If a *volunteer* ever receives the tag, it can greatly hinder his or her ministry—if not sabotage it all together. It is wise that volunteers not place themselves in situations that can raise the ominous cloud of suspicion. One way to avoid this is not to ask too many personal questions too early in the relationship. Too many questions raise flags for most inmates. Until they know they can trust you, keep personal questions to a minimum. *Never* ask questions about another inmate while that person is not present. Statements often have a way of becoming distorted in the retelling and have a way of getting back.[6]

Even though inmates may ask you to do so, never call wives or girlfriends for them. Not only is this unwise, but it is against the rules in most institutions. Most inmates are allowed to make collect phone calls. If they tell you it is necessary for you to make the call, the reason is usually not good. For example, there may be a restraining order on the inmate, and you have just helped to violate that order by making a call on their behalf. This not only can result in your eviction from the prison as a volunteer, but it can also result in the inmate picking up a new charge.

Another aspect of the inmate code is not to be too friendly with the officers. As in the army, it is part of the culture to complain about the food and the officers in charge.[7] The degree to which this occurs varies in different settings and with individual personalities, but the general rule of thumb is that "the Man" is your antagonist and your enemy. You do not fraternize with him. Conversely, this is also true for the officers; they are warned against becoming too friendly with the inmates when they go through their initial training. Security is afraid that if an inmate learns too much information about an officer's personal life, it could be used as leverage against him later on.

There are other inmate "codes" that will appear throughout the book in conjunction with the topics of other chapters, but let me touch on a few that affect the volunteer directly.

One of the most basic rules is that you *never* ask an inmate why he or she is in prison. It not only threatens the unwritten code regarding too-much-inquiry-too-early, but it could also put the resident in a very uncomfortable position. Some inmates don't want you knowing what they've done, or they just don't want to talk about it. But even apart from it being a social violation, the main reason a Christian volunteer should never ask is because that's not why we are there. Jesus Christ has sent us to represent him and to carry his message. The Lord himself did not think of his role in the flesh as bringing condemnation but to save the world from the consequences of those sins (John 3:17).

Asking inmates why they are in prison puts the focus on a particular sin. We are not sent to be their judge—they've already experienced that. Our job is to be ambassadors of Jesus Christ in the setting of a prison or jail. Our task is in the place of Christ, who continues to preach good news to the captives.[8] Jesus will come again, and it is then that he will judge the world. Until then we must be about the Father's business of salvation.

Some may ask, "What if I see or hear about something that should be reported to the security staff? Couldn't that be construed as ratting?" This is a good question and should receive more than a superficial response. Although any security briefing will tell you that you must report *any* infraction of prison rules, they are simply discharging their duty. (Which security presentation would ever tell a volunteer that there are some infractions they may ignore?) In fact, they do expect you to follow through with that injunction. They don't want volunteers deciding for themselves what is important and what isn't because, frankly, they know you are too new to the culture. They constantly worry about volunteers being taken in by inmates and, to be sure, many green volunteers *are* quite naïve. So there's certainly no way that they want you ignoring any infractions the volunteer may see or hear. Besides, they reason, a volunteer is an extra set of ears and eyes out there on the compound; why not make use of this extra help?

And what of confidentiality? Does it apply to volunteers? It may or may not, depending not only upon the rules of the institution but upon the laws of the state as well. A volunteer should find out exactly what his or her own state has determined on such issues. Sometimes the confidentiality clauses that protect chaplains do not protect volunteers. In some cases they do, if the state perceives them as coming under the umbrella of the chaplaincy and are viewed as an extension of his or her work. But I advise you not to ask a security officer what his or her take on this will be; they will always tell you that you are not covered.

Do not be intimidated by security staff who tell you that volunteers are not covered by confidentiality protections given to clergy or lawyers. Get the true legal skinny from the appropriate officials.[9] Although the security department tends to lump all volunteers into the same category, there are big differences between your role as a Christian counselor and that of, say, someone who has come in to teach mathematics. A math teacher is not likely to hear some of the painful issues that will be confided to a spiritual counselor. Your roles are different. That difference, I believe, places you in a parachaplain's position. And as such, this makes running to the administration every time you observe some minor infraction of the rules impossible for you to do your job. Let me give you a suggestion.

What you will hear from the security department and what I'm about to tell you will differ to some degree. Basically, I operate by the "major security breach" and the "bodily harm rule." In other words, there are two basic criteria that must be met before I will report an incident to the security department.

1. The information must contain a *serious* security breach (such as escape plans or an impending riot).
2. The information must contain a reasonable certainty that someone is going to be seriously hurt. (If you learn that either an officer or an inmate is in physical danger, you *must* report it.)

When sensing that I may become privy to hearing something that could encroach upon one of the two criteria mentioned above, I usually interrupt the inmate at that point in the conversation. I make it clear to him that if I am about to hear something along either of those lines, he must not tell me any more. I let him know that if that's where he is going, he will put me in a position to alert security, and that further I am bound by the Lord to do so as a Christian (Lev. 5:1; James 4:17).

This approach has proven effective over the years because it warns the inmate—before he has revealed anything specific—that he has a choice to make at this juncture. If he goes on to reveal anything further, it will be the same as if it were he who was telling the authorities. If he doesn't, I can't act upon what I am not aware of. Neither of us has been compromised at this point.

I also need to add here that the average volunteer will seldom, if ever, encounter this situation. But I have included these guidelines so you will not be caught flat-footed in the rare event that it does happen. Chaplains, on the other hand, will face this situation much more often.

Another related issue is the need that some inmates have to confess past offenses. Occasionally, an inmate will trust you to the point of wanting to confess something that still haunts him. Sometimes it is for something they were never caught or punished for. I view these situations differently from the previous one. In the former case, the information reveals some danger that is *impending*, that is, something that could take place in the future. In the latter case it involves something that *has already happened*. In this situation, I feel it is a part of our role as standing in for Christ, to fulfill John 20:23.[10]

If the inmate is not a believer, I present the gospel to him. If he is, and it seems obvious that he has come under the conviction of the Holy Spirit, I encourage him to pray for forgiveness, and I stand by as a witness. When he has finished, I pronounce him absolved in the name of Christ Jesus. I exercise this declaration not because we have the power to forgive sins but because we have been given the authority to pronounce them forgiven as ministers of his new covenant. I do not feel under any obligation to tell such confessions to anyone else. However, I have known some inmates who felt compelled by the Holy Spirit to go on and bring these past offenses to light themselves.

A final issue concerning our obligation to the security department deals with the Romans 13 question. "Shouldn't I report everything that security has asked me to report since they are my governing authority?" I leave this question to the heart of the individual Christian and would not venture to play the Holy Spirit in your life regarding it. As you are convinced, so obey (Rom. 14:22–23). It isn't within the scope of this book to present a theological treatise of my own personal interpretation of the passage (nor would it be appropriate), but if you are struggling with this issue, I encourage you to seek the wisdom of godly counselors.

The only slant I can give you here is that while you are, indeed, under the authority of the prison and its officials, they themselves have decreed that you have entered under the category of religious volunteer. You are expected to carry out the duties that are relevant to your assignment. Your immediate authority is the chaplain (if your institution has one), and you function as an extension of his or her ministry. If you are wrestling with this, you have the option of discussing this issue with your chaplain. However, once the chaplain, as your direct authority, gives you his or her ruling, you must submit to it.

I have, on occasion, come to the cell of a man who was smoking marijuana or was in possession of some jailhouse mash or other contraband food items or magazines. To report such things is not why I am there. The security department already has measures in place to discover such items. Surprise shakedowns[11] are a regular part of the regimen. If a prison is truly set back because a volunteer doesn't report such things as the occasional whiff of marijuana in the air, then they are already running at less than peak efficiency. We all have a job to do, and our combined tasks should serve to make everyone else's job easier.

Apart from an incident falling within the two major areas I outlined earlier, I have not found it necessary, or prudent, to report much else. In fact, I believe to do so would, in the long run, make it counterproductive to your ministry because the inmates would feel they can no longer confide in you. Most veteran prison administrations would concede that trust between you and the inmates is an integral element of your particular assignment, apart from which you could not function successfully.

A wise administration realizes that the value of mature Christian counselors on the tiers has an overarching effect of maintaining a peaceful environment within the prison itself. Helping to keep the lid on an otherwise potentially volatile brew, no matter where the assistance is coming from, is a value worth preserving. Navigating the swirling waters between the written and unwritten codes of the prison culture requires a wisdom that only the Holy Spirit can provide; so keep your antennae tuned to his frequency.

The Christian volunteer should be as wise as a serpent but as innocent as a dove (Matt. 10:16).

You Can Depend on Me

I HATE TOOTHACHES. The very thought of them makes me thankful for God's provision of fluoride. I met a man some time ago in maximum security who was suffering from a bad one. It had begun around midweek and had increased in painful intensity by the weekend. He knew that if the prison dentist didn't see him by Friday, he wouldn't be seen until the following Monday or Tuesday. As it turned out, the dentist did not get to him in time, so he had to endure three more days of excruciating pain. His cellmate told me that at one point he was in such torment, he had tried to extract the tooth himself by use of a razor blade. When I met up with him, he had just returned from the dentist's office and was glad that his ordeal was finally behind him.

Episodes like this highlight another aspect of prison life that inmates must constantly contend with. They live in a culture of absolute dependency. All of life's major decisions are made for them.

They do not set alarm clocks; they are told when to get up. They do not think about what to make for breakfast or supper; the choice is made for them. They are told when they may take a shower and when they can receive items from the canteen. They are assigned where they will live and who their cell mate will be. They have no choices over which neighborhood they will live in (unless they want to be sent to segregation[1]) and little choice over what they will do for work. Their clothing is issued, and the patterns and colors are predetermined. Bedding and towels arrive on set schedules; they need only have the soiled ones ready for whatever time the protocol requires.

"Count times" ensure that their presence is accounted for at fixed intervals throughout the day. Movement within the prison from one place to another cannot be made without permission, and, in most cases, it is necessary to have a pass signed by the officer supervising their last position. Independence, in this culture, is not an option.

On the outside, the average person makes hundreds, perhaps thousands, of decisions a day. Prison is a culture where decision-making, comparatively speaking, has been reduced to only a few. It is fairly easy to adapt to this facet of the experience. The issue is further compounded by the temperament of many offenders, especially among the younger inmates. Generally speaking, a sense of responsibility has not been one of their strongest suits. (It definitely wasn't one of mine.) Criminal activity, by its very nature, is an act of irresponsibility. It says: "I will do what I *want*, not what I should." When you combine this mentality with an environment that makes all your decisions for you, the result is that little is done to enhance the individual's sense of responsibility, at least during the time of his incarceration.

Then he is released to the streets.

Instantly, he is transferred from a life of total dependence to a world of near independence. It is a surreal experience, an excursion into culture shock. He is expected—in a very short amount of time—to find a job, a place to stay, and a way to get back and forth between them. He will probably have to obtain a new Social Security card and reapply for his driver's license. Before he can secure any of those things, he will probably need to obtain a copy of his birth certificate. He needs to find working capital to pay the landlord. He has to contact the electric company, the phone company, the gas or oil company.

If he intends to drive, he will need car insurance. The insurance company is only open while he is working. When will he get there? What transportation is available to him until he gets his driver's license? Who will take him around? His parole officer says he better be back home by 9:30. He can't associate with so-and-so; he's an ex-felon. Whom will he ask for help? When can it get done? New clothing is needed. Which way to the Salvation

Army? His head begins to spin from the myriad of major decisions he needs to make. "Oh yeah, I need to buy an alarm clock. . . ."

It's little wonder then that many former prisoners find the transition to the streets overwhelming. Halfway houses that enable them to transition to life on the outside play a crucial role in this adjustment. Frank Costantino, former president of COPE,[2] is also director of Bridges of America, a national movement of Christian halfway houses. In New England, the Bridge House is operated by Jim Spence, the former chaplain of MCI Walpole. In operation for over ten years now, the ministry has expanded to cover two homes and is currently involved in opening a third site. Scores of men have not only made a successful integration to the streets but also have been discipled as Christians in the process.[3]

Unfortunately, many men and women will max out and go straight from the totally dependent world of prison to the complex world of unbridled decisions and temptations on the streets.

Although life in prison can be complex in terms of relational and social dynamics, it is quite simple in terms of order. Everything must conform. Therefore, a necessary by-product of this culture of total dependence is that it creates a greater need for significance and individuality. Because there are so few opportunities to demonstrate choice over life's basic requirements such as, "What will I wear, what will I eat, where will I work, and when will I sleep?" there arises a greater need to assert one's own uniqueness. Many inmates take to writing poetry or even books. Letter-writing (in addition to the contact it provides with loved ones) also helps to preserve a sense of identity by keeping those links with the past alive. Hobby crafts, art, and music also meet essential human needs in terms of creativity and personal tastes. There is freedom in the choices, be it in the creation or in the appreciation of such things.

Where allowed, unique hairstyles and wild mustaches are often exhibited. One friend I know let his hair grow to shoulder length—on only one side of his head. The other half was shaved bald. The need for individual significance is also responsible, in part, for the popularity of tattoos.[4] Although these emblems may represent statements of rebellion in a variety of forms, their adornment still sets their owners apart. No combination is the same. They are marks of individuality, declarations of identity. In a culture that seeks to reduce everyone to a common denominator, there is a cry for individual expression.

It is important that volunteers find ways of letting the inmates do things *for* them. All too often, because volunteers are responsible for their particular program, they get into the mode of doing and running everything. But responsibility for the program does not exclude finding ways in which the participants can exercise both choice and contribution. These may be little things, but one must make a conscious effort to look for them. I usually ask different people in the group to share an experience that may demonstrate a point I am making. Or, if handouts have been prepared, I ask for a member of the group to distribute them. If you are planning a special in-prison event, perhaps posters drawn up by the residents can advertise the attraction. With so many creative people in jail, they will spend more time on the project than you ever could—and probably do a better job.

One of the things I like most about teaching an in-prison seminar for Prison Fellowship is that the content usually encourages inmate participation. Some of the leader's guides include skits that can be acted out by the participants or games that require imagination to play. I will usually ask if there are any inmates with musical ability who might like to sing or play for the group. Sometimes they will get together with other inmates back in the units and practice for a special presentation.

For example, one of the women I know at the New Hampshire State Prison for Women had played the violin when she was a girl but had not played it since. When one of the volunteers came in with just such an instrument, the young lady came up to admire it. By God's grace she was given permission by the administration (and the volunteer) to take it back to her unit that evening, and, for the first time in many years, she brought it up to her neck and began to play again. The following day, when the participants in the seminar had reassembled, she played a beautiful piece for the pleasure of the group. What a blessing it was for those of us who heard! Tears of joy united the hearts of both inmates and volunteers that day. The Lord eventually provided her with her own violin, and she continues to play it on special occasions for the church inside.

We are all members of one body. Allow the saints on the inside to share the gifts the Holy Spirit has given them whenever possible. Work hard at this. Think creatively. You will be giving them an opportunity to express their individuality as well as a sense of responsibility—the two things that are most needed in this culture of dependence. They will not only experience the joy of service, but you, in turn, will have received the benefit and blessing which the expression of *their* gift will provide.

Like most ex-hippies, I know how to strum the guitar. This ability is a great asset in prison ministry because the guitar's portability makes it one of the easiest instruments to clear security. But I have found that, in most situations, I seldom have to lead music any more. Most of the institutions I now enter have people who can play and lead music much better than I can. And even in those facilities where I may still have to lead the singing, I choose songs which engage their participation. I encourage them to clap along and teach them how to "sing arounds." I also find someone to pass out the song sheets. This assignment may seem like such a small thing, but it's another way of involving inmates. You will discover that most are eager and proud to do it.

A more important task, on your part, will be in helping them learn how to apply biblical principles to their lives and to make the responsible decisions concerning them. If any should confide personal problems with you, encourage them to make responsible choices based upon the Word of God. As highlighted in the last chapter, some of those decisions will be difficult, given their circumstances. Encourage them to take the appropriate actions. It's their responsibility as believers.

One of the greatest gifts you can leave behind as a minister of the gospel is to teach them to be dependent—upon Jesus. Because of your role in their lives, they have come to depend on you as instrumental in their Christian growth. But always remember that Christ himself is the goal. By gently weaning them off yourself and encouraging them to rely on Christ (through his Word, through prayer and through the joyful and sanctified duty of Christian obedience), you will be teaching them true and godly responsibility within the confines of this culture of dependence.

14

YESTERDAY

A LARGE PIECE OF YELLOW POSTER BOARD dominated the central portion of the cell wall opposite one inmate's bunk. To its surface he had carefully attached and arranged a collection of photographs. Smiling back at him were the glossy faces of his mom and dad, brothers and sisters, aunts and uncles, friends, and, of course, several images of pretty girls. Some of the children grinned back from the standard settings of their school pictures, while other figures posed under trees, on swing sets, or stood beside souped-up cars and motorcycles. Many of the photos were yellowed with age. My guess was that the children smiling back from those reflections of the past were now involved with children of their own.

But this was his life staring back at him, or at least the sacred part of it. Like faces forever frozen in some mysterious time warp, they existed only in a lost and faraway country, a fantasy world like the Land of Oz. This world did exist once, and in the man's memories, it still did. That poster was holy ground. I couldn't imagine how many times his eyes had come to rest upon the citizens of that other world as he lay there in a state of arrested metamorphosis, trapped in the cocoon of his own reality. How many excursions had he taken as he remembered them?

The answers to these questions depend a great deal upon how much of that world is still interactive. If there are regular visits from those same people, as well as current letters and photos, then the worlds are still running parallel and somewhat simultaneously. But even then, the types of experiences are quite different for each of them. The lines intersect only in the visiting room, or on the

113

pages of today's mail, or perhaps in the brief phone call where whispers bounce off the cement walls and echo in the ears of ever-present others.

But for those who have been down[1] for a while, the lines are fewer, and they tend to intersect all too infrequently. For some, they have ceased to touch at all.

So God uses memory to console the lonely heart. Those who dwell in this frozen time zone look back with longing to happier days. Times when things were good or at least better. Times when they had something to show for their lives. Times when that certain someone loved them, golden moments that passed away all too soon. As devastated as many of their lives were, there were patches in the quiltwork (however small) that are remembered with warmth. The bittersweet joy of memory is the stuff of poetry and the fuel of ballads. It's that strange mixture of nostalgia and pain that creates the music of the blues and separates mechanical talent from the originals. It is one of prison's primary colors.

It explains why some loyalties go very deep. When one thinks about what I would call "the great interruption" (the experience of being arrested and suddenly having the entire backdrop of life shift like stagehands moving scenery), one can begin to understand how connections with the previous props are important to them. When an inmate meets another inmate from his hometown or old neighborhood, for example, there is an immediate interest. Do they know the same people? Did they frequent the same places? Such people represent a link with the interrupted history of their former lives.

A similar dynamic exists with those on active duty in the service. I can recall during my stay in the navy how it was when one sailor met another. "Where are you from?" was usually the first question. If someone answered "Chicago" (the same area I hailed from when I joined the service), then our next question would be "Where 'bouts?" This would usually lead to an animated discussion of our old haunts. But the particular topic didn't really matter because the dialogue itself was serving a purpose. It was filling the present air with a fragrant breeze from home. A link with Camelot was being connected to the present. And whenever you saw that particular person again, there would always be this little bond between the two of you. You might call each other "Chicago" from then on, or some other personal term that identified the link.

I see this same dynamic happening in prison for the same reason. Inmates who came from the same neighborhoods or who ran in the same circles are called "homeys" or "homeboys." Gangs, in particular, like to use these terms. It identifies them; there is a common loyalty there.[2]

Contacts with the old life (as long as there were no negative ramifications) are a plus in terms of relationship. This holds true even if the person is a volunteer. One of the best questions you can ask an inmate when trying to strike up a conversation is the same one the soldiers used to ask: "Where are you from?" If you are familiar with the area, you will have something in common with them.

Posing the question about where one is from has always been a personal advantage for me because of having hitchhiked around the country so many times during my hippie days. (God uses everything!) The odds are always great that I will know something about the inmate's home area. But even in the case of total unfamiliarity, I can always ask the person to tell me something about it. Most people are happy to do this because it strikes a chord that rings of the "old country," the place of happier memories, the land before the great interruption. So for a little while the conversation itself helps them to escape. *They are talking to someone in real time about the time that was.*

This is an important service the volunteer can render, and it should not be underestimated. Like the soldiers, they will tend to remember your conversations with fondness. And if you actually *are* familiar with the "old country," think how much greater that link will be.

As for those volunteers who are ex-cons themselves, sometimes that link with the past can even include the country of the bastilles itself.

A few years ago I heard that a certain inmate had been returned to New Hampshire State Prison from the federal camp in Leavenworth, Kansas. Al LaMorey, my coworker in that prison, had met him in maximum security and discovered that the inmate knew me. It turned out that Jim had been one of the guys who had served time in New Hampshire back in the sixties—when I had been doing time. Since there was this natural tie with someone from the "old country," I decided to pay him a visit my next time in.

He had indicated that he wanted to be left alone, so they had assigned him a cell at the very end of the tier. Sometimes when the young bucks come in, they like to establish their reputations by challenging one of the older warriors to some sort of confrontation. There was no such challenge made to Jim. He had been in prison most of his life and had earned his reputation long ago. No one messed with him. He also had many more years left to serve, and that reality tends to fortify the attitude of having nothing left to lose. So the younger prisoners wisely respected this.

I appeared at his cell door one day with my usual armful of Bibles and said "hi" to him. He was glad to see me, and a very natural conversation about the "old days" ensued. We mostly spoke about the other guys we had done time with years ago. Although we had lost track of most of the men, we still knew the whereabouts of a few of them. Some were still doing time, a few others had died, and one had been murdered in prison.

At one point in the conversation, he shook his head with a smile and said, "Lennie, what happened to you? You used to be such a rip-out. What changed you?" I jumped on the opportunity to talk about the Lord and to explain to him that it was Jesus who changed me and that he was the only one who could bring about that kind of transformation. I told him that what he did for me, he could do for him.

"I'm glad it worked for you," he said, "but I'm not interested." I could tell the conversation was drawing to a close; he looked as though he wanted to get back to what he was doing. I decided to push it a little bit further, however.

"Jim, why don't you take this Bible? It can only do you good."

"No thanks," he replied. "Give it to someone who will read it. I won't."

Sometimes you get a sense from the Holy Spirit when to pursue a thing and when to leave it alone. I decided to push it a little further.

"Seriously, Jim, this book can change your life. Give it a chance. You never know."

"Look, man," he said, "I don't want to disrespect you, but I don't want it."

Sometimes you get a sense from the Holy Spirit about how far you can push a thing. I decided to give it one more try. (By this time you're *hoping* it's the leading of the Holy Spirit!)

"Jim, look, I'll tell you what. Let me put this Bible on that shelf over there, and I'll come back to see you in a couple of weeks. If you haven't read it by then, I'll take it back and give it to someone else."

He hesitated for a moment; I wasn't sure what to expect. But then, resignedly, he finally conceded with a wave of his hand and said, "OK. Put it on the shelf." (He was probably thinking that if that's what it takes to get rid of this guy, great!)

But I didn't get back to Jim for two or three months. It wasn't my intention to be that slow in returning, but I had so many other tiers to be on and so many other guys to talk to that I just wasn't able to revisit him when I had hoped.

Today I have that Bible as one of my most treasured possessions. I use it as a testimony to the power of God to change hearts. Somewhere in that three-month period, God entered Jim's cell and then entered his heart. That was nearly eight years ago. Today Jim is one of the most consistent and faithful inmates in that prison—an obvious testimony to the grace of God in conversion.

When I came back to his cell on that second meeting, the Bible had been transformed from a bright and shiny, unused book to a worn and frayed, familiar friend. It was just a paperback Bible; it was never made to withstand the kind of use it had received. You could see the imprint of his large fingers over the cover.

There was hardly a page in the entire book that had not been underlined in red and blue ink or that had not been highlighted in yellow marker. Beside his bed was a pile of yellow legal paper filled with verses. Whenever he came to a verse that was especially meaningful to him, he would write it down on the legal pad because he was afraid he wouldn't be able to find it in the Bible again. He had tabbed many pages with transparent tape that read "love" or "peace" on them. This once-violent man was now taken up with the themes of love and peace!

Months later we wound up giving him a leather-bound NIV Study Bible. He loves the Word so much that he just stood there with the new Scriptures in his hands, quietly repeating the phrase, "It's Christmas. It's Christmas." After recopying many of his favorite verses, he later insisted that we take his original Bible, the one the Holy Spirit had urged him to take on that eventful day.

I tell this story because it speaks to the power of God to change a heart. No matter where you volunteer, or no matter how little you think you can relate, or how little you sometimes feel you have to offer, remember that the battle is not yours; it is the Lord's. It is not by your power or wisdom that God transforms hearts and souls but by his power and grace alone (Zech. 4:6). There was no human representative present with Jim on the day he became a Christian. I was merely the mailman who delivered the letter about a Father's love for his errant son.

God used a previous negative experience to build a small bridge into a man's life, a bridge that had been forged long ago in the "old country" and wound up leading him into a new one.

> People who say such things show that they are looking for a country of their own. If they had been thinking of the country they had left, they would have had opportunity to return. Instead, they were longing for a better country—a heavenly one. Therefore God is not ashamed to be called their God, for he has prepared a city for them (Heb. 11:14–16).

15

The Same Ol' Same Ol'

I CAN STILL SEE HIM leaning against the door of his cell. His eyes conveyed a sense of hopelessness and unfathomable weariness. "I'm tired, man," he said. "I'm just tired. There's got to be more to life than this." He was not speaking of physical exhaustion but of the kind of plague that could, perhaps, beset a very old, sick man. He was soul-weary; he was burned out on life. He was thirty-eight years old.

I have seen that look many times since then, but for some reason that particular inmate sticks out as the epitome of them all. He is their representative, the one I think back to every time I hear another inmate echo his words. It is the weariness that comes from having spent too much time in prison, or perhaps, as is more common, having returned one too many times. Its telltale signs usually appear in the mid-thirties, a time in life when they are no longer fueled by the buoyant optimism of youthful defiance. It is a season when the empirical wisdom of age is beginning to whisper that time is passing them by—and they still have nothing to show for it. A sort of institutional midlife crisis. A tired of being tired.

Although life in the fortress continually changes in small and not-so-small ways, the *feeling* changes hardly at all. The faces are different, but the conversations are the same. How tough you were on the streets, how many girls you had, how many drugs you did or sold, how fast and cool your vehicles were, how bad an actor you could be, how loud, how strong, how mean, how quick with the tongue, and on it goes.

But it's *always the same!* The loud speakers crackle out the movement times or garble the last names of inmates with regular

119

irregularity. Bits and pieces of conversations like exploding shards of shrapnel are yelled back and forth from one cell to another; the sound of a radio or TV set, the intermittent curse or vulgarity, the taunts, the challenges, the angry outbursts—all conspire together to create an ever-present backdrop of meaningless noise.

It is hard to imagine how tiresome these sounds can become, especially to lifers[1] or repeat offenders who have reached a stage in life beyond "the foolishness." Most make the adjustment in that (for most of the time) they hardly hear the noise any more, in much the same way a person living near an elevated train can get used to the orchestrated roaring and shaking of trains passing by. Nevertheless, the constant superficiality and overarching immaturity begin to take a toll on those who seek something deeper out of life. The younger inmates, for the most part, are still into playing the macho role. They are taken up with prison life and have the energy to play the game. But for the lifers, or repeat offenders like the man I mentioned above, there is often a thirst for something deeper, something more meaningful. "There has to be more to life than this." "Like the crackling of thorns under the pot, so is the laughter of fools. This too is meaningless" (Eccles. 7:6).

Some older prisoners never break out of the immaturity of youthful braggadocio. They seem incapable of operating on a different plane. They remain older versions of their younger selves, trapped in some emotional time warp that never releases them from their teenage years. And conversely, I have known some younger inmates who were deeply thoughtful and philosophical, so I want to avoid typecasting anyone here. But generally speaking, the culture doesn't seem to allow any other channel for background noise. It's kind of like trying to hold a philosophical conversation in a ballpark full of animated fans. Like the writer of Ecclesiastes, "Everything is meaningless." And it takes its toll on everyone: guards, staff, and inmates alike.

Most prisons try to accommodate lifers. They will usually try to place them together in the same living areas. Others have "honor" tiers where, if you have behaved yourself, you can be housed in a unit that grants the inmates extra privileges. These may include such things as a single cell, extra recreation time, or even a quiet job of some sort. One of the less obvious privileges, however, can consist of the compatibility of the personalities placed there—other inmates who are quiet, not troublesome, and respectful of one another's space. In most cases, however, a kind of unspoken truce is worked out with the lifers themselves. They just agree that this is going to be a quiet tier, whether the administration orchestrates it or not. Such "agreements" are also self-policed. The community has a way of making their expectations known to those who come into it; and they have ways of getting people off the tier who refuse to comply.

Others retreat into books or writing music and poetry—far-off lands that enable them to leave the superficiality of the noise in order to satisfy the deeper longings of their souls. Many find a few trusted friends in whom they can confide. But whatever one does to find that utopia, you can be sure it will be in sharp contrast with the "same ol' same ol.'" Inmates admire genuineness. Although the noise rings with the babble of braggadocio, the clamor of angry challenges, and the endless peals of profanity, they admire the rare trait of someone who feels secure enough truly to be himself. They know this characteristic is rare in a land where image is important and weakness is shunned. It explains why the truly tough are admired and why even those who have murdered are respected—as long as there is little doubt that they would do it again. (This is because implicit in the potential threat is the commodity of authenticity.)

The art of the bluff is often exercised in this particular gaming parlor, but, unfortunately, it will often be called. Not everyone can be the baddest, and so most inmates adopt the wiser course of trying to stay out of the way. In prison, one is constantly sensitive to his or her social standing, and the attempt at ruffling as few feathers as possible is a prudent course. But remember that the noise is confrontive, negative, angry, and profane. Maneuvering through this kind of bedlam requires a restraint that is not always easy. A natural consequence is that the freedom to be oneself is greatly suppressed.

Too much effort has to be placed on navigating safely through the rocks and whirlpools of everyday life to enjoy the luxury of nonchalance. Only when one is safely in the personal lagoon of his own cell can he let his guard down. For the thousands who share living quarters, sometimes this safety can be found only within the perimeters of their own mattresses.

Christian volunteers should not underestimate the valuable contribution they can make in combating the "same ol' same ol'" syndrome. Matters of faith are deeply personal, and spiritual conversations stand out in stark contrast to the usually shallow exchanges of the tier. They are hungry for deeper conversation, and to engage in dialogue with a religious volunteer is an acceptable outlet for them. (Acceptable in the sense that since this is the volunteer's function in the institution, one would expect these people to be talking about spiritual things. We will speak more about this unique advantage of "function" in the chapter on "The Spiritual Climate of Prison.")

It used to amaze me how quickly inmates would speak to a Christian volunteer about deeply personal issues. I sometimes take it for granted, but it remains, nonetheless, a great advantage of the ministry. Part of it has to do with the role of volunteers (it's their function to talk about such things), and part of it has to do with the culture. The lives of inmates have obviously been shattered; they cannot pretend that things are going well. So the starting line for most of these discussions is already beyond the superficial "hi-world-I'm-doing-fine" level. Their lives are broken. They know it, and they know that you know it. So let's begin there.

There is no doubt that cell-to-cell ministry produces greater fruit for these kinds of discussions than do group services. Nearly all people, anywhere, will open up on a deeper, personal level in a one-on-one situation than in a group setting. But even at someone's cell, the volunteer must remember that invisible ears in the nearby cubicles not only *can* listen in but they probably are. It's not that they are eavesdroppers by nature, but remember that for them, too, this is a conversation that is traveling beyond the shallow babble of the norm. The volunteer needs to be sensitive to the fact that others may be listening in, and not lead the inmate into revealing something that may prove embarrassing to him. Otherwise, the poor soul will surely hear about it after you leave.

Suffice it to say that volunteers can meet a great need with respect to breaking through the haze of the "same ol' same ol'." Personal conversation is a humanizing activity in a very stage-prop world. Inmates look forward to seeing you when you come in. You are helping them to stay in touch with their genuine selves. "I don't get enough of this," they will often tell you. Learn to be not only a good listener but a genuine one. Each man or woman has a story to tell, and we can learn something from every one of them. Then, after a time, you will have earned the right to be heard, and the inmates themselves will want you to share about those things that are important to you.

"When he saw the crowds, he [Jesus] had compassion on them" (Matt. 9:36).

Part III
Dynamics

16

Institutionalization

"We have met the enemy, and they is us!"[1]

IN AN EARLIER CHAPTER, we spoke of the emotional pain that ensues when inmates are suddenly separated from the people and places they hold most dear. This separation includes not only being severed from their closest loved ones but also being removed from the familiar backdrop of people and places that give them a sense of self-esteem and identity. But what if that sense of self-esteem and identity is now received from the prison culture?

sEntering prison is entering a new world, and this new world has its own social life. We have already spoken about the existence of a social code, but here we are primarily interested in the society's *life*—from which the code is generated. Most of the guys I know resent the word *institutionalization,* or its sister phrase, *becoming institutionalized.* And, I think, rightly so. By its very nature it is a dehumanizing word. Prisoners view it as lumping everyone into a category of characteristics that, while perhaps of interest to sociologists, tends to erase their own uniqueness and individuality. It is also a condemnatory word when used in the courtroom. Woe to the repeat offender who hears the word "institutionalized" at his trial! He could be in danger of receiving "the Bitch."[2]

Though much overused (and misused), the term *institutionalization,* for our purposes, defines someone who has more or less adopted the prison environment as his natural world. It is the person who has learned to function more easily and comfortably on the inside than he or she does on the outside. It is the man who

127

now relates better to his friends and acquaintances behind the walls than he does to those on the streets. It is the woman who feels more socially (and successfully) able to function in a jail-house setting than she did on the outside. Ultimately, it defines the person who feels most like *himself* within this society than he does on the streets.

A sharp distinction needs to be made here between the prisoner who has successfully learned to manage his life within this culture (which he did not choose), and the inmate who can actually no longer function beyond it. The former have merely learned to make the most of it. This is not only normal; it is healthy. Such people never concede that prison is their natural environment. They see their outside life as temporarily on hold, but they are realistic enough to know that they must maneuver within their present environment as best they can. They continue to stimulate themselves intellectually and physically, but they will never accept this habitat as their own.

At first take, one may ask, "Who *would?*" But I have personally known many inmates who have. This is not to say that any of them would not jump at the opportunity of being released or even that they think of themselves as being institutionalized. But I believe many prisoners have become so acclimated to their razor-wire surroundings that they have lost (or are losing) the desire to operate beyond it.

Many "lifers" have a chance at parole. The term *lifer* can refer to someone who is serving time on a lesser sentence than actual life but has been in and out of prison so much that he or she has earned the title, for all practical purposes. A lifer is, as some have said, "doing life on the installment plan." For those who *are* serving life without the possibility of parole, the question of institutionalization is, of course, a moot point. Prison will remain their environment for the remainder of their days. One prisoner I know has been in for nearly fifty years already. He entered the state prison as a teenager. I can't begin to imagine how difficult his life would be if he were ever released.

I can still recall another man who was in his mid-sixties when I was a young prisoner. You could always find him at the pinochle tables, smoking his pipe and methodically playing out his hand. For all appearances, he seemed as content as a cat dozing on a sunspot. He certainly didn't look capable of murdering his wife, the brutal crime for which he had received a life sentence. I asked him one day in the middle of a foursome why he seemed so "at home."

He looked over the rim of his glasses, took a puff on his pipe, selected a card from his hand, and said, "Well, think of it. I'm not much interested in sex any more. I have my pipe and tobacco. I get three square meals and a place to sleep. No taxes to pay, no lawns to mow, and the best part," he added with a chilling smile, "is that I get to play cards with folks like you all day."

As he said that, I'm sure the rest of us were thinking about the details of his crime. He had blown his wife away with a shotgun because she had repeatedly nagged him while he was playing cards with a friend at his kitchen table. After the gruesome deed had been done, he calmly called the police and then told his blanched friend to sit down because they probably had time for two more hands before the squad cars arrived.

Al LaMorey[3] and I once knew a fellow with whom we had worked while he had been in prison. We met him on the streets one day—just as he was about to throw a stone through the window of a local police station. We took him to a restaurant and tried to settle him down. When we asked him why he wanted to violate his parole in this way, he said it was because he just couldn't get it going on the streets. In the prison, he knew what was expected of him and was familiar with the routine. Although he was usually in some sort of trouble, he knew his space and was comfortable with it. Even the officers knew how to deal with him because he was so much a part of the scenery.

His case is not unique. And that's what makes it all a bit scary. Our friend was content to settle for throwing a brick through a police station window. All he really wanted was to violate his parole to the extent that he would be sent back to prison to finish up his former sentence. He didn't really want to pick up a whole lot of extra time by committing a more serious offense.

But what about the person who just wants to go back to prison because that's where he or she finds life easier to cope with? A person that fits this description has entered what I would call the "free crime" category. In other words, his ultimate goal is to go back to prison. For most people, the threat of a prison sentence is something of a deterrent to wrongdoing—but this person *wants* to go back. So in his own mind he is free to commit crimes until he is caught because either way he wins. People who fall into this category create frightening implications for society.

While I admit that this is the extreme, and thankfully the minority, experience, what about the tens of thousands who have become so accustomed to the prison culture that they feel they could *handle* another trip? This is where the degree of institutionalization plays a significant role in our discussion. To the extent that a person doesn't mind spending time in prison (because it is directly related to how comfortable he or she feels there), is the degree to which one may or may not be inclined to fall back into criminal activity. I believe this is especially true for drug-related crimes. Drug addiction fuels the temptation to commit crimes in order to keep the addiction fueled and simultaneously places people in areas where evil can occur suddenly and easily. The police, therefore, eventually become involved, and arrests will be made.

But what if the criminal participants feel minimally threatened by a potential bust? While prison may not be where they want to end up, the prison environment doesn't threaten them because they are able to function well within it. In fact, the two societies are now, more than likely, *blended*. Some of the very people they are currently hanging out with on the streets probably include acquaintances with whom they've already done time. And when and if they go back to prison, some of those friends will still be with them. Thus the society they are most comfortable with—the society from which they derive self-esteem and a sense of identity—overlaps between the streets and the walls.

I'll never forget my first day out of prison. The parole officer dumped me in a town in which I had never lived because part of my parole requirement was that I could not live in the city in which I had committed my crime. So I was dropped off more than an hour away from my regular haunts, in an area where I did not have one single acquaintance. I also had two weeks in which to find a job and secure a place to stay, or I would be returned to prison on a PV.[4]

I found a rooming house that same afternoon and then immediately set out to do the two things that most men intend to do on their first day out. I was not a Christian, and therefore I immediately sought to get drunk and find the comfort of a female. There was a bar just a couple of streets from my room. When I entered the bar, squinting my eyes because of the darkness inside, I heard a voice call out from somewhere in the back of the room, "Hey Spitale!"

"Who could know me in *this* town?" I thought to myself. It turned out to be a friend I had met in prison. My time behind bars had succeeded in giving me friends all over the state! Although it is a parole violation for known felons to associate with other felons, the odds are now greater that they will run into one another from time to time because the culture is now blended. Ex-prisoners tend to gravitate to the same places and do the same things. I was to meet other ex-cons in other bars.

I soon discovered that the prison experience not only extended to friends from my own institution but to people who had done time in other prisons as well. Although I had not known these people previously, there was now an automatic bond. Like war veterans (or even Christians for that matter), the shared experience has a way of helping to identify others who have had the same experience. Once the word is out that you have done time, it has a way of attracting others who have also served time.

This magnetism extends even to those who *relate* to the criminal culture. There was a woman at the place where I was working who had dated a man who was currently in prison, and now she was interested in dating me. I already had a girlfriend by this time, but that did not deter this particular woman. Day after day, she suggested that we get together. Even though I was not interested in having a relationship with her, she felt she related to me because of the connection she felt with the culture.

While extreme institutionalization is not the category I would personally place most inmates in, the *degree* to which one identifies with the culture is a concern. Whichever term one uses to describe the process is less important than the fact that the process has begun. A trip to prison creates an exposure to a new society, and the degree to which one identifies with that society should mark the degree of concern. This dynamic has ramifications for aftercare, as well as choices of association that one will make while still *in* the prison. The challenge (for the Christian volunteer) is to make sure that those people who are seeking to grow in their Christian faith understand these dynamics as much as possible. It is often difficult for the inmates themselves to see the forest because of the trees. How does one lift his or her eyes above the culture while submersed within it?

Although the challenge is great, it is not impossible. This is especially true if prisoners have put their faith in Jesus Christ. God has now introduced them to *his* culture. The truth is that the person who was once enslaved to the dynamics of his old environment is actually gone (see Gal. 2:20; 2 Cor. 5:17). The new has come.

The volunteer must emphasize the imperative to keep the fires of this new reality burning. The basic disciplines of prayer, Bible reading, praise, confession, obedience, service—and especially fellowship with other Christians—are very important. If the volunteer serves in an institution where many of the inmates will be released within a short time, the need to find a Bible-believing, Christ-centered church for them *before* they get out is absolutely essential.

I encourage you to stay in touch with your in-prison disciples. Hold them accountable in the areas of the disciplines just mentioned; continue to encourage them. Identify other sincere Christians within the population and suggest that they meet together for Bible study and prayer. Encourage the stronger believers to seek out the weaker Christians. This gives them a much-needed sense of ministry and responsibility, as well as being of benefit to the younger sheep. There is a body of Christ—a church—within every prison. Some are in a church-planting stage, and others have actually progressed to a missionary stage, but they are still churches, nonetheless. And Christ has not held back anything they need (1 Cor. 1:4–9). Be alert for the various gifts with which the Holy Spirit has blessed his church.

Although enslavement to the dynamics of the old society has been broken by regeneration, the attachments to the former things still range deeply in the flesh—just as they do in ours. The old culture has infiltrated their lives in many areas over the years and will continually come into conflict with the new one. The prison code, for example, will challenge their young faith in many ways. The more opportunity you have to disciple the willing inmate over a long period of time, the more you will be able to assist him as he experiences his faith within the confines of his present situation.

Christian volunteers penetrate the walls of institutional society by demonstrating the reality of another; they do this both in words and actions. As your disciples have the opportunity to observe you as *you* grow, the more they will learn what it means to be a Christian in their own culture. If they are believers, the change *has* come. They are now citizens of another country, and over time, they will begin to be influenced by the Lord of that country. They have entered the society of the kingdom of God, and it transcends all cultures. It *can* be lived out in prison.

"I lift up my eyes to the hills—where does my help come from? My help comes from the LORD, the Maker of heaven and earth" (Ps. 121:1–2).

17

Workin' for the Man

IF IT'S TRUE THAT WE LEARN from our mistakes, I should be a genius by now. As I mentioned previously, one of my greatest mistakes was joining the military when I did. Exhibiting a pattern of rebellion that extended beyond my home, I was already having problems with school and municipal authorities. Now here I was joining the service—a system that was structured upon authority at every level! My greatest problem, looking back, was that I didn't recognize what my problem was.

In fact, ignorance (or denial) of the problem is one of the reasons why dealing with those who struggle with authority issues is so difficult. If you try to suggest to people that they may have a problem in that area, their very nature tells them to reject what you are saying because you come across as someone who is telling them what to do! If anger is the predominant emotion in prison, I would submit that antiauthoritarianism is the predominant attitude. The Bible refers to it as rebellion. Many inmates agree that they "wouldn't listen to anybody" when they were growing up. "No one could tell me what to do" is a refrain one often hears.

A number of inmates nurture a desire to go back to the streets after they are released—to warn young people not to take the same paths they took. They envision themselves as encouraging teenagers not to repeat the same mistakes they made. This is a noble ambition, and if they are Christians, may even hint at an early desire for ministry at some level. But inevitably, one of the other inmates will ask them, "Did *you* listen to anybody when *you* were growing up?" I have never heard anyone respond with a "yes" to this question; and the sobering silence that usually follows is a reality check for the well-meaning conquistadors.[1]

So then, prison becomes something of a paradox, or at the very least, a great challenge for those who seek to use it rehabilitatively. Whereas my choice to join the navy was voluntary (stupid perhaps, but definitely voluntary), the inmates are not in prison by choice. Society, then, is faced with the constant challenge of having stuffed hundreds of individuals with authority problems into a sardine can that is authoritarian from top to bottom. When you add the element of anger being the predominant emotion, it is a wonder that prisons run as smoothly as they do most of the time. The reason for this "success" is largely due to two major realities: (1) Most inmates want to go home at some point, so compliance is to their advantage; and (2) the security department is dedicated to a single-minded goal: stay in charge. Their sole purpose is to keep the prison under control. Anything less than this and it ceases to be a prison.

Human services,[2] on the other hand, has the more complex target. Because they are working for the betterment of the individual, the attainment of their goal is harder to quantify. It also has a much wider range of potential results. Security officers, on the other hand, need only maintain order and authority; there are no "ifs," "ands," or "buts" about it. Most officers do their jobs with professionalism and integrity, given the difficulty of the job.[3] This difficulty is driven by the paradox of the culture, which, again, is putting antiauthoritarian people in a totally authoritarian state. Most correctional officers need to be commended for doing a task that usually goes unheralded by the general public.

This means the inmates must live with the ever-present frustration of being constantly exposed to authority. "Good" adjustment takes place when the inmate accepts the authority and learns to live with it. "Bad" adjustment means you will spend most of your time in lockup or maximum security. This is just another way of saying that if one level of security isn't working for you, the degree of security you need must be increased. Security is either turned up or down, but it cannot go away. Remember, the security department operates with only one real goal.

But those who spend most of their time being sent to the Hole are also working with a singular goal: "You are not going to get over on me." Many of the rebellious activities that can occur in prison, such as throwing urine or feces, flooding cells, ripping out fixtures, physical or verbal assaults, destroying property and the like, are the bare spots along the wiring where the paradox is shorting out. These are the points of contact where the irresistible force meets the immovable object, where antiauthority meets authority. And in prison, authority cannot lose—or it ceases to be.

But the individual inmate isn't thinking in these larger terms. All he is thinking is that he is being mistreated, *again,* and he is angry about it. Something unfair is going on, and he has no recourse to address it. He is powerless to make the changes that should be made to right the wrong and correct the "abuse of power." In the end, such people tend to cling to one thing: the indomitable self. "The 'Man' may have my body, and the Man may have all the power, but he will never succeed in breaking *Me!*" This perception of his reality will be generally supported by his peers.

Don't forget that this is a culture that admires defiance. The individual's willingness to go to the Hole defending the right to his viewpoint is testimony to the standoff between authority and those under it. From Security's viewpoint, the inmate was uncooperative and had to be restrained. (Remember, only one goal.) To the inmate, his willingness to face the Hole was proof that he couldn't be broken. Authority may have placed the mustang in the corral, but it will never succeed in breaking him. In his own eyes, he wins. His unbroken spirit is, ultimately, all he has left to defend.

If an officer recognizes that this is what is at stake, he or she can do much to avoid the game by not trampling the horse. By that I mean that a wise officer will try to leave a little room for negotiation before putting an inmate in a do-or-die situation. If you leave no room for the individual to be heard, and no room for respect to be given, you are creating a potentially dangerous situation. It does no good to wait until the mustang is in a rage.

The best officers I have known over the years are those who treat the inmates with respect. Ninety-nine times out of a hundred, respect is what they will receive in return. The key to being a successful security officer is to be consistent. Consistently firm, consistently fair. An inmate needs to know that when you say something, you will stick with it. Whether it's the threat of punishment or a promise for change, your word must be trusted. The prisoner cannot leave his environment, so he wants it to be as stable as possible. This includes having officers around who will be consistent.

If rules change daily, the environment becomes unstable; the inmate doesn't know what is solid and what is shaky. If that which is permissible today may be a write-up tomorrow, an instability is created that can spread like wildfire or be as volatile as nitroglycerin bouncing around in the back of an old buckboard. Obviously, the rules in an institution must change from time to time because new or different circumstances may require it. But I am referring to those rules that are permissible one day and that are infractions the next, or the implementation of rules that appear to have no other purpose than to make the lives of inmates more miserable.[4]

Conflict and disagreement between those who have the power and those who do not will continue to exist, especially in a hierarchy of command. Soldiers in any army, for example, will always complain about the food and grumble about the decisions of their superiors. Some things just go with the territory. But what are the things we *can* change?

Christian volunteers play a bigger role in this matter of authority than most of them realize. They can be an instrument for good, or they can actually intensify the problem. Unfortunately, many volunteers contribute to the latter without realizing it.

One mistake, for example, happens most often with the clergy. Some years ago, a minister wanted to visit a relative of one of his parishioners. Under the assumption that clergy could visit whenever they wished, he showed up at a time that was not within the parameters of the jail's visiting schedule and was subsequently refused the visit. Rather than graciously accepting their timetable, he began to rant and rave about how he was a member of the clergy and had a "right" to the visit. He went on and on, even threatening to sue them for violating the inmate's civil rights. He demanded to see their superiors and insisted that the chaplain be called. The chaplain *was* called—and threw the man out himself.

Regardless of whatever "rights" we think we may have, giving the Lord a bad testimony will never be one of them.[5]

But what of regular volunteers? What role can we play in this tension with authority? Apart from preaching and teaching services, much of our time is spent providing a listening ear to hurting people. This is an important part of the ministry. But what should we do when an inmate begins to complain about the institution in a way that is counterproductive? What should we do if they are going on and on about how unfair such-and-such a condition is or how evil officer so-and-so is? Do we condone evil actions on the part of the administration, or do we tell the inmate that he should just forget about it?

Neither. For one thing, there are always two sides to every story. This holds true not only in prison but in everyday life on the outside as well. The pastor who listens to just one side of a marital conflict should know he is getting only half the story. But let us say, for the sake of the example, that the way the inmate sees it is the way it actually is. Let's say that there *has* been an abuse of authority or some unfair policy or condition that needs correcting and that the volunteer himself can actually see reasonable evidence for it. If this is the case, the person to report it to is the chaplain. He or she is your immediate authority, and it's up to the chaplain to deal with it, not you. Leave it there and trust the Lord to work through the authorities he has placed over *you*.

In the case of a volunteer who is serving in an institution that has no chaplain, and the perceived injustice seems serious enough to pursue, the matter should be reported to the appropriate authority. If the practice in question involves a line officer, the matter should be reported to his or her authority and so on up the line until someone deals with it. Never debate the issue with the offending officer while on the tier—and especially not in front of the inmates. There are appropriate channels for everything.

Volunteers are civilians and, as such, actually have greater access to higher officials than policy may permit the institution's own employees. If there is no chaplain, you are probably serving in a small facility, such as a local jail or county house of correction. A well-placed word to the *right* official, in such circumstances, may have better success in bringing about the desired change. But be wise about whom you select; be sure he or she can be trusted. Once you have made the situation known to the right person, that's probably all you can do. Never let the inmates know you have done this, even if it is for their benefit.

If you are perceived as a crusader, the word will get out. The consequences could detract from the main focus of your ministry, which is the gospel. You will run the risk of being viewed as a possible ear (or torch-bearer) for every perceived injustice the prisoners may have. Consequently, you will begin to attract those who have little or no interest in spiritual things but see you merely as a possible advocate for their cause.

If the officers, on the other hand, begin to view you in this way, you will certainly win no friends among that circle and will probably succeed in distorting the gospel's real message. As a prison volunteer, you will witness many minor injustices along the way; that too, goes with the territory. My advice to you, by and large, is not to get involved in them. It's not why you are there. You will find yourself jousting with windmills and losing sight of your real target.

Let us now examine the inmate's responsibility for a moment. Let's say that you are dialoguing with a prisoner and suddenly find yourself listening to a bitter complaint leveled at some perceived injustice by the prison or its officials. You should politely listen, not only to the content of what is being said, but also to the *manner* in which it is being said. What if you sense, after inserting a few well-placed questions of your own, that the inmate's diatribe is actually rooted in a negative, angry, antiauthoritarian pattern of behavior? How should you proceed? After giving him time to vent, it is the duty of the Christian teacher to begin to reroute the discussion and to use it as an opportunity to steer him toward scriptural principles.

If the person is an unbeliever, I generally point him or her toward the sovereignty of God. I use it as an opportunity to teach the person that God is in control of all things and that he is able to use any and every situation for his purposes. I suggest that this God may even be using the present turmoil to urge the sufferer to call out to *him* for help and deliverance. I ask questions that bring God's reality into the picture. Has he prayed about his situation? Where does she presently stand with the Lord? Does he believe that God has ultimate control?

Depending upon the answers, the Holy Spirit could direct this conversation in any number of different ways. It could be that the frustration they are experiencing *is* being allowed by God to urge them toward true peace, and you could find yourself being involved in their moment of salvation. I have witnessed many inmates surrender their hearts to Christ at such times.

If the person is already a believer, I use it as an opportunity to teach him or her about biblical authority. Don't forget that the issue of authority may be a long-standing problem for many of those with whom you will come into contact. If they became Christians in prison, why should we assume that they automatically understand what God's view of authority is? Use it as a chance to teach them. Unfortunately, too many Christians do not themselves have a good handle on this issue, as evidenced by the many sad conflicts that occur in our churches. Abusive authority by pastors, as well as congregations, is all too common. It is not within the framework of this book to go into this teaching here, but I submit that the prison volunteer, especially, should study this topic and be prepared to help inmates through it. It is a big problem area for many of them. They need to understand how God views authority and how he sovereignly works through it. Studying David's relationship to Saul is a good place to begin.

Many volunteers have contributed to the roots of rebellion without realizing it. They inadvertently feed into it by assuming that the inmate's perception of the abuse is the correct one, and they give support to his outrage by agreeing with it. This does not help him, and it only reinforces the justification he already feels in lashing out against the authority. Our "agreement," in such situations, must be limited to acknowledging how adversely the mistreatment is making him *feel*. We can empathize with the fact that it is tearing him up inside and share that anguish with him as best we can. But it is one thing to sympathize with how inmates are feeling and quite another to leave an opportunity for spiritual growth to go untouched. Use the opportunity their anger and frustration provides to instruct them in God's perspective. Take them to the Scriptures.

Do not side with them against the institution. You can agree that things are unjust (and if you have the opportunity behind the scenes to effect change by mentioning the situation to the right person, you can consider doing so), but never forget that your primary reason for being there is to help them spiritually. This does not negate doing things for their benefit, or even speaking up for them when appropriate, but you (like everyone else in that prison) have a role to play. And you yourself are under authority. Keep the focus of why you are there always in view. I find myself having to do the same thing from time to time.

It is easy, in our humanness, to get off track. Injustice *is* wrong, and there is a part of our Christian makeup that wants to address those wrongs. But it's important to realize that the platform for addressing those wrongs has not always been given to us by the Lord. If he wants to address it, he will assign someone to it. And that person may not be you. What *is* clear is that he has sent you into prison to preach the gospel, that much you know.

One practice I have found helpful in sorting out these role assignments is to ask myself the following two questions: "Who, among all these people employed by the institution, will bring Jesus' answers to this inmate? Who has been given that particular task?" If the answer is me, I'd better stick with that role.

As far as a job assignment within the prison goes, only Christians will carry the reality of the gospel and its principles to those who are confined there. It is not the warden's job to encourage them spiritually. It is not the correctional officer's job. It's not the psychologist's job. It's *your* job. By the same token, you are not there to run the institution. Nor have you been enlisted to maintain security. You have been allowed to come into the prison to provide spiritual input into the lives of the inmates. Do your job.

Teach them God's way. Teach them not to lean on their own understanding but in *all* their ways to acknowledge him. Let them know that *he* will direct their paths (Prov. 3:5–6). Teach them that he is a God who can be trusted. Teach them that no matter what is happening in their lives, he is able to turn it to the good for those who love him (Rom. 8:28). Teach them that God is big enough to work through the authorities in their lives— whether they are out to lunch or not—and is still able to bring good out of it. Teach them to love their enemies and to do them good. Teach them that prayer changes things and to pray for those in authority over them (1 Tim. 2:2). Be an instrument of righteousness in that place, and you will find yourself being used by God to bring fulfillment to those who hunger and thirst after it (Matt. 5:6).

If we as Christians do not teach these things, who will?

18

The Great Equalizer

SOME INMATES OBJECT to the idea that prisons contain a cross-section of society. "Do not lump me in with the rest of them," I can still recall one friend telling me. "I did not lead a criminal lifestyle, nor do I consider myself a criminal." He felt that he did what any husband worth his salt would do. He discovered his wife in bed with someone else and killed her lover on the spot. "That does not," he declared, "make me a criminal."

While that is debatable, I have observed that the crime of murder often does include members of society who were not engaged in a criminal lifestyle on the streets. When I was serving as a volunteer in Florida State Prison, the quietest tier in the whole place was Death Row. Some might think that this was due to the ominous weight of their impending execution, but that wasn't the major factor. A part of the reason for the quietness on this cell block was surely rooted in the fact that it was the only tier allowed to have television sets. But I believe the greater answer lay in the nature of their crimes, which usually included one or more homicides.

Murder is often a crime of passion—spontaneous and angry. Many killings, to be sure, take place in the criminal worlds of drugs or gang-related incidents, but domestic violence still accounts for the largest piece of the pie. The angry fights you hear from your neighbors next door could easily become the scene of a homicide. Jesus himself seemed to allude to the fact that anger is at the root of murder.[1]

So I understand my friend's protest that he did not want to be lumped in with the rest of the prison population. Apart from what he saw as a natural outburst of anger and passion, he had not lived a criminal lifestyle. Ultimately, however, this argument does not negate the fact that life behind the walls does reflect society in general. They are all here—the family men and the children, the bankers and the drug dealers, the computer executives, and the gangbangers. I have met ex-priests and ministers here, judges and policemen, housewives and streetwalkers, the weak and the strong, the white collar and the blue collar. They are all serving time together.

Prison is the great equalizer. It doesn't matter what you were before you came to prison. You all wear the same clothing now. You eat the same food, and you walk the same floors. The landscape is traveled by people who have all been reduced to the same singular color. This includes the wise man as well as the fool, the famous and the infamous, the corporation man and the panhandler, the Vietnam vet and the draft dodger. They all work at the same jobs, live in the same neighborhood, and sleep on the same kinds of mattresses. They have socialized medicine. They schedule no appointments, travel nowhere, and must wait to be visited. They buy the same items in the canteen and flush the same toilets. Prison life, at its basic level, has become their common denominator.

Life on the outside can seem like a vast array of Hollywood props, storefront buildings boasting a variety of window dressings. How we adorn our mannequins depends upon our values, lifestyles, and economics. Most of us go about our daily lives seldom thinking about the wide diversity of colors and choices we have. No one *seems* the same. We dress differently, live differently, and work at different levels of tasks. But, in actuality, it's only how we look. Essentially, we are all the same. Some people have the ability to project their images on larger screens; they can afford the props of fancier houses, higher education, high-powered jobs, and better neighborhoods. They *seem* bigger than life. But in reality, we are all the same size. Like little wizards of Oz, we hide behind the curtains of our illusions, huffing and puffing as we pull the levers that project the images of our lives. But we are all basically tiny.

Nowhere does this become more evident than in the naked and barren world we call prison. Here all the props and facades have been removed. The diversity of window dressings has disappeared, and the mannequins are all clothed the same. No one seems particularly larger than life anymore. The important aspects of one's history, such as education, social standing, occupation, or wealth, have all faded from view. All that remains for identification is an institutional number—a number that now serves as your new identity in this new society. It is sewn into the same location on the same uniform that everyone else is wearing. If "clothing makes the man," if facades truly have value, and if what we project is truly who we are, then everyone in prison is the same. If appearances are all that count, then everyone occupies the same rung on the ladder.

This visual impression is actually a side benefit to the Christian worker. By observing prison life, he or she is confronted with a basic theological truth that evangelicals everywhere say they believe. And this is that sin is no discriminator; we all possess its nature. We say that it doesn't matter what one looks like on the outside, we all share the same dreadful disease on the inside. "For all have sinned and fall short of the glory of God" (Rom. 3:23).

I have often been struck by how small everyone really is. Sometimes a particular case or crime gains local media attention—or even national attention, and the subjects of these spotlights become famous overnight. I recall standing next to a young woman after a service at a major women's prison in New England. I had just delivered the morning's message and, as usual, several of the women were hanging around in small groups afterwards, engaged in conversations with the volunteers. This particular young woman had been standing alone, waiting for one of her friends. I introduced myself, and after some introductory chitchat, asked her if she was a Christian. She turned with an expression of sincerity in her eyes and simply said, "I'm beginning to understand." I encouraged her to continue in her pursuit of Christ, to keep coming to the services, and to keep hanging out with her Christian friends.

On our way out of the prison, the chaplain asked me if I knew with whom I had been speaking. I confessed that I didn't. When she gave me her name, I recognized it as one that I had begun to hear about in the media. At the time, she had been there for a short while, and her case was only beginning to gain the media's attention. Over the next several months, it would ultimately command international interest. Though I seldom pay much attention to the publicity of major trials, I couldn't help but catch news updates of her case here and there. Having met her, it was hard for me to reconcile the media's portrayals with my own.

The person I met was not the bigger-than-life person who had grabbed the interest of two continents, but a quiet-speaking, almost timid girl in blue prison clothing. The chaplain later told me that she did continue to come to services and was being discipled by a faithful woman from a local church who came to visit with her each week.

What *was* a bit unsettling, however, was the way in which even a few Christians got caught up in the media hype. I actually received phone calls from people who had developed a sudden interest in prison ministry—and this young lady in particular. One woman told me that she had "received a burden from the Lord" to minister to her and wanted to know how she could get in touch with her. I told her that she was being well cared for and that if she wanted the name of some other female inmate who could benefit from a letter or a visit, I would look into it for her. She responded with genuine surprise when I told her that the girl was already being discipled, as though—apart from her intervention—it could not possibly happen. She was also not interested in discipling anyone else, and I never heard from her again.

In one nationally hyped case, a teenage boy was arrested on a highly publicized murder charge. He was eventually found guilty and sent to a nearby prison. I stopped by his cell one day as I was making my rounds and found him deeply sorrowful and penitent. Far from looking or acting like a cold-blooded movie killer, he was just a frightened boy in a cell in maximum security. On the day I met him, he was repentant and weeping. But the media fascination with his trial continued unabated until he was sentenced; he will be nearly sixty years old when he becomes eligible for parole.

I could cite other examples, but my point is to say that notoriety or fame of any sort is another false projection. People in the limelight are not bigger than life. And while people on the outside might be impressed with the projection, those who dwell in this particular canyon are not. Oh, there may be some initial curiosity when a notorious inmate first arrives at the prison, but it quickly wears off. In this land behind the gray cement walls, everyone is reduced to the same playing field. This truth is a greater testimony to the way things really are than the outside world reveals. "But the Scripture declares that the whole world is a prisoner of sin, so that what was promised, being given through faith in Jesus Christ, might be given to those who believe" (Gal. 3:22).

According to this Scripture, if we are Christians, we are all ex-convicts. It's not about our being better or different from those in prison. Sin is the common denominator. Before Christ came, we were all wearing the same prison clothing, and we were all under the same sentence of death. In the spiritual reality we were all poor; each of us, equally bankrupt. I have found this to be a hard concept (even among some Christians) to accept from an empirical standpoint. They believe it theologically, but beneath many comments I have heard is the idea that somehow prisoners are worse people than they are. They assume that because they themselves are not in prison, or were ever guilty of committing the same sorts of crimes they are somehow above those who had been convicted of crimes.

I know they wouldn't admit to this sort of thinking from a scriptural standpoint, but something feeds the perspective nonetheless. I believe that one of the headwaters for this type of thinking flows from the storefront images of the outside world. The swirling illusions of differing values, wealth, homes, jobs, and lifestyles have lulled them into making subtle comparisons on a theological plane. It has become difficult for them to realize that, as far as the sinful nature goes, they are just as naked and poor as the convicted drug dealer on J-tier.

Someone once asked the late Chaplain Ray what he thought about the death penalty. His immediate response was, "I deserve it."

If God thought that you and I were deserving of an *eternal* death penalty for the crimes we have committed, then what ultimate difference does it make whether we currently live in the Taj Mahal or in a prison cell? What, according to God, is the difference between us, since both of us are guilty of crimes that deserve the same horrendous sentence? "Lowborn men are but a breath, the highborn are but a lie; if weighed on a balance, they are nothing; together they are only a breath" (Ps. 62:9).

When Karla Faye Tucker was executed in Texas in early 1998 for her part in two gruesome murders, she became the first woman in that state to suffer that fate in many years. I had opportunity, not long after, to discuss her death with some construction workers who were building an addition for a church on Cape Cod. The church was meeting temporarily at another location, and I was to be the guest speaker that morning. Since I had arrived uncharacteristically early, I decided to stop by the work site to see the progress. I found three workers taking a morning break among all the raw lumber and scaffolding. Since the situation was ideal for bringing up a spiritual discussion (workers building a church on a Sunday morning!), we soon had a lively discussion going.

The Lord granted me the opportunity to present the way of salvation by using various bits of building material and other items useful to the illustration. After listening to me for some time, the foreman suddenly announced that someone like Karla Faye Tucker could surely not be in heaven. He had learned from all the recent media attention surrounding her case that she had claimed to have become a born-again Christian. He said there was no way she could be in heaven now, just because she had become a Christian. "She will still have to pay for her sins," he pronounced. "She did something very, very bad, and she will have to pay for that." But the youngest worker, a man named Carlos, suddenly stood up and said, "Not if you've been listening to what this man has said, she won't. He says that Jesus died for her sins and that if she is truly sorry and believes in Him, then she has nothing left to pay for!"

Grace is amazing, no matter where you find it. Whether it be in the confines of a small concrete cell or in the hollow, wooden expanse of an unfinished church building, grace is an astounding revelation. Among the lumber and the dust of a construction site, this young man had grasped its significance! The concept is foreign to the world's ears because grace can't be comprehended until one finds oneself caught in the inescapable claws of the great equalizer—sin. Only in Jesus Christ is the concept of grace truly discovered. He alone came "full of grace and truth" (John 1:14). That's why I love prison ministry so much. It is a place where all the facades of self-sufficiency have been stripped away and where it is evident to everyone within its walls that we *all*, like sheep, have gone astray. "Lowborn men are but a breath and the highborn are but a lie." We are all alike under the same sentence of death. And all of us are guilty.

Two principles could be distilled from all of this. The first is that although inmates are not awed by celebrity, *many volunteers are*. We need to be careful that we are not being lured by the sick demon of vicarious fame that spellbinds so many of those in the world. Be careful to examine the source of phrases such as "special burden" or "God told me that I was to minister specifically to so-and-so." God is no respecter of persons (Rom. 2:11). He does not care more if a person is well known to the world—and He does not care less. He sees them as they really are. Bankrupt. And wearing prison garb. If we are to be true representatives for his name's sake, in such a naked village as prison is, then we need to see *all* men's spiritual needs as the same. Inmates are quick to pick up when someone is receiving preferential treatment. An equal concern for *all* souls should be the trademark of a Christian volunteer.

Second, *your neighbor needs Christ as much as the prisoner.* In a strange twist of perspective, prison ministry volunteers can fall into what I would call the "nine-to-five" syndrome. That is, because those in prison are their primary mission field, it is sometimes easy for them to relax their evangelistic zeal once they *leave* the institution, as though they've "done their job," so to speak. But if this chapter has taught us anything, it is that *everyone* is guilty and in need of God's grace. If prison is a transparent example of this basic spiritual truth, then we in prison ministry, of all people, should be seeking uniformity in our evangelistic zeal—one that sees all men and women, alike, under the shroud of the death penalty (Isa. 25:7). Our antennae should be as alert to spiritual need on the outside as it is on the inside.

Pray that he will grant us ears to hear the cries of the brokenhearted *wherever* they may be. Our ministry grants us the blessing of recognizing that everyone is wearing prison garb—and that grace knows no bounds.

19

Hearts Behind the Mask

LIKE A KNIGHT BEHIND A SHIELD and a suit of armor, the private areas of the heart in prison are well protected. Most inmates lock their deep personal feelings away in a very private place and take them out only in the sanctity of special moments. Like treasures stored in an attic, these little boxes of dreams and memories and the bittersweet emotions attached to them are only examined when it is safe.

Consequently, these shackled souls are very guarded about sharing private and personal thoughts. Any careless moment of vulnerability—to anyone—can later provide the ammunition that may be fired back at them. Alliances can change, and even the bonds of close friendships can fray in moments of stress and tension. An old buddy could say something cruel in such unguarded moments, and though the friendship itself may survive, others probably heard what was said—others who may not have friendship as an inhibitor. Prison can be a very cruel place. Inmates do not usually provoke one another by daring to attack these private places, but sometimes the goal *is* to provoke.

When I was in prison, for example, one of the men had been convicted of murdering two young women. Throughout the years of his entire stay, he was invariably called by the first name of one of his victims. Sexual offenders are, by far, the greatest targets for this kind of abuse, but no one is really immune to it. Prison is, in itself, a hardened place where machismo reigns and hardness rules. Profanity of the vilest sort is as much a part of the culture as the walls,[1] and verbal threats are as common as the incessant flushing of toilets.

Because ears are everywhere and because social standing is based upon one's perceived image, volunteers must be careful not to place an inmate in jeopardy by some careless statement or word. An inmate's standing within the social structure may be tenuous at best. To pick up a label that could be hurtful, or to have something publicly revealed that is personally private or painful, could place him or her in a vulnerable position. Always be conscious of the actual words you are using when speaking to an inmate about private matters, and be conscious of what it may sound like to others. You must accept the reality that whatever is said, to anyone, can reach other ears. I cannot emphasize this too much.

This also applies to any statements you might make about another inmate. The best way to ensure that you are never caught in what you say is never to say anything that can catch you. Prison is a very small world. Slights are taken easily; mountains can be made out of molehills. True friendship is a precious jewel—one that can be destroyed by a single careless word. It can also occur without being verbal. For example, sometimes inmates will attempt to draw you into their beef with another inmate. If you just quietly listen to their vitriolic criticism and do nothing to temper it, the story may be circulated that you were in full agreement with it. The next time you see the other inmate who was spoken ill against, you could be surprised that your silence has come back to haunt you. Here again your best course of action is not silence but a gentle insertion of biblical perspective.

In your everyday conversations, the prudent path is never to speak negatively about anyone, no matter how secure you feel with the person with whom you are speaking. You must also be alert to what the various *interpretations* of your words might be. Can they be taken another way? When I am unsure about whether or not I have communicated something clearly, and sense that what I have said could be misconstrued, I will usually take the time to clarify it. The same rule applies to anything you may say about the institution or its staff. If you don't want the prison officials to hear that you have bad-mouthed them in any way, don't bad-mouth them in any way. Inmates have many complaints about officers and administrations, so use these opportunities to introduce spiritual principles to them.

Even being aware of all this will not prevent the occasional awkward situation that may occur between you and one of the prisoners. Chino East is one of the prisons I was assigned to in California. I would conduct services, disciple believers, and visit the units for evangelistic purposes. One of the men with whom I would meet regularly for discipleship was a guy named Steve. He was a bright young man, although a little on the hyperactive side, but seemed genuinely to appreciate the extra attention he was getting through our regular sessions. I felt he was growing spiritually and learning his weekly lessons well.

One day as I was walking around the prison yard, I happened to notice him among a small group of men hanging out on the bleachers near the ball field. I went over and soon had a theological discussion going with the whole group. These were not inmates who went to the chapel, so the discussion was a good opportunity to talk to them about the Lord. My friend was quiet throughout the dialogue until we came to an important point regarding an essential truth of Christianity. As he began to speak, the other inmates turned to listen because they recognized him as one of the Christians on the compound, and they wanted to know what his take on this particular teaching was.

To my surprise, he began to expound an off-the-wall doctrine. If I didn't correct him immediately, I knew these men would be left with a totally false impression of the gospel. I also knew that he knew better, and I couldn't understand why he was propounding such a heretical point of view at such a crucial moment. The result was that it forced me to denounce what was being said and, essentially, to rebuke him publicly for saying it. Yard time ended soon afterwards, and we did not have a chance to talk because he immediately slipped off to his unit.

A couple of weeks went by without my seeing Steve. He did not appear for our scheduled meetings and was not seen at any of the chapel events. Some suggested that his absence was probably because I had offended him. I eventually tracked him down in his unit one day, and we found a private place to talk. I asked him what had happened out on the ball field and why he had placed me in such a position. He was defensive at first but eventually the following story emerged.

It turns out that his entire life had been an experience of betrayal. Beginning with his parents, everyone he had ever attempted to trust in life had betrayed him. The consequence was that he was afraid to trust anyone; he was certain they would only betray him in the end. Early on, he developed a defense mechanism to deal with his fear. In order to avoid getting hurt, he discovered that he could turn people away by acting out extremely obnoxious behavior. (There were many in the prison who did not like him.) Whenever he found someone getting too close to him emotionally, he would resort to his backup style of self-preservation: he would set them up to reject him. He would usually do something so outrageous and so obnoxious that he would *force* the person to reject him. By striking first, he believed that if he was the initiator of the rejection, then the collapse of the relationship could come on his own terms.

Steve's example is not unusual. There are many people around us who unconsciously do the same thing. They force us to reject them because they fear being rejected. They have been so hurt in the past that they have become afraid of letting anyone get too close to them. So they insulate themselves against such people by destroying the relationship before it becomes too threatening. I know this sounds a bit elaborate, but I believe it was true in Steve's case. He and I were able to continue our studies after that meeting, and he went on to grow in his Christian faith. Slowly he began to take the risk of trusting again. Although I could not guarantee that Christians would never disappoint him, he was able to accept that the Christ in them never would. He was learning that if he were ever to experience a meaningful relationship with people, he would have to take the risk. Christians aren't perfect, but the Spirit of God within them is alone capable of agape love, the kind of love that is unconditional.

For the volunteer, the question in such cases will always be, how far does one go with someone who is driving you away? Each case is different. Some may genuinely need the space.

Others may need to be released in order to experience a few more hard lessons before they are truly receptive to change. Sometimes people will ask *you* for advice on matters like this. What will you tell them?

For example, because you are involved in prison ministry, worried parents may contact you because their son or daughter just got arrested. They want to know if they should bail him or her out. What advice will you give? Here again, every case is different. For some, the initial shock of incarceration is sufficient for the young person to learn his or her lesson—but others may need to sit there for a month or two before they feel the "ouchy." Bailing them out too early may change nothing and could actually make them cockier. Sometimes a frantic parent will rush in to bail the child out and succeed only in taking the offender off the cross to apply a Band-Aid—while God was in the process of trying to bring him to the end of himself.

It is one of the most difficult choices a parent will ever face. Do not make the decision for them. Simply walk them through the process. Help them assess the situation. Is their child receptive to change, or is this a pattern that is likely to repeat? What was he doing before he was arrested? (Sometimes parents actually breathe a sigh of relief when they hear that their son or daughter has been arrested. At least they know where they are!)

But because there will always be some like Steve, who may need that extra demonstration of God's pursuing love, there will always be a need for prayer, to seek the mind of the Lord, and to rely on the leading of the Holy Spirit. I wish I could give parents an easy rule of thumb to follow in such cases, but each situation is different. Praying for God's wisdom and seeking the counsel of wise and godly friends is the best advice I can give. There is "a time to embrace and a time to refrain" (Eccles. 3:5b).

The truth is, we do not always know which is the best course of action. When we are absolutely uncertain, however, I think it is always best to err on the side of love. It is mercy that should triumph over judgment (James 2:13b). And grace over law.

The hearts behind the masks have a great need for a friend they can trust. The private places of the heart are sanctuaries that do not easily open to others. When a Christian volunteer approaches these inner sanctums, he or she needs to realize that they are cracking this private door open, just a bit.

Proceed with care.

I Dream of Jeannie

THE ELECTRIC CHAIR at Florida State Prison is located on Q block. (At least that's where it was when I was serving there as a parachaplain in the early eighties.) When it came time for a man to be executed, he would be taken off the regular Death Row and spend his last few days on Q block. Unlike the huge, open, multi-tiered cell blocks in the other wings of the prison, here there were only half a dozen cells back-to-back on each side of a dividing wall. Most of the time, this area was used for men who were being disciplined for major infractions. Q block was the isolation area of isolation areas, a sort of a maximum-security unit within maximum security.

I was making my rounds in there one day when I met a young red-haired man who had been placed there for assaulting someone. He had a reputation for being hotheaded and was often locked up for being in fights. He was eager for conversation, and I was happy to spend some time with him. Although most of his personal property had disappeared in the wake of several cell changes over the years, he had managed to hold on to one precious bit of his past—a photograph. The tenderness with which he carefully took it out of an envelope revealed that this was his last, visible link with the outside world and his last remaining treasure.

To explain better the importance of this physical link with the past, allow me to digress briefly. One of the most recurring and nettlesome problems for inmates revolves around this issue of personal property. Since space and security measures do not permit them to have too many items in their cells, most of their personal belongings are stored in the property room. Many of the items that may have been in their possession when they entered the court system are considered "contraband"[1] in the prison setting and will not be seen again until the day they are released. These include such things as money, jewelry, and street clothing. Permissible items can be kept only in limited quantity, such as books, papers, and personal pictures.

The reason for this is that a prisoner's cell is his entire living quarters: his bathroom, bedroom, living room, and even his kitchen on occasion. There is little storage space in a cubicle of this size. When one remembers that another inmate usually shares the same quarters, one can begin to understand the impossibility of having too many possessions. Another reason, from a security point of view, is that too many items in a cell make for too many hiding places. When a shakedown occurs, the fewer items that are allowed in a cell, the fewer places that need to be searched for contraband.

Other ways to "lose" items are by theft, being strong-armed by other inmates, or by being moved from cell to cell too often. The inmate often arrives in his new "house" only to find that some of his belongings did not make the trip with him. The young man I was visiting had only one item left: a picture of his girlfriend.

Shortly after his arrival on Q block, a group of officers, similar to a SWAT team,[2] had rolled in[3] on him. (It is necessary for a prison to be able to activate such squads in an emergency.) They are the first response team in the case of a major disturbance (such as a riot) or in the case of an assaultive inmate. There are other situations that can escalate into dangerous security threats, and such tactical response teams need to be mobilized quickly. However, it is also true that human nature is human nature, and absolute power tempts men to abuse that power. I believe that this was such a case.

Because the young man had caused problems before, they wanted to "teach him a lesson." He was tough enough not to mind the physical jostling (he had been there before), but what hurt him the most was that they had taken the picture of his girlfriend and made a show of stomping on it with their boots and grinding it into the cement. He carefully lifted the limp, ragged picture and showed me the effects. Although you could still see her face, the surface was now scratched, gritty, and torn. I thought to myself that the desecration had been a very stupid thing to do—not merely for the emotional pain that it had caused this particular inmate but for the threat it posed to other officers. A simple reality in prison—or anywhere else for that matter—is that when you strip a man of everything, you put him in the dangerous position of having nothing to lose.

I recalled another fellow who had been placed on Q block not long before this young man. He was a Death Row inmate who had experienced a run-in with some officers at his cell. As a result, he swore to them that he would kill the next guard who came down the tier. They evidently thought so lightly of the threat that they neglected to tell the next shift about it. When the first unsuspecting officer from that shift came down the tier to escort him in handcuffs to the showers, the inmate made good on his threat. The mistake was that they had underestimated his emotional state and that he was already in a position of feeling he had nothing to lose. They can only execute him once, no matter how many murders he has committed.

The young man presently on Q block had not come from Death Row, but he was doing a lot of time. The officers had assaulted the inner sanctum, that private place of the heart. To my recollection he never retaliated for the desecrated photograph. He was spiritually open, and I was able to encourage him to leave the situation in the Lord's hands and in *his* ability to right all wrongs. The point of this illustration is that this young man was holding on to the dream of love, or what remained of it. That picture was the last tangible bridge across the cold river of separation between the dream and his current, harsh reality. To assault this little paper picture was to assault his last link to the dream.

As mentioned in the last chapter, the loneliness of prison life, and a culture that scoffs at needing anything or anyone, forces the inmate into his or her own private world. Most will admit that there is a face one projects to the population at large, and the "real" person one feels he or she is on the inside. This is, of course, true of society in general, but starkly obvious in prison. The culture does not permit prisoners to be too open about their need for love; it would invite the trampling of such a notion under the merciless hooves of weakness. But I have found that inmates, in general, are very respectful of one another's private thoughts. There is an inner sanctum that each man knows is holy to the other. Such things as family and mothers, girlfriends and wives, and even religious convictions are generally given a wide berth of diffident respect. Other residents tend to leave these areas alone because each knows that those things are important to him or her as well.

So there is a silent agreement in their code of ethics that does not venture into these private sanctuaries. Most inmates want to avoid confrontation with other inmates anyway. To mess with these holy places is to invite repercussions, even from the most timid of men and women. In fact, when these areas *are* attacked, it is usually done for the sole intention of provoking. Inmates who want to pick a fight, or to cause hurt, will attack these inner bastions because they *know* it will illicit a response.

Photographs and letters, news clippings of a daughter's victory at a local track meet—these are all part of the inner place of the heart. They keep alive the reality that they still have people to love—and who love them in return. You and I have the same need, but we can experience the daily ebbs and flows of a *current* relationship, which keep the tides of love flowing back and forth in a healthy way. For those in prison, the insurmountable distance of time's ocean makes it difficult for the rolling miles of months to keep their loved ones in view. There is a constant, dull ache in the heart that most inmates must adjust to.

The ache exists even for those who can no longer lay claim to having a current sweetheart waiting for them, because behind the ache is still the need to love and be loved. This common need creates the search for a balm to apply to that wound. Some prisoners look beyond the walls, seeking someone to write. They will often ask other inmates (even volunteers) if they know any girls they could write to. They will put subtle pressure on a cell mate, who is receiving visits from his girlfriend, to suggest that one of *her* friends could communicate with him. Others will actually take out ads in the personal section of local newspapers, seeking a pen pal. Others begin to look for relationships *within* the walls.

Personal observation leads me to believe that there is a higher percentage of homosexual activity in women's institutions than in men's. It at least appears to be more flagrant. Although the fabric of prison life envelops both sexes, there are some major differences between male and female inmates that have a direct bearing on their individual cultures. Ministering to each, as a result, also requires slightly different approaches. (We will speak more of this later.)

The male's culture is basically one of an emotional isolationism. He projects the lone-wolf image, the "I-don't-need-anyone" attitude that is self-reliant and macho. The woman, on the other hand, though she may project toughness as an image, is more intrinsically relational. Men who enter homosexual relationships in prison do so primarily for sex. This is not to say that the relationships do not have the trappings of emotional attachment. Many do. (As I have already mentioned, homosexual triangles are one of the chief contributors to prison homicides.) Yet, for the most part, the male's engagement is not primarily relational in its basic intention.

Women, however, tend to be highly relational, and it is a major driver in their sexual activity. For many of them on the inside, it is socially important that they "have someone." And unlike men's prisons, their culture permits it.[4] It's OK to be relational. It's OK to say you hurt. It's OK to verbalize that you miss someone. Although sex is a part of it, I don't believe sex is the primary driver for the women. They have a great need to be in a relationship. This is also true of the men, but for them it is a cultural taboo.

But cultural acceptance does not make it right. What God declares to be sinful is to be avoided and not practiced. It has always seemed to me that too big a deal is made of homosexuality as a separate issue, by both those who practice it and those who condemn it. They tend to view it as the major vortex through which all the other issues of life are swept. It always seems to be *the* issue, far outweighing—in terms of perspective and discussion—everything else. It is a sin—one of many.

For example, it is just as wrong for someone to commit a homosexual act as it is for someone to jump into bed with his girlfriend before marriage or to commit adultery. If God has said something is wrong, he commands us not to do it. That is really the bottom line. It is also irrelevant, as the case is so often made, whether one believes they "were born that way" or not. (The "homosexual gene," so to speak.) If God says not to do it, then he expects us not to do it. The heterosexual is told not to jump into bed with his neighbor's wife. One could easily say he was "born that way," because every heterosexual male is fully able to perform the act with someone other than his wife—and be sorely tempted to do so. But again, the ability (or the inclination) does not make it right. God has told us not to do it and expects his people to comply with what *he* has determined is right.

Another, less harmful, path can also be taken for the lonely man or woman who is unable to lay claim to having anyone waiting for them "out there." They can create a romance in their minds.

This can take several shapes. Pictures of beautiful, yet real-life women, be they movie stars or people they have known, can be lovingly and painstakingly drawn or painted. Fantasizing about situations in which one is experiencing a romantic episode can occupy many a thought before one falls off to sleep. The "episodes" are daydreams really, but they help to apply a temporary balm to the ache. Poetry written to a certain girl, or even writing a fictional book describing a romance that can be vicariously experienced, also helps to soothe the restless soul.

I had been married briefly before entering prison. I can still feel remorse for entangling this young woman with the selfish and irresponsible person I was at that age. She ultimately remarried and divorced again. Though married only nine months, we separated after just a few. She returned home to Chicago, and I stayed out East. A few months after arriving at the state prison, I received a single-page legal notice telling me that I had been divorced. All she had requested was to have her old name back; there were no children involved.

I recall being summoned to the control room for the reading of the notice. Two guards stood beside me as I read it. I was never quite sure why they did it that way; it's certainly not the practice now. I think they felt that they wanted to be prepared in case I took the news badly. I can recall feeling absolutely nothing. I knew the marriage had already died—and that I had effectively killed it. I handed the notice back to the guards and returned to my cell, emotionless. All I remember is contemplating what it felt like to be legally single again, something you'd think wouldn't be too difficult to imagine while sitting in prison.

But still, I had a need to be in love and to feel loved. So I resurrected a romance. I began to write poetry about a girl I'd had as a "steady" in Chicago when I was seventeen. I was twenty-two at the time of the writing and had not seen her since I'd left the midwest, but I know that the emotions being experienced while I was writing were very real to me. I found that I had convinced myself that I was in love with her all over again. The poetry was naturally drenched in a "lost love" type of syrup, and painted with the colors of mourning for magical days in the past, but they did, for a time, serve a purpose. I was experiencing those feelings again. It didn't matter that I knew she had remarried; love always hopes. In time, however, the illusion passed. It's hard to keep a fire going without logs.

Another dynamic that takes place is what I would call the "magnification of the parent role." Although a close cousin to the need for love, it has a different expression. I have observed this process particularly among the younger males. Older men and women in prison—those who have children—carry a particular pain that should always arouse our deepest compassion. Tied to missing their physical presence is the awful weight of knowing that their beloved children are growing up without them. They see the precious moments being irretrievably lost, and their longing is a pain almost too great to bear. The women are able to express this pain much more easily than the men, but

I see it in both of their eyes—a clinging sadness that never seems to go away.

The force of the dynamic in question, however, tends to affect those younger prisoners who are not too far removed from the years of childhood themselves. Many of these young men and women have had children themselves. They were usually at an irresponsible place in their lives, the consequences of which eventually brought them to prison. In many cases, the relationship with the other biological parent has long since ended, and the young person has already accepted that fact. But what is *not* accepted is that he is no longer a father or that she is no longer a mother. In addition to the need for love, the young person is also wrestling with the need for significance. This is especially true for the fledgling fathers.

For the young male in prison, having a baby scores high on the significance chart for at least five reasons:

First, it is proof, at least to himself, that he has been loved by a girl.

Second, it's further proof to him that he is needed. ("My child needs me. I'm its father!")

Third, being a father is something responsible adults do. In his own eyes he has accomplished an adult thing, committed a responsible act. The existence of the child is a reminder—at least by implication—that he has shouldered responsibility.

Fourth, fathering a baby, a real human being, is a socially important thing to do. The existence of the child is an attestation that he has done something that society not only agrees is good but is important as well.

Fifth, and this is very important within the prison culture, having a child is evidence of his sexual experience. An obvious reality for men in prison is that they do not easily experience sex with females. Although it is seldom mentioned (out of mutual deference), it is generally admitted that the longer one spends time behind bars, the less one can claim an abundance of sexual experience. Children, therefore, are reliable witnesses to their sexual testimony. Again, this tends to be more important for the younger inmates, since their youthfulness opens them up to the charge of being inexperienced.

One might think that I am exaggerating the importance of this parental dynamic in prison, but I have observed it for many years. Suddenly, the child looms large in the inmate's mind. Their incarceration brings out a renewed concern for, and an adamant defense of, their parental rights. Children that were perhaps taken for granted, and in some cases even neglected while they were on the streets, suddenly become their main concern while in prison. Although their lifestyle on the streets may have been one of total chaos and irresponsibility, they are now insulted that someone would dare to take their children away from them, or that someone else is replacing them as the father. Even if the perceived threat is the child's *mother*—and even if they were never married—it doesn't matter. "I'm the father!" he cries, "And no one is going to take him away from me. That child needs me!"

Whenever I hear such protests, I usually just listen quietly for a period of time. I find myself trying to learn if the current caretaker on the outside is the one best suited for the child's wellbeing—and praying that it is so. What generally happens is that the child winds up with some other family member (often a grandparent), and the last person any of them want to see, at this point, is the child's father. In the course of our discussions, if I can determine that the situation on the streets would be more stable if he didn't attempt to intervene, I gently try to encourage him away from any serious thoughts of reentry. In many cases, the child's mother has remarried; but that often holds little concern for the inmate who feels he's been unjustly deposed of as father of his child. "That man isn't their father, I am!" he will insist. One can easily see trouble looming on the horizon for the poor family on the streets as soon as this guy is out of jail.[5]

At this point in our encounter, I ask the Holy Spirit to assist me in helping the young man to understand that merely fathering a child does not make one a father. I explain that the *new* "dad" will have the more difficult task of training that child in the way it should go. Sometimes it is beneficial for the young man to see that his interference at this stage would actually be detrimental to the child's healthy development and that the nobler path is to love his child enough to not interfere. At first cut, you might think that this advice would not be too well received, but I have seen many young men over the years rise to this challenge. If it were merely a human effort, I would have no reasonable expectation that this, or *any* advice to the contrary, would be heeded. But we are not about human efforts. God is able.

A man at the state prison in Walpole, Massachusetts, once asked me, "How can Jesus Christ meet my needs? I need feminine companionship; I need to be able to hold someone physically. How will he meet *those* needs?" My honest answer was simply to reply that I didn't know how he would do it but that Christ was able to meet his *real* need. I do not attempt to answer for God as to how he accomplishes his will, but I remain deeply convinced that he alone is all that is necessary. And that is enough to know. I tell them that God knows how to be God, and that he knows how to do "God stuff." It's right there on his résumé: "Knows how to do the impossible." "Knows how to keep His promises." "My God will meet all your needs according to his glorious riches in Christ Jesus" (Phil. 4:19).

What should these particular dynamics of prison life mean for the volunteer? First of all, bear in mind that the basic need to love and be loved is a great one. So be careful about what you say and how you say it. (This is especially true if your ministry is writing letters to inmates.) If I were able to resurrect a childhood romance to the point of falling in love again, then a kind word from the opposite sex can easily set a hungry heart's train in motion. I have known secular counselors who were unable to maintain their professionalism when pulled by the magnetic strength of romance. The battlefield is littered with the casualties of those who were unable to resist its call upon their hearts.

I have known two separate instances in which correctional officers forfeited their jobs to marry an inmate. (Neither marriage survived.) I have a good friend whose wife left him to marry someone she met in prison while serving as a volunteer. The man was in prison for murdering his former wife. My friend was a pastor at the time and had to leave his church. By the incredible grace of God, he remarried and later became a chaplain—in a state prison. But the need to be conscious of how easy it is for inmates to read between the lines should give us pause to consider how our words or actions might possibly be misinterpreted. This is especially true in the case of cross-gender ministry.

At the same time, however, this dynamic creates a fertile field for the gospel. Like streams in the desert, the Christian volunteer brings a vial of the water that can satisfy the heart's greatest thirst. It is Christ himself who is needed. His is the love that reaches into the most hidden crevices of our lives and fills them to overflowing. There is still a balm in Gilead. For in being loved first by him, our own hearts will find their true end in worshipping him—and returning that love through a genuine desire to please and obey him. Only in a relationship with Jesus Christ does the heart find its true home.

21

Economics

HE WAS MOVING UP AND DOWN the tier making his announcement as he went. "I got only one pack of smokes left. You can each have one as far as they go." Men quickly appeared at the doors of their cell to receive their one cigarette from Kevin. This was an awaiting-trial unit and canteen supplies[1] were dwindling fast. Kevin was a nice enough guy (streetwise, to be sure), but I had never thought of him as particularly altruistic. As I watched him continue his philanthropic mission down the tier, dispensing the prized items with an air of businesslike solemnity, it suddenly occurred to me that I *was* observing a business transaction. An investment, really.

Kevin was sowing his bread upon the waters, shrewdly trusting that it would return to him some day. He was banking on the hope that his tierwide generosity would pay dividends in the future. By sacrificing his last pack of cigarettes, in a time of universal famine, he had established himself as a "good guy" on the tier and greatly increased his odds for payback in lean days to come. When the reservoirs were finally reopened and canteen supplies flowed again, who would ever refuse Kevin a cigarette? He had helped them during the drought; Kevin was one of the good guys.

Now, I am not taking anything away from Kevin's generosity because it was *still* a generous act. Whether or not the men thought he was engaged in hedging mattered little at all; he had helped them when they were down, and he deserved the same consideration in the future. He could have kept the pack for himself, but he made two other investments with his act of kindness: one was that he further established his status on the tier (which was already good), and two, kindness usually *is* repaid.

168

What I was observing was a lesson in microeconomics. The laws of supply and demand were driving the whole episode. There was even a shadow of macro-maneuvering as well. The investment of goodwill would eventually pay off in a sort of "favored-nation" status for Kevin. Sanctions, if there had ever been any, would certainly be lifted. To an outsider, one might think that economics do not play a very big role in such an overwhelmingly socialistic environment. But that would not be true. Just as in other socialistic societies, the black market thrives!

But what is the currency of this society? Cash is not allowed; and although inmates have their own financial accounts that are kept by the prison, making transfers to other accounts is a definite no-no at this particular bank. Until recently, Kevin's example demonstrated the most popular medium of exchange behind the walls. He was investing with the Bastille's money of choice: cigarettes. For years tobacco has been the coin of the realm. To a lesser degree drugs have also been used, but nowhere near as commonly, and even then, only by the few who control such activities. Tobacco has retained its dominant position in prison throughout the years. It has been legal to possess, and thus is widely used by the whole spectrum of the prison population.

But all that is changing. There is a growing movement among the nation's correctional facilities toward "smoke-free" institutions. In Massachusetts, for example, all state and county institutions have been smoke-free since 1999. What this means, economically, is that a new currency will have to emerge. I have asked the inmates what they think will replace it, and the general consensus is that it will probably be a variety of items, as opposed to any one thing. In the prison world of economics, it's as though the monopoly that the cigarette once controlled, like AT&T, will be broken up and divided among the "Baby Bells" of canteen goodies, pornography, and various favors. We will probably experience a major resurgence of the bartering system.

This trend will certainly be an interesting development to follow. While I understand the rationale behind the health and political issues, I personally favor the use of "smoke-free tiers" or designated areas, just as we do here on the outside. My basic reasons are simple: Smokers become agitated when they can't smoke. (Ask any spouse whose mate is trying to quit.) And second, one needs to consider that smoking—for those who do it—is one of the culture's few pleasures.[2]

In the past, those inmates who did not smoke were in a good position to acquire a greater cache of this island's goods. They had no need to consume the money as they used it. Although they had no personal use for tobacco, they had to be in possession of it if they were going to trade in the current markets.[3] But unlike their addicted counterparts, they did not need to deplete their supply by the temptation of self-consumption. Now that tobacco is becoming outlawed, it will join the ranks of other illegal items such as drugs or alcohol. Prohibition does not eliminate such items; it only makes them more expensive and difficult to obtain.

But apart from the topic of currency, what *kinds* of goods are traded in this society? In some cases, just about anything. Illegal activities run the gamut from drugs and alcohol to pornography and sexual favors. "Legal" items include canteen supplies or any nonpersonal items that another inmate is willing to sell. How is the money made? In most facilities a variety of jobs are offered by the institution itself. A minimal wage for hours worked is paid into the inmate's account. The inmate then buys goods from the canteen and uses these items to make other "purchases" within his or her society.

The department of corrections does its best to keep the prisoners busy. Cleaning jobs are the most common, but inmates can also work in many of the prison's various departments. The kitchen, the infirmary, the laundry, the paint or print shops, and a variety of trades such as auto repair and general maintenance are among the possibilities. But the inmates themselves also provide a flurry of underground enterprises. This world of microeconomics is full of entrepreneurs. Our friend Kevin was only one example. For example, artists can sketch or paint pictures to suit the buyer—such as images of girlfriends or of other scenes to send home as gifts. One can sell hobby crafts or intricately drawn envelopes and stationery. The tattoo parlors are always open, and so are the offices of the jailhouse lawyers.

Any natural ability or expertise can be creatively put to use. Some of the more literate prisoners compose poetry or songs for other inmates to plagiarize and send to their girlfriends, while still others are willing to sell the addresses of potential pen pals. Although most of these activities are technically illegal in terms of goods being exchanged for services, they are not serious threats to the institution. The deals that involve such major contraband items as drugs and alcohol (and now cigarettes) are the greater concerns of the security department.

But perhaps the most widespread form of acquiring illegal wealth within this empire is through the medium of gambling. Prisoners are extremely fond of this enterprise. A deck of well-worn cards is as much a part of the atmosphere as the omnipresent tattoo. Card games abound, day in and day out. The game of choice depends upon the prison's current favorite, and this can vary from institution to institution. When I was in prison, poker and pinochle were popular. Today, it is often a game of spades or rummy. Cribbage is a perennial favorite. Inmates will bet on just about anything—and usually do. One of their favorite pastimes is to wager how soon a recently released compatriot will be rearrested and brought back to prison.

Nearly all sporting events have gambling stakes behind them. Everything from a game of checkers in the yard to an international chess tournament on TV can be bet upon—from softball and basketball matches inside the walls to the broadcast of any sporting event. The big duels, such as Super Bowls and World Series, attract an even larger participation. As you can guess, where there is gambling, there is bound to be gambling debt. Many an inmate has had to take a PC to avoid the consequences of unpaid bills and IOUs. Loan-sharking is another resource that is always open for business, but the interest rates are staggering. Some fearful inmates have turned to these sources for help—only to flee from them later (see Amos 5:19). The best advice is never to engage in gambling of any kind.

Another durable racket is the perennial threat of strong-arming. This is when an inmate, or often a group of inmates, will take what they want from another inmate by force. Sometimes a physical beating will accompany the action, and there is little the victim can do. If the inmate speaks to the guards about it, he or she will be branded as a rat and probably forced to take a PC. One route that some take is the recruitment of others to avenge themselves on the perpetrators. This has the danger of escalating into something much more serious. Strong-arming has led to other crimes such as rape, and, on occasion, murder. Protection schemes, where an inmate has to make regular payments to keep himself from being victimized, is also common.

Other prisoners turn their sights outward for economic assistance. This can include a legal activity such as writing articles for publication. I have a good friend who is a regular contributor to a local newspaper. His reports are among the paper's best-read pages. Others continue to operate businesses from the inside, while still others may simply have well-heeled connections. Most depend upon the generosity of families or friends who are allowed to place money into the inmate's account.

Some inmates make financial appeals to the general public. I met one fellow in Florida State Prison who put a note in the personal sections of several southern newspapers. His ad simply read: "Lonely, white, country boy doing time in Florida. Could sure use someone to write me. If interested contact . . . " He had over eighty women respond to his ad in a short time. He showed me many of the letters he had received. It was unreal, he discovered, how many of them wanted a relationship with him and that some had even sent nude photos of themselves. Since he was getting such a good return on his investment, he would immediately hit them up for help by asking them to send money to his canteen fund. When I asked him what he did if they refused, he shrugged and said, "I pass their addresses up the tier to anyone else who wants to write them."

Others have tried to use chaplains and the chapel scene to accomplish their ends. I was once standing beside the chaplain of a major state prison while he was picking up his parcels down in the mailroom. One of the packages had the return address of a church with which neither of us was familiar. Usually his routine was to have his mail sent to his office, where it would be opened by the inmate who served as his clerk. The orderly would then sort it and neatly arrange it for him on his desk. I don't recall why he decided to open the package himself on this particular day, but I can still remember the look of bewilderment on his face when a cellophaned square of greenish-brown material emerged.

"What is this?" he queried.

"Looks like a brick of marijuana," I replied.

He looked at me in complete confusion. *"Really?"* he asked. His incredulity grew as he tried to match what he was holding in his hands with the reality that he stood just a few yards away from the control room of a major maximum security prison. But the ultimate gravity of the situation was that someone had figured out his routine and had probed a loophole in the security system. The chaplain's mail was not searched, and the chaplain did not personally open his mail; therefore, the opportunity had presented itself.

Another target can be volunteers. I say "can be," because in proportion to the vast number of volunteers who have come in over the years, this particular group has not been hit nearly as often as one might think. Two factors contribute to this. One is that most inmates genuinely appreciate the service of volunteers and do not want to risk losing the higher value of that service. The second is that seasoned volunteers learn how to field the occasional conversations they sense are beginning to head in a spurious direction. I would reiterate what I said in another chapter, and this is that most inmates are not out to con you. They appreciate your service, and most of them seldom try to manipulate volunteers for ulterior motives. But having said that, there are still some who will.

I was once talking with a friend whom I had known for many years when a man I had never met approached me and asked if I knew any single, Christian women. I must have been holding some Bibles, or perhaps he had seen me before, but it was obvious by the question that he had tagged me as a "Christian volunteer." When I replied in the affirmative, he asked if I would ask one of those women to write to him. I replied that I didn't get into finding women to correspond with men but that I knew a couple of Christian guys who would be happy to drop him a line.

At this point he became angry and launched into a verbal assault on the sincerity of my Christianity. He would have continued his tirade except that the friend I had been speaking with suddenly jumped down and put his nose right on the nose of the other man's. Poking his finger into his chest, he rebuked him for trying to lay a trip on me. When the other guy began to make excuses, my friend ominously pursued with, "Lissen up. I've knowed this guy a lot longer than I've knowed you, and when you disrespect him, you're disrespecting me." (Having been incarcerated here several times before, my friend was a popular leader among the jail's society.)

When the other guy realized which way the wind was blowing, he mumbled some apologies and took off. When I thanked my intercessor, he simply said, "No Lennie, you're my friend. When I heard him disrespecting you that was like he was disrespecting me."[4]

I mention this episode because it captures the experience of most volunteers. On one hand, you have to realize that this is a closed society. Inmates will consciously or unconsciously "test" new volunteers to see how close to the rules they are going to play it. If they see that you hedge or break rules, you will lose your impact as a Christian volunteer. (And a minority will definitely try to exploit those weaknesses.) On the other hand, you are building a relationship with those who genuinely appreciate that you are there for *them*. Someone who "comes in here positive-like" and has demonstrated that you care about them.

Volunteers should always have the rules of the institution well embedded in their minds so that when situations like this arise they will know how to respond. It is when we are caught flat-footed that the momentum swings toward the occasional manipulator. In a needs-driven economy like prison, the tentacles are constantly reaching out for new opportunities to explore; it goes with the territory. Because one is forced to operate within a very restricted area to meet these needs, exploration for new oil is always going on. It is human nature to want to "push the envelope," and inmates are no exception. They have a basic need to know where the boundaries are. Careless volunteers can set themselves up for manipulation if they do not have the rules firmly entrenched in their own minds.

But those rules also provide a built-in shelter for the Christian volunteer. As a follower of Jesus Christ, it is consistent with your own beliefs to operate legally. For example, if the rule is "nothing in—nothing out,"[5] then even bringing in so much as a postage stamp is illegal. Sometimes you will be asked by a resident to bring a letter out for him for one reason or another. Do not do this. Inmate mail is always subject to be read before leaving the institution. There can be no good reason why you, as a Christian volunteer, would want to be a part of evading this system—and few good reasons why he, as an inmate, would wish you to do so.

In such instances, reply that to do anything you have been told not to do would be wrong, and that, as a Christian, you need to obey the rules (Rom. 13:1–2). Sometimes, if inmates are persistent, I tell them that to give in to their request jeopardizes my status as a volunteer, and is it really their desire to put me in a position where I could be thrown out? This perspective usually settles things. If they persist beyond *that* point, however, then it should be clear to you that you are not being valued as a person, or that they are extremely desperate. Either way, you should end the direction of that conversation.

The Christian volunteer is in the unique position of knowing that what he or she is offering is the greatest jewel that could ever be possessed—the offer of God's forgiveness and eternal love. And it's *free!* What can compare? And when the gift is offered through the presence of a volunteer who is filled with Christ's compassion, the contrast with this economic system of a dog-eat-dog world is striking.

22

Old Friends

IT WOULD BE A MISTAKE TO THINK that in prison, which is such a cautious arena of distrust, the authentic gift of friendship rarely occurs. In a world that I have described in terms of crushing loneliness, ultimate survival, and the need to be constantly watching one's back, it is possible that the darker hues may have overshadowed the gentler, paler ones. But such friendships do occur, and with regularity.

What I have stated is that there is a need to be cautious in friendships, but not that deep friendships do not occur. There is a camaraderie that exists between men and women who find themselves in difficult situations. Stories abound of wartime friendships that create lifetime bonds. Men who have shared foxholes in life-and-death situations share an experience—and hence a relationship—that can be thicker than blood. This unspoken bond can be felt everywhere from American Legion and VFW halls to Vietnam veterans support groups.

Prison does not carry the higher sacrifice (or the honor) that the calling of a wartime experience demands—and perhaps should not be likened to it—but there is still a deep anguish here. And it is a shared anguish. When an ex-con meets an ex-con on the streets, even though they may not have been close in prison, there is the awareness of a bond. They share something in common that those around them have not experienced. This is something the participants know that cannot be adequately described to those "on the outside." How do you describe the *feeling* of prison? It is only in this sense that I draw the similarity between the two experiences; there is a connection forged between those who share them.

This "connection," in terms of a deeper friendship, is more commonplace among lifers than short-timers. Youthful offenders, who may be in prison for only a year or two, may have many acquaintances and even friends they have run with on the streets, but they seldom experience what I am attempting to describe here. I am not implying that youthful offenders and short-timers do not experience these close friendships; they can and do. But longevity of association may not be the ultimate fruit of these alliances. The lifestyles of young criminals often have them bouncing from one situation to another; loyalties are often interrupted by consequences. While these youthful short-timers may experience the "shared bond" phenomena when they meet with other ex-cons on the streets, they simply have not had the longevity to gain that silent respect for "old warhorses" that only years can create. It is a mutual respect that is harvested when one realizes that he or she has known another person for many, many years—and that those years were all experienced behind these walls.

However, the mutual experience of shared years is not sufficient in itself to create the depth of friendship that I am attempting to describe here. The vast majority of inmates remain at an emotional distance from one another no matter how many years they have shared behind the walls. They have learned how to get along with one another, and in some cases, even how to avoid one another, but there is little pretense to friendship. What I am describing is something rarer that is confined to a smaller, more exclusive number of individuals.

When one is on the lifer pods, or the cell blocks, that house lifers, one may observe this gruff friendship in action. They joke with one another in an easy, comfortable way, bringing up topics that have their own meanings behind them, in much the same way that husbands and wives use a pet phrase that conjures up a memory that is now summarized by a particular expression.

They are very protective of one another. They will risk going to the Hole to defend a buddy who has been treated unjustly. They know one another's idiosyncrasies and habits and intuitively know which areas to be sensitive to. While their blunt banter may seem to border on cruelty at times, it is so only to the casual observer. Their remarks have been honed by years of living in close proximity, and they instinctively know what is acceptable and what is not. They understand one another's moods. A joke could be made on one day that would not even be considered on another. They literally live with one another 24–7. Husbands and wives, it has been noted, spend less time together than do these prison friends.

But they do give one another space and respect one another's personal likes and dislikes. I have a friend who loves classical music. The few tapes he owns are of Bach, Handel, and Mozart. His cell mate likes country and western music. One does acrostics for amusement; the other reads comics. They are worlds apart intellectually, but they move easily in and out of their shared cubicle, comfortable in their mutual understanding of each other.

Next door is the conservative ex-special forces officer, still wrapped in the American flag, ready to discuss the latest political subterfuge at the drop of a hat. Next to him is another old warhorse, his belly now beyond the scope of his belt, but still loved and respected by his comrades. Across from him is "the professor," and the weight lifter is in the bunk below him. There's the little guy serving four life sentences and next to him the tattooed one who smiles so often you're sure he's up to something. And on it goes, each with his own story, each with his own niche.

The volunteer can never gain access to this elite club. He or she can only visit. It doesn't mean that these friends do not love the volunteer; they hold their relationship with you as special in itself and look forward to your coming. I have known some of these men for many years, and those years are not without merit. But when the volunteer enters this world, he is aware that he is only visiting; the sand is running through the hourglass in terms of minutes or hours but not in uninterrupted years. You are sharing a moment in that bubble, but it is still only a moment. The bubble floats in the air for a while and then drifts away, bursting shortly after one leaves. But for them, the old friends, the bubble continues.

If you are faithful, however, there is a fruit that appears much later on the vine. If a volunteer hangs in for the long haul, consistently showing up and keeping one's spiritual focus, there is an impact that will often be made for the sake of the gospel in the lives of these old warriors. They will respect that your faith is genuine and will be more apt to speak about such things when the Holy Spirit gives you the opportunity.

A mistake that volunteers can fall into, in these long-term friendships, is to develop a habit of seldom mentioning spiritual things with them. While we should be willing to discuss a wide variety of topics, as any true friendship should allow, we must not lose our focus. Stitches in a garment are visible half the time. By keeping the golden thread of Christ's reality weaving naturally in and out of our discussions, bringing him up in future encounters will seldom seem awkward.

The faces of so many of these dear people float before my mind as I write the conclusion of this short chapter. God has blessed me with many good friendships over the years. I have half-joked with my wife, Wendy, that most of my friends wouldn't be able to attend my funeral. (As much as they would like to!) My heart goes out to each of them in a bittersweet way. I wish their lives could be different, but at the same time I know that many of them now know Jesus Christ as their Savior. We share not only a friendship built on years of knowing one another, but one that also shares the goodness of being brothers and sisters in Christ. It is the shared experience and silent bond of Christians everywhere.

For such inmates their lives now have purpose because nothing is wasted with the Lord. They, like us, dwell in the middle of their mission field, and they have every intention of blooming where they are planted.

They have discovered what a wonderful friend they have in Jesus.

23

The Intimacy of Forgiveness

"I COULD NEVER forgive him for what he did!"

These words were expressed by an inmate at a woman's prison who was trying hard to come to grips with an essential doctrine of Christian faith—the issue of forgiveness. There was no way I could conjure up the dark images I'm sure she was recalling and that, for her, were too horrible to describe adequately. I sympathized with her. For many victims the memories of the past include people who have been the source of such incredible pain that forgiving them seems impossible. There is simply too much hurt and anger.

Society tends to think of the person in prison as someone who needs to *ask* for forgiveness, not someone who needs to *grant* it. The people of this culture are viewed primarily as the "hurters," not the hurt. But they are often both. Many people in prison have been predator *and* prey, criminal *and* victim. The issue of forgiveness, then, will play a frequent role in the counsel of volunteers, from both sides of the coin—and from both sides of the walls.

I have known families of victims (some of them Christians for many years), who can barely bring themselves to consider forgiveness, let alone be able to exercise it with any degree of long-lasting success. One such family, upon receiving a letter from the man who had been convicted of murdering a family member, felt all the nightmarish feelings surrounding the event come flooding back at just the sight of the name on the envelope. What made it even harder for them was that the man said he had become a believer and was writing to ask them for forgiveness. It was all they could do to send a card with a short note saying they would grant him the forgiveness he sought but—please—don't ever write to them again.

The victim of a crime is often the forgotten face of prison ministry. For every crime committed by one individual, there are often several persons who were directly hurt by it. Most prison volunteers I know are sympathetic to the plight of the victims, but they will have little opportunity to minister to them. Usually the last person the victim ever wants to see is the person who hurt him, and this aversion extends to anyone who is perceived as being associated with the criminal. As a volunteer you must honor this and pray that God will send other comforters to them. If you have been assigned the field of laboring among prisoners, you must accept the fact that you will seldom, if ever, be called to minister to their victims.

True forgiveness is an elusive quarry; the painful emotions keep returning. Like a rubber ball on an elastic string, they strike the paddle of our hearts again and again with renewed pain. The alternating flashes of hurt and anger lead the victim to believe they can never forgive, no matter how hard they try. They forget that emotions were not created to think; they were only created to feel. They enable us to experience love, compassion, empathy, sorrow, or any of the other noble expressions of children made in the image of God.

But sin has so drenched the world in its all-encompassing stain that we are awash in a sea of tragedy, assault, and evil. When these events touch our lives, we respond to them with an attending flurry of reactions that suddenly burst upon our hearts without preparation. Emotions do not reason; they react. They do not rationalize; they are triggered. They do not think; they feel. And everything about the nightmarish event floods us with emotional pain. The feelings fluctuate wildly between the mixed colors of numbness, hurt, anger, hatred, and revenge. I have known some inmates who are serving their entire prison sentence on the fuel of the latter two feelings: hatred and revenge.

For those inmates who become Christians, the radical concepts of Jesus Christ regarding forgiveness challenge them in two ways: First, they know he expects it of his disciples; and, second, they don't know if they can be truly genuine about it. The double-edged dilemma that obedience creates for those who desire to follow Christ is that they intellectually comprehend the command to forgive but find themselves emotionally incapable. They know, in their hearts, that the smoldering fires of pain still burn. Many of them realize that while they may have *verbalized* a commitment to forgive, they still experience deep hurt and anger whenever they think about that certain incident or individual.

The result is that they feel they have failed as Christians and failed at forgiveness. They come again and again to Jesus' words in Matthew 6:14–15: "For if you forgive men when they sin against you, your heavenly Father will also forgive you. But if you do not forgive men their sins, your Father will not forgive your sins."

They feel like spiritual washouts, or even worse, that perhaps they aren't Christians at all. But I believe the problem lies not so much in their Christian *desire* to forgive as it does in the inability of their emotions to separate what they are feeling from what they believe. Just because a person still finds himself or herself experiencing deep feelings of hurt, shame, guilt, or anger doesn't mean that the commitment to forgive wasn't sincere. In fact, many who struggle in this area will admit that feelings of *hatred* still burn in their hearts.

So what gives? How can this be? Aren't we commanded to *love* our enemies? It will always be important, for those who have never been the victims of horrendous actions, to extend great compassion and understanding toward those who have.

Many great saints and theologians, far wiser than I, have written on the topic of forgiveness. Several excellent books on the subject have been written, and those who struggle in this area should seek all the assistance they can find. The genuine expression of this defining Christian characteristic has been conveyed in the biographies of saintly men and women throughout the centuries. Wonderful examples in our own time exist, such as those of Corrie Ten Boom, Elizabeth Eliot, and others. I can add little to this great cloud of witnesses. But I have discovered a little principle that has helped me greatly in this area of practical forgiveness, and I would like to pass it on to you. I call it the "intimacy of forgiveness" and perhaps it will be helpful to you as you seek to lead others out of pain's discouraging bondage.

Not long after I became a Christian, a woman (who was also a believer) had said something demeaning to me about my wife. I have long forgotten what it was, but I can still remember how I felt. I was angry. I went off to work the following day with her words still gnawing at me. As the day wore on, the insult had so escalated in my mind that I couldn't wait until I saw her again so I could launch my well-rehearsed words of vengeance upon her. My long workday, though greatly preoccupied by this carousel of repeating scenes, was consoled only by the fact that I was going to let her have it. (In a Christian way, of course. I would make certain that my words were draped in the robes of biblical self-righteousness. That nothing of the sort existed did not occur to me; revenge finds many costumes.)

Driving home from work that evening, still rehearsing my words, the Lord pierced my heart with a concept that, for me, was totally new. It was so striking that I can still remember, to this day, exactly where on the road I was traveling when it came. A picture of the crucified Christ came before me, and the reality of the unspeakable *price* of his forgiveness registered in a way that it had never done before. The kernel of truth that was revealed to me at that moment was this: *at the cross Jesus agreed to take the pain!*

Essentially, God, in his desire to forgive us, agreed to take the pain. The forgiveness for our own atrocious acts lay in the fact that he, under his own initiative, agreed to take the full punishment for our sins. And further, he did not bring them up to us again. I suddenly realized that forgiveness was a contract, not a whim. A process, not an event. A commitment to suffer, that we might be released.

This process involves the combined activity of our mind, will, and emotions. As Christians, we first use our minds to acknowledge that God's way is right. In this case it is forgiveness that is right because it is clearly taught by God—and clearly demonstrated by him as well. It is within his character to love so much that he is inclined toward forgiving the objects of his affection. With my mind, therefore, I acknowledge—and agree with—this reality. Second, as an act of obedience toward this clear teaching, I *decide* to forgive and *choose* to do so. I make it an act of my will. But the third reality is that my emotions are involved, and it is precisely here that many well-meaning Christians have fallen upon their own swords. They fall into the trap of believing that reexperiencing the old, negative feeling *after* their decision to forgive must mean that they have not truly forgiven, or else they wouldn't be feeling this way. But this conclusion misinterprets the way emotions work.

Emotions do not think. They weren't designed to think. They are headless, winged creatures that sink their talons deep into our hearts whenever they are triggered by certain external stimuli or by old memories. But they have nothing to do with a rational and obedient decision we have made with our heads and hearts. Experiencing old feelings of anger or revenge—and yes, even hatred—does not mean we were not sincere in our desire or commitment to forgive; it simply means we still carry the lingering *pain* of those emotions.

And forgiveness, simply put, is an agreement to take the pain. I knew immediately that I had to forgive this woman. Not just theoretically, but in actuality. And I also understood, in that moment, what the price tag would be. It meant that all the hurt and indignation I was feeling over the unkind comments she had made about Wendy had to be endured by me, and that further, all the carefully rehearsed phrases of revenge I had planned must never find the light of day. It was not a denial of the anger but rather a subjugation of it.

I think we must be honest in admitting we *feel* a certain way; otherwise we are deceiving ourselves by denying the existence of emotions we know we are experiencing. But emotions always lag behind the truth and, like ripples on the surface of a pond, tend to remain long after the rock was thrown. They are not always in sync with current events. The "current events" in this case were my obedience to the Lord's command to forgive and my decision to release the offending party.

But what to do with those emotions? Where do I bring them? How do I handle the recurring pain? The answer is, We take them to the cross. But what does *that* mean? Is this just another attempt at self-denial by using some "Christianese" lingo that is supposed mysteriously to whisk all the pain away? No. As a matter of fact, the pain lingers. So what do I mean by "taking it to the cross"? I mean it literally—and this is where we get to the heart of practical forgiveness.

When I realized that God was asking me to forgive this woman—and that as a part of that process I was to absorb the pain of the personal hurt I was feeling—I suddenly realized that I was sharing, in a small way, what Jesus had experienced at the cross. He had died alone. He could have retaliated by saying, "You have truly hurt me. I'm hanging here for *you,* but all you can do is mock me and hate me." But he said none of those things. In fact, he simply said, through all his monumental pain, "Father, forgive them, for they do not know what they are doing" (Luke 23:34). The cost of forgiveness was that he agreed to absorb the pain.

It's hard to explain what I felt at that moment. It was as though I was sharing an unbelievably intimate moment with my Lord and Savior. I was sharing an intimacy with Christ that could only be gained through the pain of forgiveness. I felt I was participating in a divine, almost mystic, principle. Suddenly, I almost began to revel in my pain, not in any masochistic way but in an identification with the Jesus who loved me so much that he agreed to take *my* pain.

And I understood him better—no, more than that—I felt a bond with him. The pain of my injury had caused me to travel the pathway his own heart had traveled. The forgiveness I was choosing to extend for that slight injury was, in a very small way, closely related to that great act of love—Christ at the cross. I felt that he understood my hurt and that he had allowed me to enter a special communion with him by reminding me that he too had experienced that particular pain. When he forgave me, he never brought my sin up to me again. He had truly let it go. But not without enduring the injury of it all.

I have shared this principle with many inmates over the years. It's a principle only Christians can understand or participate in. By bringing our emotional pain to him (this shared experience of hurt) and by *enduring* it, we travel the same road our Savior has traveled. It doesn't make the pain go away immediately, because the pain is, in itself, the way *into* the intimacy. It is the emotional turmoil itself that we bring to Christ and share with him. And in the process we experience something deeply sweet and spiritual. In the holy recesses of that secret place, we discover that although the Via Dolorosa is paved with thorns, we find *him* there.

And if we will tread that path each time those old feelings are triggered, we will discover that these emotions slowly catch up with the new reality: that we *have* forgiven. These winged creatures will not hurt us so much in the future as they do today. Will they reappear from time to time? Yes, that's the nature of emotions; they are triggered. But over time, they will not appear as often or hurt as much.

The *choice* to forgive can be an immediate, point-in-time act of faith, but the emotions will still linger. Bring them to the cross of Jesus each time they rear their ugly heads and share them with him. Absorb the pain of the hurt, the anger, the desire to retaliate—and release the offender again. And again. It's the price you agreed to pay as the forgiver. Then understand, in a new and fresh way, the price of *his* forgiveness, and enter into an intimacy with him that this whole, awful experience has somehow provided for you. And even if the person you have chosen to forgive never accepts it or even cares, it doesn't matter. Jesus understands. He's been there. He is there still. And he will wait for you.

"Now I rejoice in what was suffered for you, and I fill up in my flesh what is still lacking in regard to Christ's afflictions, for the sake of his body, which is the church. I have become its servant by the commission God gave me to present to you the word of God in its fullness—the mystery that has been kept hidden for ages and generations, but is now disclosed to the saints. To them God has chosen to make known among the Gentiles the glorious riches of this mystery, which is Christ in you, the hope of glory" (Col. 1:24–27).

Part IV
Engaging the Culture

The Spiritual Climate
of Prisons and Jails

THE PREVIOUS THREE SECTIONS of this book presented us with an inside-out view of the prisoner's world; we attempted to scratch at the surface of how it feels to live in his or her shoes. In this final section, we will begin to engage the culture itself. I've provided some basic guidelines and practical tips for getting started, but let us set the stage by first considering the spiritual climate of the institutional world you are entering and your own role as one of those "smiley-faced Christians" within it.

On the tiers of one of our local prisons, I heard someone yell: "Hey Padre! Could you come over and talk to me after you're done talking to him?" This request came from about three doors down on the opposite side of the cell block. To speak with the men on this particular tier, one must stoop down and talk through a small rectangular opening that is built only wide enough to pass food trays through. The fellow who had called out to me was not a believer and was one of the rowdiest guys on the tier. When I went over to see him, he joked around a little but was genuinely curious about what I was doing. The conversation soon turned to spiritual things in earnest, a scenario that is common for a Christian ministering on the tiers.

A religious volunteer can expect to be addressed by a wide variety of titles on the cell blocks. I have been called everything from "rabbi" and "father" to "reverend" and "preacher boy." Most recently, I am referred to as "the Christian dude." By God's wonderful grace, I have had literally thousands of conversations with inmates over the years, and the vast majority of those discussions have centered on spiritual realities. Countless numbers have prayed with me to receive Christ, and many have broken down in tears of repentance for the things they have done.

I do not know of any more fertile ground for the gospel in all of the United States than our jails and prisons. I make that statement unequivocally and without reservation. If you are looking for a more fruitful harvest field, apart from leaving the country, you will be hard-pressed to find it. I received this letter from an inmate in Florida: "Our largest home mission field with the greatest need seems to be our prisons and jails. Of course some of the absolute best Christians I have met are behind fences and walls and will be for the rest of their lives. Praise God He uses us no matter where we are or what we have done!"

Think of the following scenario: Where else can you find so many for whom the facade of self-sufficiency has been stripped away? Where else can you enter a place that is filled from top to bottom with people who know they have done wrong and, in most cases, readily admit it?[1] Where else can you find so many who are genuinely sorry for what they have done? Where else can you find so many broken, hurting, lonely people all collected together in one small space? Where else can you enter a community where so many of its members have been humbled? (I am not saying that they are all humble; I am saying that they have *been* humbled.) Where else can you enter an arena where every unbeliever understands that your *function* is to talk about God? And further, that they *expect* you to bring him up?[2]

Where else can you strike up conversations with strangers and have over 90 percent of the people you encounter willing to speak to you? And, due to the overcrowded conditions in most facilities, not only does his cellmate get to hear the gospel, but so do all those listening in from the cells around you. Where else, when you are done speaking of spiritual things at one location, can you simply move two or three steps in either direction and start the conversation all over again with someone else?

Think about this! What I have described is a razor-wire beehive filled with humbled souls who know they have done wrong, who are often broken and repentant over their condition, and who are now giving you their full attention. I often ask them, "How many of you would have given me two minutes of your time when you were out on the streets?" The answer, almost always, is none of them. Then I announce that God, in his great mercy and compassion, has slowed them down long enough to consider the claims of the gospel and has put them in a gracious state to receive it! "For God has bound all men over to disobedience so that he may have mercy on them all. Oh, the depth of the riches of the wisdom and knowledge of God! How unsearchable his judgments, and his paths beyond tracing out!" (Rom. 11:32–33).

The gospel in prison carries a missionary flavor that crosses many ethnic and cultural divides. For example, there is a virtual revolution going on among many Hispanic inmates who are encountering the message of grace. Many of them have already had a high degree of religious exposure, and most are still very sensitive to religious things. Like Paul's description of the Jews in Romans 10:2, they have long had a zeal for God, but it was not based on knowledge. When they encounter the Christ of the Gospels, there is a fire to their conversion that virtually explodes in the worship services. Being passionate by nature, they worship and preach passionately.

It is a joy and a privilege to partake in a worship service behind the walls. The blend of ethnic cultures brings a richness to the worship that can be appreciated by all who participate. We also have a growing number of Asian inmates in our correctional facilities. Many of them are hearing the gospel for the very first time, and it penetrates with a freshness that is exhilarating to witness.

I remember one young Cambodian man named Lourm who began to attend our Bible studies. He had been a member of one of three major Oriental gangs that operated in a nearby city in Massachusetts. His parents had fled the genocide that was occurring in their country during the Khmer Rouge purge and had settled in this city, where there was a burgeoning Cambodian population. Lourm grew up on the streets and eventually wound up going to prison.

During the early days of his incarceration, while he was still awaiting trial, he met and received Jesus Christ as his Lord and Savior. He was one of those "seeds sown in fertile soil." He not only attended all the Bible studies and services faithfully; he became a lover of the Book. Everywhere he went, he carried his Bible and was gifted with a sincere heart for the lost. Wherever they placed him, he began to have an influence on the other inmates, especially those of Asian background. It was common to see him show up at the Bible studies with a few other guys in tow, many who could not speak English. Grinning in embarrassment at first, they arrived with Lourm and would soon take part in the studies. Laotian, Vietnamese, Thai, and Cambodian—all learning about Jesus.

I had to send away for literature in these various languages to keep up with them, and I trusted that the evangelical organizations I was writing to were sending me stuff that was theologically sound. *I* certainly couldn't make sense of the spaghettilike scrolls that filled the pages! I once asked an inmate what the booklets and tracts actually said as I passed them out to him. He examined the covers with a studious frown and then broke into a huge smile. Singling out a specific spaghetti strand, he announced, "This one say 'Jesus!'"

Lourm was released after about four years, and though he is still awaiting deportation, he is now active in a good Cambodian fellowship in his neighborhood. He has reached out to his family, and some of them are now attending the church. His mother also has become a Christian.

I tell Lourm's story because I want to illustrate how extensive God's great love for us truly is. Who could have known that out of the tragic circumstances in a country on the other side of the world that God would use the flames of war to drive a family to another country? And that out of the pain of trying to fit into another culture, a young man would get involved in gangs and drugs and wind up going to prison? And further, who could have foreseen that in a jail cell on another continent, he would come to Christ and eventually lead his family to a knowledge of the Savior? Praise him for His love and sovereignty!

Those tired old tiers that are trod by hopeless, helpless people continue to be a rich harvest field for the gospel. I stood in front of the cell of one man, who, as it turned out, just wanted to argue about religion. When I realized that he wasn't serious and only wanted to debate, I brought the conversation to a close and began to turn away. As I did so, his cell mate, whom I hadn't previously seen because they kept their cell so dark, suddenly leaped off the top bunk and said, "Wait! *I* want to hear more about this!" Not only was he sincere in his desire to hear more; he wound up praying to receive Christ before the surprised eyes of his argumentative cell mate!

Many inmates are endowed with a good sense of humor. It is beneficial for them to be able to laugh in spite of their circumstances. Those who can do so tend to fare better than those who cannot. The impish child still resides in many, and they enjoy a good prank or a humorous set of circumstances. They also seem to respect those who can dish it out as well as take it, including volunteers and chaplains.

A classic incident occurred with Pastor Bud Wood, who has been the chaplain at the Middlesex County Jail in Billerica, Massachusetts, for two decades. Once, while he was in the middle of a sermon to nearly two hundred guys in the cafeteria, he noticed that a solitary inmate had risen from his seat and was slowly making his way up front. Bud kept preaching, but he was conscious of the man's steady progress along the side wall. When the inmate came to the front, he walked toward Bud and did not stop until he stood directly beside him. He was a big man and taller than Bud, who is not a small man himself. Since Bud could no longer ignore his presence, he turned and met the man's eyes. The stranger was glaring directly at him and asked in an ominous tone, "Who are you?"

Attempting to dispel the tenseness that everyone was beginning to feel, the minister responded with a lighthearted, "Hi, I'm Bud. I'm the Protestant chaplain here. Who are you?"

Expressionless, the man intoned, "I'm Jesus Christ." Then he repeated, even more darkly than before, "Who are *you*?"

"You're Jesus Christ?" Bud asked.

"Yes," came the rigid reply. And then again, "Who are *you?*"

It was clear by now that the man had severe psychological problems, but with two hundred inmates looking on, and no guards in sight, the chaplain had to ease the situation somehow. Without missing a beat, Bud replied in mock astonishment, "If you're Jesus Christ, how is it that you don't know me? You mean I've been working for you all these years and you don't know who I am? How can that be?"

At this, the whole place broke into laughter, and the tension of the moment was immediately broken. The man himself seemed unruffled by the remark; he was obviously in his own time zone. At this juncture the guards appeared and ushered the poor fellow off to the infirmary. He was sent to Bridgewater[3] the next day for treatment and observation.

On the tiers, the potential for encountering all sorts of strange situations and sights is enormous. The inmates take these things in their stride, but volunteers have to be a bit more prepared for the unexpected. The best defense I can recommend is to stay spiritually in tune yourself; then your responses are more likely to be the appropriate ones. If you stay close to the Lord in terms of your own devotional life, he will often impress you with just the right actions or words.

When holding a Bible study on the tier, I like to go to each man's cell before we begin and invite him to attend. I can remember one fellow who replied cryptically, "I already read a bible." I was encouraged to hear this until he continued, "I read Satan's bible!" He then attempted to give me a brief discourse on the merits of a satanic bible he had been reading. I interrupted his soliloquy by saying, "Why do you want to be on the losing side?"

"What do you mean?" he challenged.

"Jesus has already defeated Satan, and he's going to crush him completely in the end. You're on the losing team."

"Satan takes care of me," he growled.

At this I took a few steps back and made a dramatic show of surveying his surroundings. "Satan takes care of you?" I observed. "I really like his hotel accommodations!"

"Whattya mean?" he sneered.

"Don't you get it?" I asked. "Look where he has you! He's got you in jail, taken everything away from you, and in the end he wants to kill you and steal your soul. And you still think he's doing you a favor?"

He countered with a few more theological objections but then, almost sheepishly, said that maybe he would come out to the study just to see what I had to say. He wound up coming to the Bible study that week and the following week as well. On the third week he bowed his head at the table with the other inmates and prayed to receive Christ, renouncing his old allegiance to the enemy.

Prison ministry is like being involved in the Book of Acts all over again. Every trip to prison is etched in the continuing work of the Holy Spirit. God uses these "houses of mourning" (see Eccles.7:2) to bring rebellious people to the end of themselves by allowing them to experience their own brokenness and their own inability to make their lives work. He humbles them and slows them down long enough to consider *his* answer for their lives— the forgiveness of their sins through the shed blood of Jesus Christ at the cross. The average prisoner sitting in his or her cell isn't really interested in lofty opinions about theology. "My life is broken. How do I fix it?" is the basic question he asks. "If you say it's God, tell me how that works."

But I also do not want to paint a picture that the fruit is just falling off the trees throughout the prison systems; that also would not be true. In our American culture, one can no longer assume even a rudimentary acquaintance with the Bible or the claims of Christ. Many young people coming into prison today have never even *heard* that Jesus died on the cross for their sins. This may sound incredible to many, but it is the truth. Even in the case of many African-Americans, who have long been the beneficiaries of a rich, Christian heritage in our country, the old assumptions can no longer be made.

As little as ten to fifteen years ago, I could approach the cell of a black man and almost count on the fact that he had a Christian mother or grandmother who had raised him. In fact, I would often use that very premise as an avenue to speak about spiritual things. I would simply ask, "Do you have someone on the streets praying for you?" Invariably the answer would come back through a sheepish smile, "Yeah, Ma's praying for me," or "Gramma's been praying for me my whole life." Then I usually announced, "Well, I'm standing here in answer to her prayers!" This usually drew a laugh because they knew Grandma would agree.

But today this scenario is getting more and more rare. There has been a basic decline in biblical instruction among families of all races, and Islam has made significant inroads among the black populations of our prisons. It is offered primarily from a nationalistic appeal. "Christianity," their teachers espouse, "is the white man's religion." Thus they attempt to make Uncle Toms of those inmates who try to follow the old paths.

And yet, by God's power and grace, some of the strongest Christian inmates I know are those dear, black brothers who stand strong in the gap for the Lord Jesus Christ. And wherever they are present, I find the opposition unable to make a lasting beachhead. The strength of their commitments encourages those other men who still remember the past echoes of their Christian heritage, and the church always tends to grow in numbers wherever they are present. They are warriors in my estimation—modern-day Eleazars standing in their fields of barley and turning the tide of battle for the Lord's people (see 1 Chron. 11:12–14).

In a Bible study at a women's prison not long ago, a young woman who had been listening to the Word as it was being preached suddenly broke into sobbing. As the other girls in the circle tried to comfort her, she kept repeating, "I didn't know it was wrong! I didn't know it was wrong!" When they were finally able to ascertain what it was that had been so "wrong," they discovered that she had been referring to her involvement in prostitution! She knew that it was a criminal act as far as the state was concerned, but she had never thought about it as being a sin against a personal God.

I know there are some who may read this and wonder how she could not possibly know that her prostitution was a sin, but I offer it as further evidence of the current dearth of biblical instruction among many American families. Her life had been a history of sexual abuse that, in her case, led to the easy transition of selling her body for profit. The absence of biblical values, combined with her daily exposure to a society that promotes immorality at every level, sent the message that the only punishment for prostitution is dispensed by a state court, not a heavenly one. When she found herself in a 1 Corinthians 14:24–25 type of situation, she was convicted by the goodness of God's Word and a deep sense of her own sinfulness. Only then was the balm of Christ applied to the wound in her heart as she asked him for his forgiveness.

Every faithful jail and prison worker can give you many other testimonies of his wonderful power and grace. The fields are truly white unto harvest. For the present, God is keeping the doors to these dark places wide open to the gospel—and for those who will venture forth with it. Whether or not you are (or plan on becoming) involved in prison ministry, I would ask that you remember to pray for the prisoners as Hebrews 13:3 instructs us—"as if you yourselves were suffering."

A final example of prayer and the power of God to keep these doors open is told by my coworker and mentor, Don Moberger. He relates how several years ago, a sheriff in one of the county jails in central Massachusetts decided to eliminate all Christian Bible studies and services at his jail. He banned the volunteers from coming in and put an end to their activities. The little group of volunteers called Don, and he went out to meet with them. He also tried to speak to the sheriff, but he was unrelenting. The small band of volunteers then met together for fervent prayer. At one point during the evening, Don prayed, "Lord, we ask that you will either change this man's heart or take him out of the way so that your gospel can go back into this jail." Within a week, the sheriff had died of a heart attack!

The sheriff who replaced him was much more open to having Bible studies and services, and the gospel was soon being declared at the jail as before. To this day, Don is still sobered by the timing of events and the manner in which that prayer was answered. But there is little doubt in either of our minds that God is serious about having the message of his Son reach the ears and hearts of prisoners—and woe to anyone who thinks he can hinder that work! I also know that he wants us to pray continually and never to take for granted that *he* is the one who is holding those doors open for us.

"Nevertheless, there will be no more gloom for those who were in distress. In the past he humbled the land of Zebulun and the land of Naphtali, but in the future he will honor Galilee of the Gentiles, by the way of the sea, along the Jordan—the people walking in darkness have seen a great light; on those living in the land of the shadow of death a light has dawned" (Isa. 9:1–2).

25

Smiley-Faced Christians

IT IS A TRIBUTE to the power and love of God that he has sent—and continues to send—so many faithful volunteers to minister behind prison walls. The number of men and women has been so great and so all-encompassing that Christian volunteers have *themselves* become a recognizable part of the culture. Seasoned prisoners have come to accept these seemingly naïve, smiley-faced people as part of the common fabric of their prison experience. For that testimony in itself, God must be praised for his great and persistent love for prisoners!

When a distraught parent calls to tell me that his rebellious son or daughter has been picked up by the police and is now sitting in some lockup, I inwardly praise God. Finally, they are in a position to listen to someone. Finally, they have been interrupted in their reckless race toward self-destruction. Finally, the parent knows where they are at night. Finally, the continual threats and damage they were wreaking in the lives of others have been suspended. And now, finally, they will be put in an optimum place to hear the gospel!

In New England there is scarcely a county jail, prison, youth facility, or lockup where the gospel is not being preached by Jesus-loving, Bible-believing Christians at least once a week. At Vision New England we saw that goal reached in 1986, and the work continues to gain strength as more and more church-based volunteers are added each year.

The Coalition of Prison Evangelists (COPE) has hundreds of prison ministries on their mailing lists, both nationally and internationally, and the well-known ministry of Prison Fellowship is global. When one adds the innumerable, individual ministries that are constantly and quietly being carried out by faithful men and women from local churches throughout the world, the numbers are staggering.

In the majority of institutions I am familiar with, religious volunteers far and away outnumber all other types of volunteers. It is not unusual for the number of religious volunteers in any given institution to exceed 50 percent of *all* volunteers entering that facility. And even though the term "religious volunteer" includes non-Christian spiritual groups, the percentage of Christians who give their time in this way still exceeds all the others. Men and women returning to prison know that among the scores of administrative officials, guards, counselors, social workers, and other paid staff they will encounter, they also know they will probably run into those "smiley-faced Christians."

Volunteers from all backgrounds flood the prisons of our country on a daily basis. Old and young alike, retired individuals or parents of young families, college students or business professionals, men, women, ex-prisoners, and people from virtually every tribe and nation take part in this gospel invasion of our American prison system.

It is always a little bit baffling to most convicts that volunteers will use their free time to do this. I recall one Christmas Eve, while serving my sentence at New Hampshire State Prison, when a group of about a dozen men and women from the Salvation Army came to minister to us. We all filed into the chow hall as they sang Christmas carols and passed out little hard candies to us in paper cupcake holders. On our way back to our cells, we jokingly threw several of the candies against the cold, stone walls of the cellblock to watch them explode. (Our way of saying we were too cool for little candies. But I'm certain all of us counted to see how many we had left when we got back to our cells.)

Later that evening, in the darkness of the night, I lay on my bunk and wondered what kind of people would give up their Christmas Eves to come into a prison and sing to a bunch of inmates they didn't even know. It was a foreign concept to me because I knew that *I* would never do such a thing. And even though I was not to come to Christ for another eight years, I was seldom able to pass a red Salvation Army bucket from that point on without throwing something into it. Although I didn't remember any verbal message they delivered, they had touched me with something else—an expression of love that was above and beyond the ordinary.

Prison is a scary place for new volunteers. All they know is what they have seen in the movies or on TV, which always panders to the sensational aspects of life in the "Big House." I have taken many volunteers into prison for their first experience, and I usually tell them that it is quite normal for them to be experiencing some apprehension. It always provides a wonderful opportunity to have prayer with them and to bring to mind the all-sustaining grace and presence of God. Jesus brought this reminder home to me once when I was standing outside the Green Unit.

The Green Unit was a part of Raiford State Prison in Florida, just down the road and across the county line from the East Unit of Florida State Prison in Starke. This particular section of Raiford had been condemned for some time, but they were still housing inmates in it. At the time, it was being used as the disciplinary wing for their hard cases. Raiford already had a national reputation as a tough prison, and my first time on the tier of this unit felt portentous. As I stood at the entrance, looking through the faded green bars of the last door separating me from the inmates, I experienced a rising sense of apprehension.

I had no contacts on this tier and was conscious that everyone on the cell block was suddenly conscious of me. The graveyard quietness of the afternoon was shattered as the guard unlocked the gate for me. The brash rattle of his keys, the metallic clinking of the lock as it turned, and the harsh clang of the door slamming shut behind me left everyone aware of my presence. As the guard walked away, I stood there alone, looking down that long, cement catwalk. My perspective did not permit me to see a single person, but I was aware that everyone on the tier could see me. This was accomplished by the use of little shards of mirror that were suddenly thrust through the bars of each cell. To them

I looked like one of those smiley-faced Christians, but for me the view was one eyeball after another peering back at me from all those little bits of glass.

To add to the sense of foreboding that I was already feeling, a voice at the end announced, "God's on the tier!" Several others burst out laughing. They must have observed the Bibles in my hand and had pegged me as a religious volunteer.

But God used that man in a way I'm sure he never intended. The Lord had me think about the words that had so dramatically broken the silence: "God's on the tier."

God is on the tier!

It was exactly what I needed to be reminded of at just that moment! God *was* on the tier! He was with me then as surely as he always is! Up until that moment I had been feeling very alone. But suddenly the truth that I *wasn't* alone came flooding back to me. My courage returned and, filled with a sense of power and confidence, I began to move forward down the cell block. I found myself thinking, *That's right! God is on the tier. Watch out tier!*

And the Lord brought about a wonderful victory that day. I had meaningful, spiritual conversations with several men that afternoon. These were to continue into the days ahead. Many of them wanted me to come back. They told me that virtually no one came to that tier to see them, and they were grateful for my visit and the Bibles that I brought. But the greatest triumph was the victory the Lord had won in my own heart; I never forgot the lesson. I would need it many more times in the future, and there are still times when I need it today. But the reality stays with me: "God is on the tier."

To every volunteer who ventures beyond those walls by faith, I say to you that the Lord will be with you. He promised (see Isa. 43:2; Matt. 28:20b; Heb. 13:5b). And because of your faith and your willingness to follow him wherever he leads, you will see great and awesome things that you never would have seen otherwise. Keep on keepin' on—the view from Mount Pisgah (see Deut. 34:1) is breathtaking! And God is on the tier!

"Faith is the victory! Faith is the victory!
O glorious victory that overcomes the world."[1]

26

Getting Started

AMONG THE MOST FREQUENTLY ASKED QUESTIONS posed by interested Christians about prison ministry are the following:

- "I'm interested in prison ministry, but I'm not sure it's for me. How can I find out without making a long-term commitment?"
- "How do I get involved in prison ministry? How would I go about it?"
- "I'm not a great Bible teacher, but is there anything else I could do?"
- "My friends and I have a musical group; is there a chance we could play at the prison?"
- "I'd like to go, but I'm not sure I can relate to the prisoners. Should I try to be involved anyway?"

If you have asked these or similar questions, it is my hope that we will answer them to your satisfaction in this chapter.

Prison ministry is similar to any other "home mission" ministry with two glaring exceptions: *accessibility* and *exposure*. In most other ministries, we can easily observe—and interact with—the target group. For example, we observe elderly people all around us, so we are well acquainted with the population. We see children or teenagers and know what it's like to interact with them. We also know, through this same interaction and exposure, whether or not we are particularly drawn to these people as a group. I know one young lady in her early twenties, for instance, whose heart is particularly drawn to the elderly. She enjoys their company and loves to visit them. She has since become involved in a nursing-home ministry. She loves them and they, in turn, love her back for her kindness and bubbly enthusiasm. Her frequent visits fill the lonely hours of the elderly and express the comfort of Christ to them.

In these cases, we don't have to make a commitment to the ministry before deciding whether or not we have a heart for it. Our exposure gives us a pretty good clue. But how do we experience that exposure with prisoners locked behind concrete walls? Many Christians have never been inside a prison, let alone interacted with its inhabitants. The media has colored their perceptions of inmates. They are also aware (as this book has pointed out) that the culture of incarceration is very different from the daily world they are accustomed to on the outside. Potential volunteers may question whether or not they would be able to minister effectively within this culture. How would they be accepted? How would they relate? Such questions would be reasonable to ask, given the volunteers' lack of exposure.

The solution would be to reverse the unique challenges of accessibility and exposure. We need access not only to the environment but also to the prisoners themselves. We must give them the opportunity to step out from the shadows of our own minds and into the light of day—where we discover that they are no different than we are.

Exposure Without Commitment

The best place to begin is to participate in some form of prison ministry activity that does not require us to make a further commitment. It is exposure to the people and the place that is needed first. I recommend three ways to go about this:

1. Literature
2. Conferences
3. Special in-prison events

Chances are, you have already been reading *something* that pertains to prison ministry. Or perhaps you heard a testimony that inspired you. Perhaps you know someone who is involved in prison ministry. You may even know a particular inmate.

Whatever the case, something has sparked an interest on your part or, at the very least, a curiosity regarding it. Whatever it was, it began to demystify the concept of prison ministry and brought it into the realm of possibility for you.

I would encourage you, therefore, to continue reading about this ministry whenever you can. Many denominational publications print articles about their involvement in jail and prison ministry, and there are many stories and testimonies of people whose lives have been changed behind those concrete walls. The newsletters of major prison ministry organizations such as COPE or Prison Fellowship keep their readers aware of the powerful things God is doing behind the razor wire and in the lives of individual prisoners. Even the small newsletter that Wendy and I have been sending out to our support team for over twenty years has brought our readers closer to those dear faces behind the walls. As a result, they have become acquainted with them in a way that transcends the common media perspective that the world is communicating. They are not afraid of inmates; they pray for them.

I would also encourage you to attend prison ministry conferences. The Coalition of Prison Evangelists host national and international conferences each year. (Information and addresses regarding ministries are in the back of the book.) Among COPE's many materials you can purchase a copy of *Effective Jail & Prison Ministry for the 21st Century* by Dr. W. Thomas Beckner and Jeff Park, an excellent compilation of various aspects of prison ministry by those with expertise in their fields.

Chuck Colson's Prison Fellowship has a wide assortment of materials and information that can assist the prison ministry volunteer. They have training sessions available in most states for those who are interested in participating in their ministries. Visiting their Web site can supply you with the name and number of your state's director.

Kairos Prison Ministry is another national organization that provides an excellent opportunity to be exposed to the ministry without necessarily making a long-term commitment to it. They host in-prison weekends of fellowship and teaching that are based on "listening and loving." These events are followed up by monthly reunions with those inmates who participated in the main event.

If you are in the New England area, you may contact Vision New England at (603) 881–7704. We hold two or three annual prison ministry gatherings for volunteers and interested parties. We call them our "Caleb Conferences" and we host them regionally. These gatherings, and others like them, go a long way toward exposing individuals to the various facets of prison ministry. There are workshops on related topics, testimonies of ex-prisoners, major speakers, and a large number of volunteers and chaplains from the various facilities in the area.

The third avenue I would encourage you to take is to participate in a special event that is held at the local jail or prison nearest you. It is possible that an existing ministry may be able to get you cleared to participate in their regular service. Or you may be able to take part in a special musical event being performed at the institution, such as a Christmas or Easter cantata. Prison Fellowship also conducts three-day in-prison seminars in which volunteers are recruited to participate. Usually held on a weekend and led by a trained instructor, the new volunteer is exposed to the ministry in a nonthreatening way and will take an active part by being involved with a small group that includes a mixture of volunteers and inmates. These are excellent forums for getting to know the residents on a deeper, more personal level. I highly recommend them.

For those of you who have musical ability, many ministries welcome the opportunity to have you come and share your gifts. You may be part of a band or a singing group. Clearance is usually extended without too much hassle for these types of special events. (Try to keep your equipment needs to a minimum, however. Too much gear tends to slow the entry process. All equipment must be cleared ahead of time.)

Any opportunity that permits you to be exposed to the culture without having to make a more involved commitment is helpful. If possible, try to ensure that your entry is under the auspices of a credible and established ministry.

How to Begin

Let us say that you have been sufficiently exposed to the culture to realize that you have developed a heart for those in prison. You have come to the place of making a commitment on a more regular basis and would like to get something started. There are basically six routes you can take.

1. Contact an Established Prison Ministry Organization

Why reinvent the wheel? It is highly possible that you may have an outreach in your area that is specializing in prison ministry. For example, Vision New England's scope of responsibility covers the six New England states. By God's grace we not only have a list of all the correctional facilities in our area but a record of most of the chaplains and workers who are currently going into them. If someone in this region wanted to be involved in a ministry to prisoners, we inform them of the institutions nearest to where they live and inform them of possible opportunities. If this information is unknown to us, we can direct them to the people who oversee the ministries of those particular institutions.

The Coalition of Prison Evangelists has a booklet that contains all its member ministries as well as the names of most of the correctional facilities in each state. By joining the membership of COPE, this extremely helpful tool can be made available to you. When I want to follow-up with an inmate in another state, this list has provided me with the names of ministries that may be working in those institutions. Contacting the local state director of Prison Fellowship is also helpful in terms of possible ministry follow-up of inmates.

If you live in Canada, the obvious contact that is available to you is the national ministry of Bridges of Canada, which is directed by Monty Lewis. Formerly known as Cons for Christ, this ministry has been so blessed by the Lord that it now operates with the full support of the Canadian government.

Many local ministries have expanded to the point where their jurisdiction now covers several institutions within a given area or state. The people who oversee these ministries are usually well known locally. If you contact them, they may be able to direct you further. Such ministries are usually encouraged to hear from people who may be interested in assisting the work. It helps them to expand their efforts to provide more services, both inside and outside the prison.

2. Contact the Chaplain

If you are considering ministry in an institution that has a chaplain, it is mandatory that you make contact with this person. He or she is the one who must approve any religious activity that takes place within his or her institution. In a large facility that houses hundreds or even thousands of inmates, the scheduling of religious events is a full-time job. The state recognizes this and has employed these people to oversee the responsibility. Normally, any request for involvement is responded to in a professional and expedient manner. Occasionally, however, there are so many programs going on that chaplains may be reluctant to upset the administration by submitting requests for new ones—even if they have a time slot available.

Potential volunteers can experience frustration in trying to get in because their requests appear to go unheeded or they are delayed. Other chaplains serve under regimes that restrict religious meetings. The chaplain may *want* additional help, but the powers-that-be make it extremely difficult. In this case, you might consider joining an existing ministry effort.

If the institution to which you are applying has a chaplain, this is the person to whom you must make your requests. In a large institution, the chaplain needs to be cautious about the quality of volunteer he is bringing in. Speaking with you over the phone seldom gives him enough information about your character, maturity, and demeanor. You have a couple of options for overcoming this. The first is to ask for an interview. (They will often require this anyway.) The second is to give the reference of a friend or acquaintance who is already known to the chaplain. (Be sure they are in good standing with him!) The latter choice is preferable, if it is available to you.

Beyond this, if you know someone who is already ministering as a volunteer at the prison, ask him or her to inquire of the chaplain *for* you. This can usually be done informally. Since the current volunteer is an acquaintance, the chaplain can be open and honest with him in terms of existing opportunities.

If you do get an interview, bring references. Be sure to include the name and phone number of your pastor. (Involvement in a local church fellowship is imperative.) If you are accepted, most institutions require that you go through some form of orientation process they conduct for new volunteers. You will usually find these meetings to be interesting and helpful.

3. Join an Existing Ministry

This is usually one of the best avenues you can take, and it is especially helpful in facilities that do not employ chaplains—such as many county jails or city lockups. It gives you the opportunity to be exposed to the ministry as well as providing some much needed encouragement for the existing team. If you are aware of a group that is going into the local jail, consider contacting it. Sometimes this "group" often consists of little more than one or two faithful people who go in week after week. Ask them if it would be OK to join them some evening. In most cases they will welcome your participation.

Occasionally, joining the ministry that is part of another church can result in varying doctrinal views. They may not hold the same beliefs you have on some minor points. The rule of thumb here is that if you are the one joining the group, do not seek to impose your view on theirs. They were there first. If what they teach is too uncomfortable for you, then it would probably be best not to join them. (I am speaking here of *nonessential* doctrine—not unorthodoxy.) Most veteran prison ministry volunteers do not get too hung up on the minor differences of doctrine that can divide Christians on the outside; they tend to focus on Jesus Christ and him crucified. But if the differences lie in the area of worship styles, I would encourage you to continue with them for a while. When sincere Christian hearts unite to worship the Lord, we can learn much from one another as we expand our horizons in learning to declare his praises. The inmates will also benefit as they are exposed to a wider variety of worship experiences.

4. Approach the Administration Yourself

In the event that the facility you desire to enter has neither a chaplain *nor* an existing prison ministry, then you will be breaking new ground. This endeavor has several steps attached to it.

Among the first things you must do is make your desire known to the church and ask them to pray about it. Ask friends to be praying for you. (It is assumed that prayer has been an integral part of *all* these options, but especially so in this case.) Two of the specific things you are praying for are that you will be received favorably by the jail administration and that the enemy will not succeed in preventing your entry. Another important request is for a partner.

It is good that you have it on your heart to visit the prisoners, but solo ministry can become very discouraging at times. (The enemy will not be happy that you have been given permission to go in, so he will attempt to discourage you in a variety of ways.) The Lord Jesus knew what he was doing when he encouraged the disciples to go out two by two. A great antidote to discouragement is the company of a like-minded fellow worker.

Next, obtain the approval of your pastor or elders. This is important not only as a confirmation, but also it will prove helpful to you when you make your pitch to the jail's officials. It's important for an administration to know that a local church is supporting you in this effort and that you are there as a direct result of their wishes. Most jails and county facilities like to maintain good relationships with the communities of which they are a part; this includes churches. When they realize that an entire congregation of people (some of whom may even be neighbors of theirs) knows that you are making this request of them, it helps to make them more open to your petition.

Finally, contact the prison. Do *not* make your request to the first person who answers the phone. Ask to speak directly to the head official of the facility. In the case of a county jail, this title can vary. The person may be known as "sheriff" or "superintendent," or even "administrator." Make sure you know the correct title before you call as well as his or her personal name. If the officer answering the initial call asks who's calling, give him your name *and* the name of the church you are representing. In small towns, someone in the congregation may know the person in charge personally. A well-placed comment by them, to the effect that you will be dropping by to speak with him, can be suggested informally. In most cases, the pastor himself should call ahead to let the administrator know that a member of his congregation is interested in meeting with him. This can be very helpful in terms of paving the way for you. Do not be afraid to utilize the natural connections the Lord has already provided.

Many Christians have assumed that these institutions do not want anything like a church service or a Bible study going on at their facility. But just the opposite is often true. From my phone in Massachusetts, I have contacted jails as far away as Northern Maine on behalf of a local congregation, only to have the sheriff respond with, "We'd love to have something like that in here! The guys have been asking for a service, but I didn't know who to contact." The dear saints living only a few miles away from the jail assumed that the administration would be closed to their efforts, so they never approached them. Meanwhile, a man living 250 miles away makes one phone call and the door is thrown wide open!

Don Moberger, head of Vision New England's field staff, had a similar experience in Maine. He once visited with the former chaplain at the state prison in Thomaston many years ago. The guy was not known for being very evangelical, but Don went ahead anyway, suggesting the possibility of someone coming in to do a worship service. The man responded with enthusiasm to the idea but didn't know of anyone who might be interested. When Don walked out of the facility, he noticed a small Assembly of God church right across the street from the prison. The pastor was at home and, after listening to Don, couldn't believe what he was hearing. "I've been trying to get in there for years!" he exclaimed. And he pounced on the opportunity. The pastor began a Saturday evening service at the prison that he faithfully conducted for over twenty years before retiring.

If you have a desire to start a ministry in a jail or prison that has little or nothing going on, pray and knock. Pray that the timing of the Holy Spirit will open the door for you—and then go out there and knock on it. Never assume that the door is closed.

5. Consider Using Your Gifts and Talents in a Nonreligious Program

Sometimes volunteering for spiritual opportunities may not be available at the prison you want to serve in. Or, you may have expertise in other areas. I am aware of many Christian volunteers who are serving in a "Dorcas" kind of ministry within the prison (see Acts 9:36–42). That is, they are helping prisoners by teaching them skills and abilities through the uses of their own. For example, the program department of a prison may have a great need volunteers to donate their time to help inmates improve their reading skills. Christians have been able to share their faith in a low-key way just by building relationships and demonstrating the compassion of Christ as they assist them in this vital area.

Others I know have offered to do seminars on financial planning, while still others have shared basic marriage and parenting principles. Some volunteers have imparted vocational skills like woodworking, plumbing, computer training, and mechanics. Others have supplied materials for sewing projects, ceramics, and other crafts. Bilingual Christians have a tremendous opportunity to teach second-language skills. Christians with musical talents have many options available to them and are often permitted to teach in some capacity, perhaps a particular instrument or even music theory.

These skills and talents open doors that may be closed to a more traditional approach to prison ministry. While it is expected that proselytizing will not be part of your agenda in such cases (and you must honor this), the fact that you are a Christian will speak a good word in itself. The inmates will often make a comment about your faith while you are working beside them, thereby opening the door for you to give the reason for the hope that you have.

6. Consider the Needs of Aftercare and Family Ministry

Finally, let me take the opportunity to widen the range of potential prison ministry options for you. The possibility of ministry *outside* the prison walls does not occur to most inquirers at first. But the needs of aftercare, as well as ministry to the families of prisoners, are just as important as the efforts going on inside the prison. In many ways, they are even more urgent. Potential volunteers should seriously consider lending a hand in these two areas; you will be involved in meeting a great need. There are, comparatively speaking, very few volunteers ministering in these arenas at present. Very few volunteers have caught the vision (although it is steadily increasing) for ministry to the families of inmates as well as to the diverse opportunities that aftercare provides.

Each of these, in turn, is a broad heading under which many related ministries could take place. For example, under the heading of family ministry, there is a need for counseling, transportation, baby-sitting, big brothers and big sisters, food, clothing, and even safe living quarters. There is a need for friendship, a listening ear, a pat on the shoulder, a hand in a hand. Effective discipleship and fellowship can be provided through the godly sacrifice of shifting one's personal schedule.

The church can involve the prisoner's children in activities they already have going on for children and find creative ways to introduce them to wholesome playmates and activities. If it is true that the spiritual well-being of the wife is important to the man in prison, the presence of good people around her children are important to the mother. Who is better equipped to provide this than the church?

There are so many other things that could be done. The many facets of prison ministry provide compassionate Christians with a wide variety of opportunities to express the love of Christ. There is ample room for visionaries and dreamers to find creative ways to meet the many needs that exist. There are others who are financially able to assist those good works that are already going on under the name of prison ministry. There is room for preachers like Peter and servers like Dorcas. We need them both.

I thank you so much that your concern for those in prison has led you to read even this far. May the Lord bless you in whatever you do for his sake—and wherever he might lead you to do it.

27

Dos and Don'ts

GIVING A STICK OF GUM or a ballpoint pen to another person are normal gestures in outside society. Both activities are illegal behind prison walls.[1]

Orientation processes that inform volunteers about the rules of the institution are common in most state and federal correctional facilities. Some do a better job of this than others. County institutions, on the other hand, are less formal and do not usually conduct such meetings. Nevertheless, it is extremely important that volunteers understand what they are allowed to do while inside the walls, and perhaps more importantly—what they are *not* allowed to do. Their continued access to the institution depends upon it.

Following is a list of basic "dos and don'ts" for prison volunteers. If you are new to ministering in prisons or jails, I strongly suggest that you familiarize yourself with these concepts. While I stop short of describing them as canonical, most institutions would ordain them as such. Nor does it hurt "veteran" prison ministers to review them periodically.

While a few of these rules listed may be permissible in some institutions, they will be the exceptions rather than the rule. Some places allow their seasoned volunteers to get away with certain activities that are technically not allowed, but this permissiveness is usually due to a long, developed relationship of mutual trust rather than legislative prudence.

The following listing is not exhaustive. It should be used as a *supplement* to your institution's own list of rules and regulations for volunteers and *not in place of it*. If there are discrepancies between this list and that of your institution's rules, always defer to theirs. But if your facility offers no such list, you will find this one helpful. Some institutions would add items that are perhaps more pertinent to the logistics of their own facility, while others may have an even shorter list. All would probably agree that this lineup includes the essentials. I have taken the liberty of giving a brief philosophy underlying each regulation. Sometimes a decree is better remembered when the reasoning *behind* the ordinance is explained.

Nothing In—Nothing Out

This is usually rule number one. Do not bring any unauthorized material into—or out of—the institution. "When in doubt, leave it out." Most places have lockers where you can place items like watches, wallets, cash, or jewelry. If this makes you uncomfortable, lock these items in your car. Normally, wedding rings are allowed but no other jewelry. This rule is directed toward bringing items into the institution that you may leave behind and taking items out that you did not bring in. Do *nothing* like this. Ever. Not stamps, not writing paper—nothing! *Never* take a letter out for an inmate, no matter how sympathetic you may be to the reason behind it.

Christian volunteers are allowed to bring their own Bibles in, and usually paperback Bibles for distribution. Most places will allow certain other kinds of Christian literature, but *all* items must be approved by the prison. If you are sitting there wondering whether or not such and such an item would be allowed, my best response to you would be: Don't bring it in until you find out.

Lock Your Car While on Institutional Property

In case an inmate escapes, the prison does not want to make his getaway too easy for him. (That some of them could probably get into your locked car more quickly than you could with a key is irrelevant. It would at least slow a few of them down.) The rule also exists because some inmates are allowed to work outside the prison walls. Contraband items could be stolen from your vehicle. Another perceived threat behind this regulation is the possibility that you could have arranged a situation whereby an inmate working outside could stop by your car and pick up contraband while you were inside.

Request a Copy of Your Institution's Rules for Volunteers and Memorize It

This will remove a lot of doubt for you, and it also sends a message of responsibility to the institution.

Always Demonstrate Courtesy and Respect to Prison Officials

It is the Lord Jesus you are representing.

In the Case of a Conflict with Correctional Staff, Do Not Argue but Comply Immediately

This is a must. Whether you think that a particular action by a correctional employee was appropriate or not, be respectful and comply immediately. Volunteers must never forget that they are in a prison. Correctional staff may have to do some things you don't understand. If something is happening in the institution that is of an urgent nature, they do not have time to stop and explain it to you. But regardless of how you interpret any action, what you must do—*at the time*—is comply.

You are free to pursue your complaint with his or her supervisors later on if you thought something was inappropriate, but a better course of action may be first to speak to the person at the earliest convenience and discuss the matter with him or her. I find that officers often feel guilty for an insensitive encounter with a volunteer and desire to have a chance to explain themselves later. Pursue the former course only if the problem persists.

Caution: I am not referring to such nominal things as waiting in front of doors for what seems like an interminably long time for some unseen officer in some unseen control room to pop the door for you. Such things go with the territory. I don't know of anyone who has not had this experience—including the staff and the officers themselves! But again, if you feel the problem is persisting and is beginning to interfere with your approved schedule, then respectfully saying something to the right person at the right time may be in order.

Do Not Get Involved in an Inmate's Legal Problems

You can be sympathetic to the things that trouble inmates. Compassion is a part of who we are as Christians. But we are not inside that institution to be their legal angels; there are lawyers for that. You must draw the line at such things. The institution believes you are in their domain to provide spiritual comfort and guidance for the inmates. To do otherwise may jeopardize your volunteer status. If you get the lines blurred, the administration may force you to decide which role you want to play. Do you want to be a legal advocate or a Christian volunteer? They will usually not allow you to be both.

This strict definition of your role is actually a safeguard for you. It enables you to stay focused on the main reason you are there and to provide a valid reason for not becoming personally involved in prisoners' legal matters. Those who do so run the risk of losing their focus, diluting their message, and jeopardizing their ministries.

Do Not Reinforce Negativity Toward the Administration

This is not only counterproductive with regard to your continued good standing as a volunteer; it reinforces the works of the flesh. Bitterness, hatred, lack of forgiveness—and especially rebellion against authority—are all reinforced by your willingness to play into such sentiments. You are present to reflect *and teach* the life and fruit of the Holy Spirit—not the works of the flesh (Gal. 5:16–26).

Dress Appropriately

This is a two-part instruction for the Christian volunteer. The first part has to do with the required dress code for volunteers. The institution will quickly apprise you of what is permitted and what isn't. If you are wearing the latter, you simply will not be permitted inside the institution. The rules partly revolve around what is considered "the inmate uniform." The volunteer cannot wear anything that can be too easily mistaken for the clothing that is worn by the inmates of that particular institution. For example, one prison I know requires inmates to wear white shirts and black pants. Consequently, volunteers cannot wear either. In many places, jeans are common apparel for inmates. Thus volunteers showing up in jeans will be barred from the institution.

The thinking behind this is driven by two security reasons: The first is that in the case of a disturbance (such as a riot), prison officials want to be able to identify civilians quickly. If everyone looks the same, this would make the situation extremely difficult in a chaotic atmosphere. The second is the threat of escape. If volunteers are allowed to enter the institution looking like an inmate, then it is conceivable that an inmate could leave the institution looking like a volunteer. The inaccessibility of "street clothing" to inmates is an essential slice of the security pie.

The second instruction for Christian volunteers is centered on wearing apparel that is suggestive to the opposite sex. Halter tops, thin dresses, and short shorts are not permitted in most houses of correction, but for any *Christian* to come into a prison environment wearing something that could cause another to stumble is, I think, a great sin. What may be borderline acceptable for a Christian to wear on the streets may be totally inappropriate in this deprived arena. Male volunteers in women's institutions and female volunteers in men's institutions need to be extremely careful about this.

Always Bring a Picture Identification with You

Basically, unless you have something like your driver's license in your possession, you don't get in. The institution *must* know who you are.

Do Not Make Unauthorized Public Statements Regarding Inmates

This is extremely important—and often violated. Many volunteers have gone back to their churches and told stories about certain prisoners *by name*, for the purpose of prayer or testimony. Unless the inmate has given written consent to do this, it is not allowed. (Most institutions do not permit this even if the inmate agrees to it.) The risk that some private bit of information could be released to the wrong people is a grave danger, not only from a security point of view but also from the perspective of physical danger. The possible scenarios are many. Some inmates are often moved around to different institutions for their own protection; no one is supposed to know where they are. Some churches have friends of—or even family members of—the victims. Think how they would feel if they suddenly received surprise news about the perpetrator of their pain while they were sitting in church![2]

Still other volunteers fall victim to the media frenzy surrounding notorious inmates they may have met. Statements made in public could easily wind up on the evening news—especially if they reveal some new slant that the lawyers on both sides may be interested in. At the very least, the integrity of the volunteer has been tarnished.

Never Make Public Statements Regarding the Transportation of Inmates

This seemingly innocuous activity can result in someone either escaping or getting killed. There are people on the outside who would love to have a chance to bring their own vigilante justice down upon the heads of certain inmates. If they knew when and where they could—they would. But the greater threat is the risk of escape. There are some inmates who have enough power and influence to arrange for others to free them by intercepting their mode of transportation. Such inmates are usually moved at the last moment, without giving them a chance to alert others about the plans.

In one situation I heard about while in California, a volunteer was asked by such an inmate to call his family to let them know he was being moved. "So they wouldn't make the long trip to visit for nothing." Fortunately, the volunteer asked an officer about it and was immediately told why it would not have been a very good idea. As unlikely as some of these potential dangers seem, and as infrequently as they might occur, their *possibility* makes it mandatory to keep them on the list of don'ts for volunteers.

Do Not Pass Anything from One Inmate to Another; Do Not Carry Messages Back and Forth

Prisoners are extremely creative in their ability to get messages to one another and to pass items back and forth. Some of these are contraband items such as drugs and mash[3] or even ordinary things like soap or cigarettes. That old magazine you pass from one inmate to another may contain something hidden in the pages that is against the rules; but whether the item is permissible or not, volunteers are generally not permitted to act as runners.[4] Again, because *some* items may be contraband, or perhaps messages of an ill nature might be conveyed (such as plans to do bodily harm on someone else), the rule is kept simple for volunteers: don't do it.

Occasionally, a volunteer may be trusted to pass harmless items from one inmate to another while on the tiers, but this must always be done with the authorization of the officer on duty. When in doubt, tell the inmate you will have to ask for the officer's permission. His reaction will usually let you know whether his request was innocent or not.

Do Not Ask Inmates About Their Crimes

This could never serve any good purpose that I can see. First, as Christian volunteers, it is not the reason we are there. Our assignment is not to judge prisoners for a particular sin, but to bring the remedy *for* sin. Second, there are very few inmates who would want to be asked such a question, especially by people they do not know very well. If, in the course of a developing friendship, the inmate wants to volunteer the information, that is up to him. Third, it is a terrible icebreaker. There are many better conversation starters.

Do Not Enter into Any Business Dealings

One would think I wouldn't even have to state this, but such offers will occasionally appear in different forms, and the volunteer must be ready with a quick response. Sometimes the offer seems innocent enough; it may even be something as small as their being willing to pay you for running off some copies of their poems for them. Even if something like this were permissible at your institution, do *not* do it for reimbursement of any kind. A good rule of thumb is *never* to accept financial compensation—in any form—from an inmate. Authorities do not want to open any door that could lead to volunteers being caught in a scam of some kind.

Do Not Run

Except for authorized sporting events, there can be *no* good reason for running to take place inside a prison. Inmates are not allowed to run—even if they are late for something. So if one is seen doing so, the reason must be for something like fleeing from bodily harm, intending bodily harm, or escaping. If guards run, it is because some situation has required their immediate presence, which is seldom a good sign. If a civilian employee, staff member, or volunteer runs, the officers think someone is in trouble. Running in a prison is like a barking dog at night; it's a warning that something must be amiss.

Do Be Consistent

The inmates look forward to special activities they have become aligned with. Special events like Bible studies and worship services are highlights of the week for them. For a volunteer to treat such a commitment lightly reveals a gross underestimation of how important that event has become to the prisoners. If you know you are not going to be present at your appointed time, let the inmates know the week before. The participants will be disappointed but not let down.

Be Honest

Do not make promises you cannot keep. No matter how small the promise might seem in your own eyes, it will be greatly anticipated by them.

Be Adequately Prepared

Do not treat your commitment lightly; Christ deserves excellence. Be as diligent in preparing for your prison event as you would be for any similar forum on the outside.

Use Prudence in Letter-Writing

Unless you knew the person before his incarceration, a principle that should *not* be ignored is that men should write to men and women to women. Do not write the "friend of a friend." Join, or inquire about, the established letter-writing program of a credible prison ministry.

Do Not "Bad-Mouth" Other Groups

Do not be party to speaking negatively about any other group of volunteers—religious or otherwise. If they are not Christians, let the Scriptures themselves testify to the truth. If they *are* Christians, demonstrate a spirit of unity. In both cases, let your demeanor testify to the character of the Christ you serve. Inquiring inmates initially put much more weight on how individuals *act*, as opposed to what they teach.

Arrive on Time and Leave on Time

Prisons run on schedules. All activities are carefully planned around inmate movement times. Every activity has a set time and place to occur. If you do not arrive on time, schedules are thrown off in terms of when inmates can legally move from place to place within the prison. This not only affects the residents but the correctional staff as well. Officers also have to be in set places at set times. If you are not where you are supposed to be when you are supposed to be there, why should they wait for you?

Just as important, *leave* when you are supposed to. Many Christian volunteers, who are accustomed to going overtime in prayer meetings at their own churches, think nothing about going over in this setting as well. Do not do this. The same restrictions of movement that applied at the beginning of your activity apply just as strictly at the conclusion. Inmates will generally take their cue from the volunteers, whom they regard as having authority over them. If the volunteer keeps them too long, who are *they* to say anything? This is not only detrimental from an administrative point of view; it can also result in a write-up for the inmate who is now in danger of being out of place or even missing count—both of which require disciplinary action.

Set a good example by observing your time allotment exactly. This teaches the principle of obedience to the inmates you are desiring to impact and also makes the officers who must oversee your activity more inclined to be favorable toward you.

When in Doubt—Ask!

This final bit of instruction catches anything else we may have missed. If you are ever in doubt about any rule or procedure, ask someone with the proper authority and knowledge. Be selective about who you ask because you may get different answers from different people. A line officer who is concerned about security—and thus minimizing excess movement and activity—may give you a different response from someone in human services who is favorably disposed toward programs.

If you are considered a "religious" volunteer and the institution in which you are serving has a chaplain, then he or she is the person you should always consult first. As far as the administration is concerned, the chaplain is the one they are paying to oversee religious responsibilities; and he or she is recognized as the proper chain of command for issues concerning their volunteers. If the facility has no chaplain, then I suggest going right to the top. Since there is no identifiable chain of command for you, it will not seem improper if a volunteer asks to speak to the sheriff or the superintendent, whichever the case may be. If you deem that the person in this office is unfavorable toward you or your program, then select someone in between who also has some authority and who may be more amenable.

The reason you must be wise in selecting the right person first is that once you are given an answer, it is difficult to get it rescinded. Any attempt to do so could be perceived as trying to "go around" the first person. This is a no-win situation for you. Even if you do succeed in getting the order rescinded, you will have made the first person look bad, and he or she will not be inclined to make things easier for you from then on.

"I am sending you out like sheep among wolves. Therefore be as shrewd as snakes and as innocent as doves" (Matt. 10:16).

28

Conducting an In-Prison Bible Study or Service

THE MAIN PURPOSE of this book is to give the volunteer a sense of what the culture *feels* like to those who live there. Although the how-tos of Bible studies or services are not my primary objective, I have offered this chapter (and the next) as a quick reference guide for you. Other ministries, such as those listed in the back of the book, will also provide excellent guidelines for you. The following is a list of questions that volunteers have often asked regarding how they should conduct such activities, along with a brief response to them.

How Is Leading a Bible Study in Prison Different from Leading One on the Streets?

Basically the procedure is the same, with these possible differences:

- Unless you are working with a small core group of disciples, most Bible studies and services in prison will usually have a higher number of unbelievers present.
- In a jail setting you will have new faces on a regular—and sometimes weekly—basis.
- Their motives for attending your study may differ. (Such as: curiosity; be with their buddies; get out of their cells; have some fun; etc.)
- The questions and comments they make will tend to be very straightforward (blunt, actually). This is the nature of the place, but sometimes it is just to test you. Inmates do not get to observe your private life. To them your main reason for being there is to share information. Sometimes

they do or say something startling because they want to know how much of what you are saying can be demonstrated in your own life.

- The setting for your study will usually be very different from someone's living room. (1) The study could be held in a "day room,"[1] a chapel, a tier, a cell, a cafeteria, or even sitting on a toilet bowl. (2) It may be very noisy and disruptive. If you happen to be on the tiers, you will likely hear radios blaring, people yelling, multiple conversations, clanging doors, and intermittent announcements over the intercom. (3) Inmates may be in and out at will. (Bible study may be one of the few places they can exercise freedom of movement and choice. Although, in many cases once they sign up for the event, or have received a pass to go, they are generally stuck there until the service ends.) (4) Profanity may be occasionally uttered. (5) Interruptions are common. (Officers may need to call people out of your group for various reasons. Even the study can be suddenly ended due to some unforeseen circumstance. Stay flexible.)

In What Ways Is Conducting a Bible Study Similar?

- They are similar in terms of group dynamics. Being familiar with basic Bible study skills is still important. For example, knowing how to draw out quiet or shy people, or dealing with people from different religious backgrounds, handling "talkers" and others who might tend to dominate a group—all these are common experiences.
- The Bible is still your bottom-line authority.

Which Curriculum or Materials Should I Use?

- The Bible is always best, especially in settings where there is a high turnover of inmates—such as a county jail. You want to demonstrate visibly where you get your information and what you rely on as authoritative truth.
- Inmates do not generally do well with traditional, "fill-in-the-blank," or homework types of studies. Each session

should be able to stand on its own, without the partici-pant's needing to be present at last week's study. (Again, this will be different if you are working with a more com-mitted, long-term group of disciples.)

- This does not preclude those teachers who like to come prepared with a number of copies containing an outline of the day's teaching. But in gatherings that contain dif-ferent ethnic groups, this approach will not always be practical—unless you are prepared to make translations! It also runs the risk of embarrassing those who do not read well. It is has been my experience that the learning styles of some cultures do not incorporate a lot of pencil-and-paper work. They may respond better to stories or real-life examples.
- Learn to be rich in illustrations and stories that support the principles you are teaching. *All* inmates tend to relate to these and enjoy them. (But keep this in balance—do not overdo it. If you are just a storyteller, you run the risk of diminishing, to some degree, the role the Bible needs to play in their lives.)
- In addition to a couple of "whole" Bibles, learn to carry a supply of New Testaments in with you. Their smaller size enables you to have more books with you, and it is always useful to start seekers off in the New Testament anyway—especially if you can leave it with them.

Which Books of the Bible Are Best to Start With?

- The Gospels are best (especially John or Mark). In set-tings of high turnover or frequent attendance by seekers, you want them dealing with the person of Jesus Christ immediately. Watching Jesus in action is the most fruitful method in such situations. It keeps the study focused on the main thing.
- If the majority of your group's participants have been through a Gospel with you, you may go on to Acts, Romans, or one of the smaller epistles such as Philippians or James.

- Inmates—like many other seekers—have often heard of Revelation and are fascinated with it because of its symbolic end-times imagery. (This has been true especially since the tragic events of September 11, 2001.) They may suggest it to you as a book to study. While this has value as an attention-getter (and may increase your attendance), it has an additional challenge attached to it. If they leave the institution without clearly understanding the gospel, you did not do your job as well as you might have. While it is true that Jesus and the gospel can be clearly presented from Revelation, you will have to work much harder at it due to the numerous discussions that the imagery and the prophetic ramifications will ignite.
- Avoid starting studies that teach the "pet doctrines" of your particular denomination or group. This practice tends to divide the church inside because teachers from other denominations may be coming in as well. This would be similar to having elders from another church coming into your fellowship and teaching your people their own particular pet issues. If you wouldn't want this to happen in your own church, why would you want to encourage it in the inmate's church? Focus on Jesus!

Should the Time Be Spent Only on Bible Study?

- This depends largely on how much time you have.
- If time permits, singing is always a good way to start. Having a team member who plays the guitar is a big help. Inmates love to sing songs—once you get them going. The more uninhibited you are about singing, the more apt they will be to join you.
- Prayer should be a part of every Bible study. Taking prayer requests is also a good idea if you have time. (Remember to ask about possible answers to prayer at the next study. Pray about these things at home.) It is always good to begin and end with prayer. If you have a person who is growing steadily in his commitment to Christ, you may ask at some point if he would like to

open or close in prayer. This is a way of teaching the others that Christians "grow" in their faith. But be sure to get his permission privately first.

What Is an Adequate Amount of Time for a Bible Study in Prison?

- An hour to one and one-half hours is best.
- If all the time you are permitted is half an hour, this can still be adequate. But be sure to stay focused on the Word; you will have to cut down on the amount of informal chitchat.
- Be flexible! The amount of time you have will not always go according to schedule.

Which Bible Translation Should I Use?

- A modern, easy-to-read translation is best. Scripture Press puts out an excellent New Testament called *The New Life Study Testament*. It has extra study helps and is very easy to read. You can get the New King James Version (NKJV) from the American Bible Society and the International Bible Society has an edition called *Free on the Inside,* which is now the New International Reader's Version (NIRV). (This particular translation has articles that are relevant for inmates.) They also supply the popular New International Version (NIV), which is also good. There are others; find one that you are comfortable with.
- Although an excellent translation, the King James Version (KJV) creates an unnecessary barrier in a place where reading problems abound. For those of you who cut your teeth on the King James, I would recommend using the New King James Version.
- Spanish ministers still tend to favor the Reina-Valera over the more modern translations, but the inmates themselves tend to favor the latter, such as the Versión Popular.
- Whichever version you use, try to have everyone using the same translation. If you have different inmates trying to follow along in different translations, it brings an

unnecessary confusion to the Bible study or service. If everyone has the same translation, you can also refer to the page numbers to help everyone find the text you are teaching out of. This is also an aid against making them feel embarrassed about their Bible knowledge. If you have Hispanic inmates attending, it would be worth your while to bring a dual translation version for yourself.

How Much Previous Bible Knowledge Should I Presume Inmates Have?

- None. (Those who do have some previous acquaintance with the Scriptures will quickly reveal themselves.) But the percentage of inmates who come to prison with little or no acquaintance with the Bible is growing rapidly. You can no longer assume even the most basic familiarity. This will be less true in longer-term facilities.

- You should periodically explain the basics of the Bible to your group. (1) What it is and how it came to be. (2) The difference between the Old and New testaments. (3) Familiarize them with the table of contents. (4) How to read "chapter" and "verse." (5) Explain why some of the titles have the names they have. (This helps to diffuse some of the mystique and fear they may have regarding the Bible.) (6) Teach them how to look up passages for themselves.

- Use page numbers when turning to different passages, but always cite the book, chapter, and verse along with it. This helps to familiarize them with the names and how things are found.

- Always wait until everyone has found your teaching text before you begin.

- It is generally better to stick to the exposition of one passage. This will keep you from "hopping around" too much, making it difficult for them to keep up with you.

Should My Bible Study Be Inductive or Mostly Lecturing?

- Inductive. Learn to ask key questions. You want them involved.
- Read a small section of your text and then go back and ask pertinent, leading questions regarding the key points of the passage.
- In the event of being pressed for time, or of having a "talker" or other disruptive member in the group, you may have to do more lecturing.

Should I "Go Around," Having Each of them Read a Section or Verse in Turn?

- No. While this is a good idea for getting them involved, it will be threatening for those who feel they do not read well. You run the risk of embarrassing them before the whole group. Some are so sensitive about their reading skills that they will actually avoid the study in the future for fear you might call on them.
- It is always best to ask if anyone would like to volunteer to read.
- If there are different ethnic groups involved, you may ask if one of them would like to read the passage in their own language (providing they have the Scriptures in their own language).
- Use an inmate interpreter if necessary. This is a wonderful (and useful) way to involve them.

Should the Bible Study Always Be Evangelistic, or Should I Gear It More Toward Christian Growth and Discipleship?

- This depends on: (1) the type of institution (long-term or short-term) and (2) the makeup of your particular group.
- If you tend to have new people every week, you will have to keep it evangelistic.
- If you have a combination of both, look for alternative ways to feed the disciples (Christian books, correspondence

courses, Bible memorization, evangelism, one-on-one meetings, etc.). Usually, a good Bible study leader will (with the
help of the Holy Spirit) find ways to feed both the seekers
and the Christians during the course of the same study.

What If I Have a Disruptive Member?

- Take control. (The other inmates will respect you for this,
  and they need you to do it because they don't have the
  authority.)
- Deal with it gently but firmly.
- Never get angry or quarrelsome. Don't argue (2 Tim.
  2:23–26).
- If he continues to be uncooperative, warn him once. If he
  persists, ask him to return to his cell. If he still refuses,
  contact the nearest officer in charge. (While this hardly
  ever happens, you need to be prepared to use this ultimate tool if it becomes necessary, for the sake of the
  study.)
- Even though you don't want to lose this person, you will
  eventually lose the others if you don't do anything about
  it.
- Some other options may include: (1) Telling him you will
  be happy to speak about his particular issues later, one on
  one. (2) Being open to the suggestions of some of the
  other guys. (3) Assessing if his issues are relevant for the
  rest of the group. (4) Wisely letting an influential
  inmate—who does want to listen and learn—"correct"
  the disruptive member. Occasionally such individuals can
  fix the situation better than you can and say things you
  can't. But be cautious in this. Never instigate this tactic
  yourself and don't let it become an angry exchange
  between the participants. (5) Pray in the Spirit at all
  times.

What If I Have a "Talker" Who Keeps Dominating the Discussion?

- The methods used would be similar to those you would use on the outside: (1) Direct your questions to others. ("Does anyone else have any ideas about this?") (2) Take the person into your confidence later and affirm his level of knowledge. Then explain to him how he can actually assist the Bible study by giving others a chance to answer questions. I have found that most inmates will readily respond to this. (3) Sometimes just sensitively ignoring him may be the best remedy.
- If it's a short-term prison, there's always the chance he may be gone by next week.

What If I Have an Active Member of Some Other Religion or Cult in the Group?

- Gently instruct him.
- Allow a brief time to insert a teaching around an orthodox view of the person and work of Jesus Christ as a natural part of your study. State clearly who Jesus is and support it with a couple of clear Bible references. *He* is the issue; and it will be around the person and work of Jesus that other false systems will depart.
- Remember that although this person is free to attend the meeting, he has chosen a *Christian* Bible study. Christian doctrine is what will be taught—and is the viewpoint that will be expressed.
- Do not let him turn it into a platform for his own erroneous doctrine.
- Do not argue with him; the Bible says it ruins those others who listen (2 Tim. 2:14).
- Remember that *you* are the one who has been assigned the authority here.
- The ones who stand to benefit most directly from this exchange (beside yourself) will probably not be the cult member but those others who are listening. They will be judging not only your words but most especially your

reactions. It is an opportunity for them to see how a Christian responds to such situations. If you are under the Holy Spirit's leading during this time, the cult member usually reveals himself as the one who acts most poorly and with less love.

- As in the case of the disruptive member, the inmates are expecting you to take charge.

What Do I Do If I Feel the Discussion Has Gotten Too Far Off Track or Out of Hand?

- Keep firm control. This is *your* responsibility, not theirs.
- Not all discussions that "stray" are unprofitable. Some are extremely relevant to where many of your listeners may be. You must ask the Holy Spirit for guidance as to whether or not the particular topic you have wandered into is important for their growth at this time. It may be an issue that many of them are dealing with or a topic that many of them want to pursue further. Sometimes just asking the inmates is the best thing to do in such cases. A helpful question might be, Is this something the rest of you want to spend time pursuing right now? Doing so also demonstrates flexibility and sensitivity on your part.
- Straying is a natural tendency, and each situation must be weighed as to its relevancy. Inmates often want, and need, to share; but sometimes the sharing leads to personal stories or topics that may be irrelevant or uninteresting to the rest of the group. In this case, you need gently to bring it back on course at the earliest opportunity. But do this with gentleness and respect.
- Remember that this is a *group* Bible study. Your concern is not only for the individual but for the group as a whole. Your repeated reluctance to curb these "excursions" can jeopardize the whole study. The others came to learn, and if they sense that you are not maintaining order by keeping the study on track, they will conclude that every week will be a repeat performance and will eventually quit coming.

What Should I Do If the Prison Staff Gives Us a Hard Time?

- Pray.
- Make sure you know what your prearranged guidelines were and gently remind the officer that you were designated these parameters when you were given the OK at the beginning. For example, an officer may occasionally take it upon himself to end the Bible study ahead of time and send everyone back to their units. You must always obey this command when it is given. Later on, however, you should approach the officer and ask him why he took this action. Sometimes there are valid security reasons for doing so, and you must always give them the benefit of the doubt regarding these eventualities, even if they do not seem apparent to you.

  If you notice, however, that the same officer has a tendency to do the same thing over and over again, you can be sure he is being antagonistic. In such cases, remind him that you were designated a particular time slot. If he is late in getting you started (or early in breaking you up), he is not complying with the guidelines that were approved by the administration for your scheduled event. He will need a good reason for explaining why he took the action he did when you bring it to his supervisor's attention. If the supervisor is unsympathetic, go over *his* head.

- If the institution has a chaplain, this is the first place you must take the complaint. The chaplain who is over your program is also the one who is immediately over you in the "chain of command." It will be up to him or her to take the appropriate action.

- If the chaplain is unsympathetic, be careful how you proceed. If you go "over his head" on this or try to go around him, he may tag you as a troublemaker. In situations like these, you must pray for the Lord to remedy the situation in his own unique way. Be patient and open.

The Lord may be developing *your* character through those he has placed in authority over you.

- Don't forget that you are there entirely by grace. Do not be perceived as someone who "demands his rights." Such an attitude will only get you escorted off the grounds or at least succeed in making your ministry much more difficult.

- I have found that if you treat the guards with politeness and respectful obedience, they will, over time, generally come to return the respect, and you will experience far less adversity in the long run. I usually tell new volunteers to weather these storms patiently and respectfully, and after six months or so, they will usually notice a big change in the way the officers treat them.

Should We Open and Close in Prayer?

- Yes, always open and close in prayer. They have chosen to sign up for a Christian Bible study. Christians pray.

- Do not assign any person to pray until you are sure he or she is ready to pray in public. If you sense someone is getting close to this stage, ask in private how he would feel about the possibility of your calling on him to pray.

Should I Always Extend an Invitation?

- If you are in a situation where there is someone new every week, then every week should at least include a clear presentation of the gospel and an opportunity for those who are ready to respond to it by praying along with you.

- If you later have the chance to follow up people privately (whom you feel might be open), this is usually best. One-on-one gospel-sharing tends to produce the most lasting fruit.

- If there has been a response to the gospel, provide practical follow-up instruction for them. For example, you may be permitted to provide good discipleship material or be able to plug them into other Christian inmates. Give them some basic instructions on how to read the Bible on their own. If they are being released soon, ask them if they know of a good Christian church on the streets. (You will be surprised to find that many of them do. Some have friends on the streets whom they know are Christians. Encourage them to contact them.) If they don't know of any churches in their area, *you* find them one. If they don't know any Christians on the streets, *you* arrange for someone to get in touch with them. If it is close to where you live, go yourself.

• While you should never assume that everyone at your study is a Christian, neither should you presume that everyone is an unbeliever. Some Christians in prison get a little discouraged—and sometimes annoyed—that all they get is evangelistic messages because the guest speakers assume they are nothing but heathens. Many know the Bible better than we do.

What About Bringing Female Volunteers into Male Prisons to Take Part in the Bible Study or Service? Or Vice Versa?

• This is not a good idea. (Follow the rule of thumb: male volunteers in male prisons; female volunteers in female prisons.)

• Some exceptions can be made for mature Christian men and women who are over sixty years old.

• It builds barriers to the gospel that need not be there.

• Motives may be cloudy on the volunteer's part, consciously or unconsciously.

• Emotional attachments can begin much too easily in this intense environment, especially if the volunteer is coming in week after week.

• If you are already in this situation, stay with the other members of the group at all times. Do not engage in private discussions. Do not engage in counseling situations.

What If an Inmate Asks for a Special Favor?

- As a general rule of thumb, say no. Inmates will occasionally ask you to do them a favor such as mail a letter, bring a special item in (or out), or even make a phone call for them. Oftentimes, a volunteer will feel awkward about such requests. They "feel" like they shouldn't but don't want to convey that they aren't willing to help. But there are basically two good reasons for saying no: (1) It is usually illegal. You can jeopardize the whole ministry for one small favor. The inmates know the rules better than you do, but sometimes they'll just try anyway. This is not usually because they are intent on conning you, but in a world where you can't do *anything,* the temptation to keep pushing the boundaries is always there. This often comes as an unpremeditated request—just to see if there are any openings that weren't there before. So you shouldn't take these attempts too personally or think that the prisoners are being particularly devious. A few *may* be trying to slip one past you, but I find that most are just trying to read the landscape to see where all their options lie. (2) If it gets around that you are a "soft touch," you increase the odds of having insincere people at your Bible study.
- Your primary purpose for being there is spiritual. Don't lose your focus.
- Some volunteer groups *are* focused primarily on meeting social and material needs. You must be clear about what God has *you* there for and stick to it.
- If you have been a volunteer in the same institution for many years, you will eventually gain a greater level of trust and rapport with the staff. Some things that were stated as taboo for all volunteers may begin to have slight exceptions in your case. But always be sure you have authority to do what you are doing. After you have been given the OK for a certain exception, chances are you will be allowed to do it again. But this last advice is given

only to those "veteran" volunteers who have been around a long time, and have proven—by years of faithful, untroubled service to the prison staff—that they can be trusted.

- Read your institution's regulations for volunteers over again every year. This is always a healthy practice.

How Should I Conclude My Bible Study or Worship Service?

- On time. (I recommend closing the service a little bit earlier than scheduled if you desire some informal chitchat time afterwards.)
- In some institutions the inmates can be written up for being out of place if they return to their units beyond the designated time. Your insensitivity in this area can result in a disciplinary action against them. In most cases the administration will not blame *you* for the tardiness; they will blame the inmates.
- Your obedience is a testimony to the correctional staff about the manner in which the servants of Jesus Christ go about their duties.
- If you are consistently careless about ending on time, you will succeed in alienating the staff and be guilty of teaching irresponsibility to the inmates (not to mention disobedience).
- Many volunteers wait for the staff to break the meeting up, but this is your responsibility. If you are good about this, you make it unnecessary for the officer to interrupt the meeting, and most of them will appreciate you for it.
- Conclude with a prayer. (If your message has been evangelistic, you will want to give those who may be ready an opportunity to respond to the message.)
- Because this is such a fishbowl society, everything you do becomes a testimony for Jesus Christ. You have the high honor—and responsibility—of modeling *him* under the lens of this type of scrutiny.

29

Cell-to-Cell Ministry

IN MANY PRISONS, cell-to-cell ministry is a privilege generally reserved for chaplains only. But never assume that this privilege cannot be extended to you as a volunteer.

Along the scenic coast of "downeast" Maine, I knew a wonderful volunteer who did a weekly Bible study at the local county jail. Every Monday night he would make the trip for the few men who would come out for the meeting. During one particularly discouraging season, not a single inmate came out for almost six months! (I still bless God's name for his example of faithfulness.) But as he was driving through the snow on his way to the jail one cold January evening, he found himself praying, "Lord, I've tried to be faithful in this, and I'll keep going if you want me to, but I need a sign from you. If no one comes out tonight, I'll take it that you want me to stop going in and that the season for this ministry is over."

That evening one lonely soul made his way out to the Bible study. The first one in six months! And in the beautiful way that God has in making a point—the young man prayed to receive Christ that very night! Like the visit to a certain stable one wintry eve long ago, this also proved to be a pivotal moment. From then on, this faithful volunteer always had at least a few inmates heed the call for Bible study.

Shortly after this, I was able to join this dear saint for one of his evenings at the jail and share in his ministry with the men. But when I observed how the Bible study was announced, I could see why the enemy hindered the turnout. A non-Christian officer would go back on the cell block and verbally announce the meeting. I learned later that sometimes these officers would subtly—and sometimes not so subtly—mock the thought of any of these men going to a "churchy event." The inmates would pick up this attitude, and the prevailing winds would soon make it difficult for any potential seeker to buck the trend. Jail was hard enough without the inmates being labeled as "religious weirdos."

Even when the event was announced without bias, the procedure lacked the personal touch that a volunteer could bring to it. I asked my friend why he didn't go back on the tier himself to announce the study. He said he didn't think it would be allowed, and, because of his presupposition, he had never asked. The ironic thing was that he knew the sheriff well; they had grown up together in that small town. I suggested a meeting with the sheriff. On the following day we went to see him. It turned out that the jail was indeed reluctant to permit such a thing, but the sheriff said he would think it over. The official word came back about a week later. The Lord had touched the sheriff's heart so deeply that he passed the decree that my friend would be permitted to announce the Bible study back on the cell blocks by himself!

This ability to get back where the inmates lived had an immediate effect on the attendance numbers. This volunteer began getting about a dozen or more men out to the Bible study each week. And what's more, the Holy Spirit began a small revival there at the jail! Men were coming to the Lord on a regular basis. What my friend discovered was that in just the few minutes he was permitted to get back among the inmates, he was able to have personal conversations with people who could suddenly see a real face connected with this "religious stuff," and further, that he appeared to be "an all-right guy." Their collective curiosity now motivated them to come out to the study. Once the social stigma against attending the meeting was removed, others felt free to attend as well.

There is no substitute for personal one-on-one contact with inmates. Not only does it enable the volunteer to hone in on a particular inmate's issues, but it puts him in contact with those who would have never entertained the idea of going out to a "church thing." I have seen many men come to Christ who, I am fairly certain, would never have been caught dead in the chapel—or at something called a "Bible study meeting." I am not putting down group meetings and services; they will always be necessary and are usually all that the institution will permit. But there is just no substitute for personal contact.

While group meetings often have many who respond to the gospel by raising their hands or "coming forward," the personal work of discipleship and affirming what they have just done is usually left to someone else. And if this is all the follow-up they receive, these new initiates are likely to be the same ones who will raise their hands at the next evangelistic service.

The other consideration is: "How, then, can they call on the one they have not believed in? And how can they believe in the one of whom they have not heard? And how can they hear without someone preaching to them?" (Rom. 10:14). If there are people up on the tier who would never come to a Bible study, how will they hear? The short answer, of course, is through the witness of Christian inmates. And while this does occur to varying degrees through these faithful people, the social pressures of prison dynamics still make it difficult for the unbeliever to break through his stereotypes about "religion." This sort of back-on-the-unit witnessing by Christian inmates is often more effective in long-term institutions such as state or federal prisons, rather than in county jails. This is true because the disciple has a longer time to grow and mature and he has a longer time to display the change that has come.

Another dynamic is the social standing of the inmate who has come to the Lord. If one is low on the totem pole's pecking order, there may also be a low response to anything he or she attends. On the other hand, if a socially powerful inmate becomes a Christian, the very opposite can occur. I have seen occasions where such individuals have been successful in motivating the entire tier to come down to Bible study! While this is primarily based on the sheer strength of his personality and social standing, I smile at the way the Holy Spirit uses such people. Due to

244 ENGAGING THE CULTURE

the hierarchical caste system that exists in prison, the conversion of an influential inmate can have a significant impact on the way Christianity is perceived by the population at large.

Again, I want it to be clear that I am not minimizing the importance of group Bible studies and services. I regularly engage in them myself. Nor do I want to take away from the fruitful work of those dear prisoners who have earned, by their long faithfulness, an impact on the other inmates back on the tiers. (That, ideally, is how it *should* work!) Such men and women are the true backbone of the ministry inside. But they are the elders in these places; and just as on the outside, there are only a few such people in any church. If it is a short-term facility, the chances are even less likely that there will be many inmates who have gained this kind of maturity.

Augmenting Bible studies or services with cell-to-cell work makes for a very effective and fruitful prison ministry. If this is something that you would be interested in adding to your present effort, I would encourage you first to pray about it and ask the Holy Spirit to open doors *and* hearts. (I should also emphasize here that I am *not* recommending cross-gender ministry. Male volunteers should *never* be ministering one-on-one back in the living areas of female correctional facilities—and vice versa. As previously mentioned, a wise rule of thumb is that they not even volunteer in institutions for the opposite sex.)

If you have a chaplain at your institution who is open to such cell-block activity, mention your interest to him or her. (Such ministry can lighten the chaplain's visitation load.) If there is no such person at your facility, ask for a meeting with the superintendent or warden. Do not start on the lower rungs with this request. Security personnel will almost always say no, and even the program department is skeptical about allowing civilians ("nonprofessionals") back on the tiers.

Your approach with the warden or superintendent should be based on the grounds that your presence on the units will serve to keep the place peaceful because you will be providing "spiritual comfort." You will also be augmenting the work of the professional counselors because you will be providing free counsel to troubled individuals. Such words as *peaceful, counsel,* and especially *without cost* are music to a warden's ears. And if you have already demonstrated that you are a responsible and courteous volunteer who obeys the rules, the powers-that-be will feel much more secure about allowing you on the cell blocks. In fact, I don't encourage you to make this request without having first demonstrated—over time—that you can be trusted. There is a season for everything. Choose your season wisely.

I met one inmate at Florida State Prison, an unbeliever at the time, who observed: "You know, when you Christians come on the block, the place seems to get lighter. I can almost see darkness retreating down the tier as you approach." Others have said, "It doesn't seem so depressing when you folks are here." Never underestimate the value of your presence in the lives of the inmates, whether you are confined to the chapel or permitted back on the tiers. They genuinely look forward to your arrival.

If, by God's grace, your institution allows you to minister in the cell areas, let me give you some practical guidelines about how to proceed while you are back there.

Maintain a Consistent Devotional Life

You must be Spirit filled. By this I mean that you cannot be running your spiritual life on automatic pilot. Many times we feel that we can get away with this during the normal routine of our lives on the outside (it's not true, of course, but we often deceive ourselves into thinking so). But, if you plan on ministering to inmates in their own living areas, being led by the Spirit is an absolute must. You will encounter many unexpected situations and attitudes, from both correctional officers and inmates alike. You will see and hear things that, while they are a normal part of this culture, they are not a normal part of yours. You will sometimes be caught flat-footed in terms of an appropriate response or reply.

You will occasionally feel alone or overawed by the feel of your surroundings. The need to be "prayed up, read up, and filled up" is a must for the volunteer. I do not recommend going in if your spiritual life has not had a devotional consistency. I am not saying you must be perfect (inmates learn from our struggles as well as our victories), but you must be intentionally consistent in your devotional life.

Follow the Rules

If the chapter in this book on "Dos and Don'ts" applies to prison ministry in general, they apply doubly here. Read them again, become very familiar with them—and obey them.

Develop Good Relationships

Correctional employees can make your ministry difficult or easier. The best way to develop a good relationship with the prison's staff is to see them as Jesus does. Always remember that they need him, too. Don't be pushy or carry a demand-your-own-rights attitude. This is not only un-Christian; it will get you nowhere (except maybe off the tier). Correctional officers are people made in the image of God. They perform a difficult job with little public respect for performing it. In my opinion, society owes them a huge debt. But when is the last time you have heard society commend them for what they do? Many officers operate under huge stresses from which it is not easy to disentangle themselves when they come home to their families. But while society may not honor them, you can—by the way you respectfully interact with them.

Do not be surprised, however, if at first the correctional officers don't seem too friendly. Their initial assessment of you will be that you are a naïve, gullible, do-gooder who will always side with the inmates against them. (Unfortunately, many green volunteers throughout the years have done little to correct this misperception.) Give them time to observe your ministry and demeanor. You are Christ's ambassadors, displaying what he is like to *all* people, not just to some. As you represent Him faithfully, the day will come when most of the staff will respect both you and your ministry. Be patient.

Use Wholesome Materials

The Bible is your primary weapon. When I am greeted by correctional officers or inmates on the tiers who ask me how I'm doing, I often respond in the words of that old wartime song, "I'm praising the Lord and passing the ammunition!" Although they laugh at this, I mean it literally. I *am* praising God, and I *am* passing the ammunition—the Word of God. Because your work on the tiers is a mobile activity, you can't be weighed down with too much stuff, so be selective about what you bring.

I usually carry a stack of New Testaments because you can carry a greater number than "whole" Bibles, thus enabling you to give away more material. You also want inmates (who may have little knowledge of who Jesus is) beginning with the New Testament anyway. But in case your discussions lead you into defending the faith from the Old Testament, you should also have a copy or two of the entire Bible. For this reason, some ministers like to bring in their personal Bibles because they are more familiar with where everything is. This is OK, but it's also carrying in something that can't be given away. Personally, I like to leave the prison empty-handed.

If you can carry additional material, good Christian literature makes great icebreakers. Following are some of the better suggestions for you: Chaplain Ray's testimony books are perennial favorites. Many inmates have come to Christ by reading these stories of ex-offenders. Christian magazines such as Billy Graham's *Decision,* or RBC's *Daily Bread,* and the numerous publications of LifeWay Christian Resources including *Open Windows* are also popular. Prison Fellowship's newspaper, *Inside Journal,* is a great resource and is well received among the inmates. Relevant "spiritual life" or discipleship books are helpful for those who have become Christians, but be sensitive to reading levels. Many Christian colleges such as Emmaus and Moody offer correspondence courses. Compile a list of these organizations and ministries; they will be a great asset to you and help you network with others. Also become familiar with a quick, concise way of sharing the gospel, such as "the Bridge" illustration or the use of a favorite tract.[1]

Initial Contacts and Introductory Statements

If you already have contacts in the cell or dorm areas, see these inmates first. You will meet others through them. Inmates are naturally curious about new things going on in their living rooms. (Wouldn't *you* be?) If you have no previous contacts, just walk on to the tier until you make good eye contact with someone and then stop and speak to that person. (Remember, you are walking in the power of the Lord—or should be! Count on him to direct you to the people he wants you to meet.) Take the initiative; be friendly. I have seen God use a simple smile to break down some of the stoniest exteriors.

After initial eye contact is made, greet them and give them your name. Always extend your hand for a handshake. Most inmates will automatically respond in kind by receiving your hand and supplying their names as well. The stack of Bibles in your arms will probably give you away, but if there is still some doubt about what you are doing there, identify yourself as a Christian volunteer. This will define your "function" in the institution and give the inmates a more comfortable framework from which to perceive you. It will surprise you how many are willing to speak with you. But if these initial exchanges don't stimulate a conversation, begin by asking a few nonthreatening questions, such as: "What's your name?" Or, "Where are you from?" I find that this is the most natural. If you happen to be familiar with the area they are from, you can discuss it with them. If not, you can ask them what it's like.

It is generally OK to ask, "How much longer do you have to be here?" or its counterpart, "How long have you been here?" Most inmates do not mind these questions, but if they answer "for life" or some other incredibly long time, sympathize with them but make *no* comments about why. (It's possible that a few inmates may be sensitive to these questions, feeling that they are indicators of the seriousness of their crimes, but I have not personally found this to be the case.) However, you may prefer the next question: "How are you doing with the Lord these days?" This is a legitimate inquiry for you to make, considering your function in the institution. And it very often leads to a spiritual discussion.

Female volunteers working among women prisoners have found it helpful to say something like, "Hi, I'm so-and-so. I'm a Christian volunteer. Would you like a visit?" While male inmates would not relate to this, women find it quite natural to "visit" or to sit and chat. This also leaves accepting the invitation up to them. But never ask what they have done for which they have been sent to prison.

Don't become anxious over an awkward silence; it's OK. Most inmates know that what you are doing is not an easy thing. Sometimes the silence has a way of prompting *them* to speak. Be discerning. You may be interrupting something personal, or he or she may *not* want to talk to you. Most inmates are polite about this, usually responding with a wave of the hand and saying something like, "I'm all set." You must always respect this response and keep on moving. If you come to someone's cell while they are on the toilet or sleeping, keep on traveling in these cases as well. You wouldn't want some stranger to walk uninvited into *your* bathroom, would you? This is their home; respect it as such.

Make it easy on yourself by learning to be a good listener; I can't emphasize this too much. If you listen, the Holy Spirit can grant you better insight into where the inmates are coming from, enabling you to minister with more focused effectiveness. In addition, you will have earned the right to be heard. By *really* listening, and not just pretending to listen, you respect their uniqueness as persons, and they will respond in kind. Displaying genuine interest sends the message that the God you represent is *also* genuinely interested. Always esteem them as people made in the image of God. Your respect for their value is not determined by whether or not they are spiritually open to you. They are people—not scalps to be taken.

If you are organizationally minded, try to keep a notebook of contacts, conversations, and progress. Remembering names, requests, and past discussions goes a long way with the prisoners in terms of relationship building. Spend your time wisely. Try to resist spending all your time with one or two inmates. This can cause jealousy among some of the others and also stir up rumors. It may feel safer, but it prevents you from meeting other inmates, which is part of the goal of cell-to-cell work. The enemy will also try to throw "time-stealers" in your path as well—those people who have little spiritual interest but just want to take up your time with some fruitless argument or discussion. Pray for discernment and sensitivity on how to draw these types of dialogues to a close. They could be hindering you from meeting the next person, who may be very spiritually open.

Discipleship is also important and necessary. It's OK to spend a little extra time with someone who is growing in the Lord, but remember to keep it in balance. Prudent time spent with a sincere disciple will reap eternal benefits by reproducing Christ in others. They, in turn, will impact other inmates.

Be consistent. If you said you would be there once a week at a certain time—be there. Things that may seem small to you are big to them. Keep your promises or don't make them. Most of all, walk in the Spirit of the Lord and trust in his sovereignty. All these suggestions will be purely mechanical unless the Spirit of Jesus is bringing supernatural energy to them through you.

Cell-to-cell ministry is like being a part of writing Acts 29— you will witness many amazing things and experience the power of God as he goes before you. Depend upon his wisdom; be a student of his Word; and pray in the power of the Holy Spirit on all occasions. The environment can seem threatening at times (even the officers can occasionally make you feel more uncomfortable than the inmates will), but remember that God is with you. His intent is to spread his fragrance into every nook and cranny of this dark dungeon. How exciting that you are on the frontiers of this movement!

"With this in mind, we constantly pray for you, that our God may count you worthy of his calling, and that by his power he may fulfill every good purpose of yours and every act prompted by your faith" (2 Thess. 1:11).

30

The One-Year Rule

"YOU SHOULD COME and hear his testimony. It's dynamic!"

The event was a men's breakfast, and the speaker was to be a man who had been saved in prison and released the previous month. The enthusiastic invitation came from one of the volunteers who had worked with him on the inside. He was anxious for me to come and hear the man speak.

The scenario is a common one. Volunteers desire other Christians to know more about the exciting things God is doing in prison. One of the most dramatic ways to do this is to hear the testimonies of these wonderful trophies of God's grace. The speaking forums are usually set up by well-meaning people or ministries that want to encourage other Christians with real-life examples of God's power. The desire is understandable, and the testimonies given often *are* very encouraging. So what's the problem?

While this scenario is common, it is also a common mistake. One of the worst things a volunteer or a church can do for a person who is just coming out of prison is to put him into the spotlight too early. They are usually unaware that what they are doing can destroy the person they are attempting to encourage.

I realize this topic is more a facet of aftercare than inside-prison culture. However, the principle behind it is so important and the violation of it is so common that I believe it would be a disservice to potential volunteers—and ex-prisoners—not to warn them of it. To better understand this principle, one must go back to the dynamics of the in-prison culture itself.

If the person in question was not a Christian when he went into prison but was saved while incarcerated, he has little familiarity with the church culture *as it exists on the streets*. His born-again, ecclesiastical experience has been with the inside church, and he may even have occupied a significant position within its society. He has been looking forward to the day when he can participate in a church on the outside. (And rightly so. This should be the aim of all of us who profess to be Christian volunteers.) But in the heart of this new member is also a strong desire to be accepted within his new church setting. The desire not only to fit in but to be met with approval by his new congregation is extremely important to him.

For the better part of their lives, people who wind up in prison have carried a sense that society, in general, has viewed them as failures and outcasts. Their backgrounds are often the streets, and their past associations are those who were doing the same negative things they were doing. They have been spending the last several months, or perhaps even years, in a place they know is at the bottom of society's list of preferable habitations. They have been branded as "convicts," "misfits," "ne'er-do-wells," or some other form of "lowlife." And now, suddenly, they have all these upright Christian people holding them in high esteem. Nay—more than that—they want the ex-offender to *speak* to them!

Such an individual feels like he is being lifted up to a position of honor, esteemed by those *he* perceives to be the cream of society's crop—upstanding church people. Ostensibly successful citizens. They want *him* to speak! He who was once *avoided* by such people is now being accorded a near-celebrity status among them.

He is asked to speak to youth groups in the hopes that his dramatic experience will serve as an example of the power of God at work. The adults are also hoping that the kids will relate to him and want to stay away from the devilish things that almost destroyed him. For his part, he may even have harbored the secret aspiration of speaking to young people when he got out and now sees it as God fulfilling his dream. He is finally able to use his negative experience for good! After listening to him, the church members are impressed and want him to speak to other groups. First this one, and then another. Soon he is a regular guest at men's meetings and women's clubs—all who want to hear him give his testimony.

It is simply too much to bear and way too soon. Eventually, a dangerous fork in the road may appear. One path finds the newly released pilgrim shouldering an increasingly heavy load of pressures and expectations. Anxiety and insecurity begins to set in. Can the current level of popularity be maintained? Will the esteem continue? In moments of doubt, the temptation to revisit the old people and places where he *really* feels comfortable begins to be felt. If drugs or alcohol played a part in the past, the urge to relieve the pressures in these old time-tested ways becomes even greater.

Or another, more subtle path may be taken—the warning given to the elders in 1 Timothy 3:6: "He must not be a recent convert, or he may become conceited and fall under the same judgment as the devil."

What can happen is that the sudden fame begins to go slowly to their heads and they become top-heavy. They begin to perceive themselves as ministers. Such a person may think to himself, *After all, isn't it me they always want to hear? Isn't it me they are always putting forth as an example of God's power?* Since these people (whom he perceives as having had their spiritual acts together for so long) see no problem in putting him into all these visible roles, it must be further confirmation of God's calling on his life! Sooner or later the subtle deceitfulness of sin can cause him to become less and less submissive to authority. "After all," he reasons to himself, "hasn't the church recognized me as a spokesman?" *He* knows what he's doing; he's a leader in the church!

The situation is further complicated by the way in which the average church person perceives the ex-prisoner. He or she is often viewed as streetwise and tough, a rugged person who knows the ropes. Some of the men, for example, *are* physically impressive. Others do have strong personalities. Some preach the gospel with deep conviction and passion. And even though the church knows the offender's past sins have been forgiven, the mental imaginations of what they must have been like are still fresh in their minds. (By now, the congregation is all too familiar with his or her testimony.)

In reality, the average churchgoer is *afraid* to correct the person. "After all," comes the conclusion, "who is going to correct *him* with any forcefulness?" Even those who should be holding him accountable, such as the elders or the pastor, are also reluctant to confront the person. In the meantime, the one who probably has the greatest influence over him (the volunteer who worked with him while he was in prison) has become so caught up in this new dynamic of vicarious fame that he doesn't see the danger coming until it's too late.

And just what is that danger? The danger is that we will unwittingly become a part of causing these ex-prisoners to stumble—and possibly get back into a life of crime. We do this by never giving them the wise encouragement of taking the necessary time to get their feet planted firmly on the ground. Leaving prison for the streets is a big enough adjustment as it is, let alone entering a culture they have never experienced—the outside church.

Enter the One-Year Rule. This is a principle we have adopted at Vision New England and implemented for over two decades. Because we work directly with inmates and have been training others to work with them as well, the principle has proven to be a sound one over time. When a Christian man or woman is preparing to leave prison, we instruct them to become involved with a local church. But we also advise them to stay virtually out of sight when it comes to any sort of public ministry for at least one year. (Some aftercare ministries, such as New England Aftercare Ministries in Framingham, Massachusetts, actually recommend *two* years.)

By "public" ministry, we mean any sort of activity that puts them, as individuals, into the limelight. This includes *any* public speaking or giving of their testimonies—not even at a men's breakfast. Nor should they be encouraged to speak to youth groups or go back into a prison to share their story.[1] They should be instructed to politely refuse any such offers that may come their way—even if they come from well-meaning church people.

They can *attend* such functions as men's meetings, Christian concerts, retreats, potluck dinners, etc., and we encourage them to do so, but they are to play no visible role. I usually tell them that if they want to serve in their church in that first year, they should look for a quiet, out-of-the-way ministry such as cleaning the church or working on the grounds. Joining work projects with the other men of the church is also ideal. They need the fellowship and desperately need to build relationships, especially with other Christian men. If the newly released person is a female, the same principle holds true, the only difference being that her primary discipleship should come from mature Christian women.

It is to be understood, of course, that in no way does this prohibition include worship services, Bible studies, or other group ministries of the church. They can participate in evangelism teams or any other ministry that has them sharing the load with others. What I am addressing here is the more visible ministries that tend to push former prisoners, as individuals, into the spotlight.

I also instruct them that their priorities should include finding a job, getting settled, ordering the affairs of their lives, and seeking any other group reinforcement they may need. Attendance at meetings such as Christian twelve-step programs, counseling sessions, or any other support that may be pertinent to their specific temptations, are important safeguards. If they have families whom they have reunited with, they must major on becoming responsible spouses, parents, sons, or daughters. We strongly encourage them to hook up with others of the same sex who will both disciple them and take them under their wing. Such mentors are greatly needed for those young Christians coming out of the correctional facilities. They must also be willing to submit to the godly counsel of such individuals—as well as to that of their church. Beware of those who do not have teachable, submissive spirits. They *will* eventually become a problem. It is not a matter of *if*; it is a matter of *when*.

If, after a full year, they have walked before the Lord in this quiet, submissive way, they can then begin to be exposed to more visible ministry. The testimony of a man or woman who has been out of prison for over a year, without any major mishaps, is a greater testimony to God's power than the untested witness of only a few weeks. It is also a safeguard for them. If they happen to stumble during that year, do not put them under a pile of guilt for it. Let them know that they must start recounting their year from the point of stumbling.

How will we know if they have been successful in this or not? I tell them that I will confirm their journey with their pastor. If the pastor can tell me, after a year of faithful involvement with his church, that the former prisoner has been doing well and has been a faithful and regular attendee at the church, then the person will not only be assisted toward more visible ministry, but he or she *deserves* to be. The pastor's confirmation also ensures the individual's participation in the life of a local fellowship. This is extremely important. Without continuous, active participation in the life of the same church, there is no way of ensuring the person's spiritual stability. Be wary of church-hoppers; it may signify other problems.

Ideally, the One-Year Rule is introduced to the prospective members *before* they leave prison. I feel that we owe it to the churches that will be receiving them to prepare the inmates as much as we can before their release dates. This will also help us to determine (to the best degree possible) how they are really doing spiritually. Sometimes they do not always react as well as you would hope. A few have said, "I'm sorry Lennie, but I must obey God rather than man. Who are you to tell me that I can't minister in a certain way for a year? *God* has sent me to tell young people to stay out of places like this. *God* has told me to give my testimony and to preach. I will not do what you say; I must obey *him!*"

While this argument sounds spiritually impressive on the surface (after all, who can argue with a commissioning by God?), I believe that its general tone reflects a lack of submission to any earthly authority. It also reveals a continued strain of rebellion.

At its root is pride, and it runs counter to the advice of the Scriptures, which tell us to seek the counsel of other godly men. It is not that I set myself up as the last authority in their lives, but if I have been involved in their growth while on the inside, then I do have a role to perform in terms of preparing them for the streets.

The One-Year Rule is a principle I firmly believe in; and I frame it in the form of counsel that I am convinced would be in their best interest. At the very least, I certainly have the right to ask it of anyone who wants me to help him or her when they are on the outside.

In over twenty-five years of prison ministry, I can honestly say that *without exception* every inmate who refused that counsel flaked out within their first year of freedom. Furthermore, most of them got into trouble again and went back to prison. This is not because I am a prophet but because the principle works as a test for the heart. Those who had so much pride that they would not come under anyone's authority revealed a heart with some serious liabilities in terms of spiritual growth.

I can also state that for every former prisoner who humbly *received* the counsel, every one of them went on to do well. Not only did they stay out of prison, but they became integral parts of their local fellowships. I can still recall one young man who called me up exactly one year later—to the day—and said, "Okay Lennie, my year is up. Can I start going into the prisons with you?" Others have even gone into ministry or on to seminary. Some of our country's most powerful preachers and teachers served time in prison.

Newly released people need *time* to get their feet on the ground. They have to establish a foundation on the streets that builds a routine of normalcy into their lives. This includes a new pattern of dealing with life's basic requirements. They need time to make the adjustment from the old culture to the new, and this includes things like paying bills, going to work, fellowshipping in the life of a local church, building a new support base of the right people in their lives, developing healthy relationships, and taking on the normal responsibilities of life. With the advice of wise volunteers and godly counselors around them—and the persistent love and compassion of the church—they can do it.

The heart that is willing to submit to this One-Year Rule is exhibiting a trust and a humility that will be essential for its spiritual growth. We do former prisoners a great harm, I believe, by not giving them time to adjust. The weight of responsibility is on *us* to exercise this prudence; they are too unfamiliar with the cultural pitfalls to see them coming for themselves. Unfortunately, many well-meaning volunteers are oblivious to this danger as well. Be firm in this and you will reap its benefits later on. So will the disciples you are attempting to help and the churches they attend.

These dear people, if nurtured correctly, will turn out to be powerful assets to any church that receives them—to the praise of *God's* life-changing glory!

31

Stitches in Time

A MAN'S HAND, holding a needle and thread, suddenly appeared directly in front of my face. There was nothing to be seen beyond the forearm. But unlike the image that struck such terror into the heart of Belshazzar (see Dan. 5:5–6), the appearance of this hand had a perfectly natural explanation.

I had just entered the hallway of a long, narrow tier with two rows of cells stretching out before me on either side. The row of cells on the left was called "K" side, and the series on the right was labeled "L." Each individual cell had a number. Since all the cells looked alike, these "addresses" were essential for determining exactly where an inmate had been assigned to live.

As I entered the tier, the hand holding the needle and thread was suddenly thrust through the small, barred window of L-5, the fifth cell on the right. The voice accompanying the apparition made this request: "Could you give these to the guy in K-13?"

My reason for being on that particular tier was to visit a certain inmate way down in the neighborhood of L-25, but since it was no problem for me to drop the thread off on my way, I collected them from "the hand" and proceeded over to K-13. (The tier officer had given me permission to pass such items.)

When I arrived at the steel door and peered through the bars of the small window, I saw a man sitting, yoga-style, on the top bunk. He had a book opened between his knees and was studying it with a puzzled frown of consternation. The book was the Bible.

"Hey, that's pretty good reading you've got there!" I said.

"Yeah, I just picked it up," he mumbled, with obvious agitation in his voice. And without looking up he added, "I thought maybe there was something in here that could help me control my anger."

I asked him what the trouble was, and as the story unfolded, I learned that he had just been locked up again for getting into a fight that very morning. "I just can't seem to control my anger," he scowled. "It's always getting me into trouble. So I picked this up wondering if *it* had any answers for me."

"So what are you finding out?" I asked.

"Aw," he replied with obvious frustration, "I can't seem to understand what it's talking about."

Then feeling very much like Philip with the Ethiopian eunuch, I began to instruct him about Jesus. And since he is the same Spirit who led Philip two thousand years ago, he still knows the perfect time to send his messengers alongside other "chariots" today. This prisoner had been prepared for the arrival of this visit as surely as the eunuch had been prepared so many years before. And like his forerunner, he also prayed to receive Christ as his Savior!

I went on my way rejoicing as I continued my journey down to L-25. The Lord had interrupted my own plans by redirecting me with his. In his own unique fashion, he had accomplished it all with a needle and thread! Afterward, I reflected on just a fraction of the many events that had to be in place to set that cycle in motion. A rip here, a tear there. A spool of thread being passed from cell to cell—without any apparent design or pattern. An unexpected visit by a Christian volunteer at a certain time. A completed sewing task, a new request by an inmate next in line to repair a tattered garment. A flare-up of anger, a fight, a lockdown. A moment of final despair and frustration culminating in the realization that one's life is out of control. A "book" in a cell, long ignored. Hopelessness everywhere else. A visit by Philip.

"A stitch in time saves nine." So goes the old adage. That's exactly how the gospel in prison strikes me on occasion. Prisons are all about time; and the Lord uses this sanctified hiatus to gather his tattered children to himself and stitches their broken hearts with the golden threads of grace, love, and forgiveness. He repairs their wounded lives and sews up the tear between his holiness and their filth—and cleanses them with the water and blood of Jesus Christ, the master tailor.

Prisons and jails abound with stories such as that about the man in K-13. They ring out as testimonies to God's grace. They are stories that declare his glory and his wisdom, his indescribable love for sinners. They are indeed stitches in time.

Since becoming a Christian in 1975, I have been given the grace to observe God's power in many wonderful instances. I have witnessed miraculous answers to prayer and have been permitted to be involved in the salvation of hundreds of people. He gave me a love for his Word from the very beginning and continues to lead me each day into its wonderful treasury rooms and awesome vistas. I have seen God open doors and make a way when there was no way. I have, on occasion, been washed with the sheer love of God and experienced tender moments that were uniquely his and mine.

He has caused the boundary lines of my life to fall in pleasant places and remains the God-Who-Found-My-Children-on-the-Mountain. He has given me gifts and the privilege of having platforms to use them. He has blessed me with a godly wife whose wisdom has kept her Mr. Magoo on track throughout many an unguarded time. He has granted me two sons who make me proud, as well as many godly friends. He lets me preach his gospel! I could fill the pages with his countless blessings to me.

But his specific calling on my life was unique because it happened only once.

As a new Christian volunteering at the local jail one day, I found myself standing in front of the cell of a young man who had just prayed to receive Christ. He was the first man I can ever remember leading to Jesus. As I stood there watching the tears that trickled down his cheeks, I suddenly sensed the Lord's presence on the tier behind me. It was so vivid and so real that I can even tell you where he was standing. It was behind me and a little to my right. I also sensed that he had his hand upon my shoulder. It was my right shoulder. And I heard him say to my heart, "This is what I want you doing."

I do not recall being afraid or even surprised. It just seemed so natural at the time. I am still in touch with that particular inmate, although he is now over twenty years older. He has remained in prison all this time. He has had his struggles, but he is still walking with the Lord.

The experience was unique, and the calling was clear. I have never looked back. My heart's desire is that I will never be disobedient to that calling. As God continues to make a way, I will continue to walk through those steel doors. If he ever changes that direction, he will have to make it as clear as he did in the beginning. Until then, we have a kind of mutual agreement: I keep going until God changes the orders.

As a result of that calling, I have wound up doing more time as a Christian than I ever did as an unbeliever! There are many stories I could relate to you about how God has worked miracles in the hearts of so many men and women, boys and girls who sat in the darkness of their hopelessness and despair, only to discover that there *is* a Father who loves them dearly. Stories of miracles and *amazing* grace. I have tried, throughout this book, to pick those examples that spoke most closely to the various points I was trying to make. But if you are reading this as a volunteer yourself, then you have witnessed your own miracles. You have your own stories. You have beheld the power to change hearts that God still has.

If you haven't gone behind the walls yet and are contemplating prison ministry in some form, I hope this book has been helpful to you. Should you decide to step out, you will be entering one of God's most highly blessed arenas. You will find yourself on the cutting edge of ministry—an Acts 29 sort of adventure. The benefits are many. Your faith will grow. Your knowledge of the Word will increase. Your prayer life will be recharged. You will behold miracles. You will gain new and lasting friendships. You will discover spiritual warfare. You will see the devil unmasked, and he will attempt to unmask you. You will be a weapon in the hands of a holy God against forces of evil. You will be tested, tried, challenged, sneered at, turned away, and rejected—but you will remain victorious.

You will bear witness to the destruction of lives and families. You will see others snatched from the fires of hell and watch them go on to be shining witnesses of God's mercy. You will hear many a sad and tragic story and stand in the gap as a minister of prayer and a soldier of hope as tears of despair are shed before you. You will witness lives reborn. You will receive blessings and ministry from the very people you came to bless. You will declare the praises of him who called you out of darkness into his wonderful light—and all the while you will count yourself blessed for being a part of it all.

You will find yourself being used as a vessel of Christ's compassion. No matter whether you received a specific, unique calling, as I did, or whether you went out of simple obedience and found yourself liking it, this matters little—as long as your primary motivation remains the love of Christ. That is what counts. "For Christ's love compels us, because we are convinced that one died for all, and therefore all died" (2 Cor. 5:14).

Volunteers are themselves trophies of God's grace. Each of *you* has a story to share, no matter how big or little you think it is. All of us, as Christians, are testimonies to the miraculous power of the living God because none of us had the ability to wake ourselves up from the dead. You may recall, in an earlier chapter, that I said I would tell you the story of Patti, the woman at the well. Here it is:

Part of my responsibilities includes checking in on the labors of various prison ministry volunteers throughout a six-state area. Since we played a small part in many of their start-ups, I stop by once in a while to see how the ministry is going and to encourage them. I recall joining a group of volunteers from Maine who were doing a weekly service at the Cumberland County jail in downtown Portland. Accompanying them on this particular night was a woman in her thirties whom I had not met before. She was a little on the robust side, and she wore a gray sweatshirt with the phrase "I've been born again!" emblazoned across the front. We met outside the prison and entered as a group.

While we were being processed through, I couldn't help but notice how animated this particular woman was. Or how outspoken! All the way through the control area she would speak to every guard we met. "Hi! Have you been born again? *I've* been born again! Do you know Jesus? You need to know Jesus! It is *so* great knowing Jesus!" As we were processed into a small alcove where visitors were waiting, I noticed that a half-smile of bewilderment had crossed the faces of the officers in the control room as they pushed the buttons to let us through the sliding doors. When we entered the alcove, she greeted every tired mother and kootchie-cooed every surprised child. "Hi! Have you been born again? *I've* been born again! You need to accept Jesus as your Savior. He's *wonderful!*"

And on and on this went. She spoke to anything that moved as we were led down to the cafeteria in the basement where the evening service would be held. As I glanced behind us, the scene bore a resemblance to that old "white tornado" commercial. People seemed to have been picked up and dropped back down in astonishment wherever this woman had been.

She had an opportunity, as did the other volunteers, to speak to the inmates as they filed in. The prisoners were a pretty radical group that night. Among the participants was a muscular, heavily tattooed biker still wearing his colors and another guy who had been picked up for revolutionary activities. He had one arm fitted with a prosthesis, since his limb had been blown off transporting explosives. They and the other inmates were swept into the path of the tornado as our friend continued her relentless rendition of "I've been born again."

I can't say that her theology was square on the mark in every area, but there was no denying her exuberance over the good news of salvation! As a result, the men softened up considerably and were later open to the gospel message I gave. We had opportunity to speak with them afterwards, and it was quite evident that they were much more interested in spiritual things than they had been when they first came down.

As we left the building after the service, I asked about the source of her exuberance. She was happy to relate to me the following remarkable story. It revolved around the fact that she had once been very hostile toward God—and Christianity in particular. She had kept God at arm's length and wanted nothing to do with him. Her life had been that of a Proverbs 7:11 woman: wanton, drunken, and defiant. She had bounced from man to man, had been married four times, and eventually settled into a live-in relationship with a guy. She had consistently shaken her fist at God until one day, a few years before my encounter with her, a Christian friend had dropped in on her and had succeeded in opening the Bible with her. Her friend brought her to the fourth chapter of John. As she heard the account of the woman at the well, the Holy Spirit began to awaken a spark of hope within her. She thought to herself, "If God could forgive *this* woman, who had had one more marriage than *I've* had, and who was also shacking up with someone when Jesus met her, then perhaps it's possible that He could forgive *me* as well!"

It turned out that the basic reason she had rejected God all those years was that she was certain he would reject *her* for the life she had led. She had come to believe that God could never want someone like her, so she made a great pretense of not wanting God! When she discovered, through the brave visit of her faithful friend, that God not only wanted to forgive her but that he *loved* her—the truth was too much for her stony heart to bear. She reached out for the extended hand of grace and had been rejoicing ever since! And like her counterpart of old, she was going back into the village and shouting to anyone who would listen, "Come see a man who told me everything I ever did! I've been born again! Have *you?*"

I have told this story many times since that evening. It speaks so directly to the appropriate response to grace. I tell audiences that Patti is the name of the woman at the well. I met her at the Cumberland County Jail one night, many years ago. I tell the story because that, essentially, is why we go into prison. The love of Christ *compels* us! And those who have been forgiven much—love much.

I have seen many gentle-hearted volunteers do prison ministry over the years; some so unassuming that an observer might be tempted to ask, "How can such seemingly naïve people relate to these hardened individuals?" From men and women in their eighties to young men who look as though they are better suited to teach physics; they have come in all sizes and shapes. But they have one thing in common: they love Jesus, and they have an overwhelming love for people in prison.

I tell potential volunteers that although they need to be realistic about their expectations and wise about the environment in which they are operating, they must *never* underestimate what God can do. Not only in *their* lives but also in the lives of those to whom they have come to minister. Occasionally, there is a tendency among some volunteers to view the inmates as seldom becoming little more than they are now—babes in Christ. To view them in such a limiting way is to make the mistake of seeing them only as the world sees them. Thank the Lord that he never viewed *us* in that way! Perhaps that is one of the advantages of having been a prisoner myself; I'm fully convinced of what God can do.

It often occurs to me, as I am working among the inmates, that any one of them could go on and do great things for God— far greater things than I could ever dream of. They are tomorrow's leaders, tomorrow's preachers, and tomorrow's evangelists. They are tomorrow's fathers and husbands—stars shining in the universe as they hold out the word of life, blameless and pure, children of God without fault in a crooked and depraved generation (Phil. 2:15).

Jesus came to seek and to save those who are lost. We have more value in his eyes than all the created wonders of the universe combined. If the Father sent the Son to die for us, we have infinite worth in his eyes. The Father still watches the road for his sons and daughters to return. He found us while we were still in darkness, ignorance, and arrogance. And he sends us out now to find those other sheep who still walk in darkness. Prisons are not unique in this. The whole world is a prisoner of sin (Gal. 3:22). But like Patti, many of those who sit in our country's prisons and jails find the message of grace exceedingly good news. "Where meek souls will receive Him still, the dear Christ enters in."[1]

Prison ministry also provides many glimpses into what a deadly game the enemy is playing. Sometimes he overplays his hand, and we gape briefly into the dark depths of his ferocity and hatred where its intensity jolts us. Were it not for the protection of God over his saints, we would be destroyed in an instant. Were it not for the pursuing love of God for his sheep, we would never step a single foot behind those walls. Does it not seem curious that we currently have more freedom in this country to speak the name of Jesus behind prison walls than we do in our public schools? Society doesn't see the ironic corollary. Why is it so surprised that the children it insisted on training without moral absolutes grow up to be lawless adults?

As prison ministry now forges ahead into the twenty-first century, new challenges will provide new opportunities. We have a great need to stay abreast of new developments. State-paid chaplains may become a thing of the past. Do we have church-sponsored missionaries ready to take their places? High-security prisons will become more computer driven and technologically secure. Movement will be more restrictive, both for inmates as well as volunteers. Access to the areas where inmates live will be denied in most cases. How will we reach them?

Part of the answer will be to convince prison administrations of the necessity to maintain a physical presence inside the walls. Christian volunteers still bring a calming effect to the environment, no matter how modern the prison may be. As inmates become more and more isolated from the outside world and from one another (isolated units is a current trend in new prisons), tensions will increase. Frustration levels will also increase as anger becomes fueled over the robotic living conditions in a high-tech, sterile age. Security will be so tight that there will be little opportunity for the prisoners to vent, at least in any cohesive, collective way. Although mass rioting will become less of a threat, violence upon individuals will increase, both against officers and certainly between inmates.

It is a wise administration that will recognize the value of Christian volunteers operating within the living areas of their prison. Ministries that provide good Christian literature will also play a larger role. Visual and audio communication will continue to be important, where permitted. I recently heard of a radio station whose broadcasts are directed entirely toward people in prison. Mothers and wives send brief messages to their loved ones behind the walls, while programming is geared toward the issues that inmates face. But whatever the changes, volunteers must keep believing that God will continue to empower and "fulfill every good purpose of yours and every act prompted by your faith" (2 Thess. 1:11).

In closing, I'd like to quote a short letter by Bob Sawyer, an inmate in Vermont. Printed here with his permission, this letter is addressed to prison ministry volunteers everywhere.

> Sometimes, when folks come to visit, they ask me what they can do. They usually mean they want to buy something for me, to provide something tangible. I like to tell them what I'm going to tell you this afternoon. I ask that they let the outside world know that the body of Christ is alive and well inside here. Tell them there is a remnant seeking God's face, who has repented of the sins that put them in here and who has asked the Creator to help them stay free in Him so that there will be no further need of incarceration. Tell them that life goes on for those in the Lord.
>
> Satan's press wants the public to be afraid of us. The secular media focuses on what terrible things have been done by those of us living in here. The public does not know the whole story. You can help. The Lord needs you, we need you, to help balance the record. Please tell the world that Christ lives in prison. Please tell the prayer warriors in your community to lift up inmates in their regular prayers. Lives have changed in this facility and places like it all over the world. Please tell people about it. You will be blessed for your efforts.

Endnotes

Chapter 1

1. The names of inmates and former inmates have been changed for the sake of privacy.

2. The term *jail* usually refers to a city or county facility. It generally refers to an "awaiting trial" status. "Houses of correction" are also used for other short-term facilities. *Prison* or *penitentiary* is normally reserved for long-term state institutions. Federal facilities are sometimes referred to as "camps" and "penitentiaries" as well as prisons. But with regard to appropriate terminology, calling a prison a "jail" is much the same as calling a "boat" a "ship."

3. We will speak more of this in the chapter entitled, "I Dream of Jeannie."

Chapter 2

1. Time taken off one's sentence for good behavior.

2. The average sentence nationally is around twenty-seven months (*Los Angeles Times,* 16 August 1999).

3. A short inmate is one who will be released soon.

4. William Shakespeare, Sonnet 77.

5. High school equivalency diplomas.

6. Emmaus Correspondence School, 2570 Asbury Rd., Dubuque IA 52001. (Phone) 1-800-397-2425.

7. Gospel Express, P.O. Box 131, Gordonville, PA 17529.

8. "I am not saying this because I am in need, for I have learned to be content whatever the circumstances. I know what it is to be in need, and I know what it is to have plenty. I have learned the secret of being content in any and every situation, whether well fed or hungry, whether living in plenty or in want. I can do everything through him who gives me strength" (Phil. 4:11–13).

Chapter 3

1. TV is obviously a major contributor to the sociological development of young people. The latest statistics reveal that a child watches twenty-five acts of violence in one hour of TV (CNN 1/99).

2. To "max out" means that an inmate has served the absolute limit of his sentence. For example, a three- to five-year sentence means that three is the minimum time to serve and five is the maximum time to serve. Such a sentence means that the inmate would become eligible for parole after the minimum three years has been served and, if released, would have two years of parole supervision left. If an inmate's behavior has been such that no "good time" is awarded for good behavior, he or she risks staying in prison until the maximum sentence has been served. In this case, maxing out would mean serving the top end of the sentence, a full five years.

3. Usually a minimum security residential house where inmates can be sent just prior to their full release. Although still under the jurisdiction of the Department of Corrections, the residents can work in the community and make a more normal transition into society.

4. A failed drug test. Usually randomly taken for parolees.

5. Department of Corrections.

6. Rehabilitation clinics or groups.

7. "You were taught, with regard to your former way of life, to put off your old self, which is being corrupted by its deceitful desires; to be made new in the attitude of your minds; and to put on the new self, created to be like God in true righteousness and holiness" (Eph. 4:22–24).

Chapter 4

1. "Woe to those who call evil good and good evil, who put darkness for light and light for darkness, who put bitter for sweet and sweet for bitter" (Isa. 5:20).

2. Riots usually occur after months of long frustration and burst out as suddenly as a spark to gasoline, often over the smallest incidents.

3. Department of Corrections. The penal arm of a state government. At the national level this is known as the Federal Bureau of Prisons.

4. The length of such programs differs from state to state, but average stays are anywhere from three months to a year.

5. Most states allow only one chance at the shock program as an alternative to regular prison time.

Chapter 5

1. Usually a surprise and thorough inspection of an inmate's cell, or an entire cell block. Individual persons can also be "shaken down."

Chapter 6

1. A segregation tier for disciplinary cases. Also referred to as "Segregation" or "the Hole."

2. In recent years, it has come to light that this has occurred in much greater numbers among young boys than previously thought or suspected.

3. A national ministry specializing in working with troubled youth. For more information call (508) 616-9286 or write: Straight Ahead Ministries, 43 Hopkinton Rd., Westborough, MA 01581-2103.

4. Carol was a dear sister in the Lord who worked as a staff person in a juvenile center in Boston and was on the board of Straight Ahead Ministries. She died in her mid-thirties of cancer in 1994.

5. Department of Social Services (for youth being troubled by others).

6. Department of Youth Services (for youth getting into trouble).

Chapter 7

1. Occasionally I run across an inmate who is prone to saying such things as, "They're out to get me," or "They're messing with my food." This "messing" can include everything from believing that spit or semen has been mixed into his meal to being convinced that the food has been poisoned. Inmates with this problem begin to eat only what is sealed or can pass a close inspection. Slowly they lose touch with reality. The monster of fear has immobilized them with its paralyzing sting and reduced them to helpless victims awaiting some agonizing end. Their minds become obsessed with things that a healthier outlook may take in stride. If this fixation continues to grow, the results can lead to illusion, fantasy, obsession, paranoia, schizophrenia, or thoughts of suicide.

2. Occasionally, an officer takes a personal disliking to an inmate that is beyond the inmate's control. But the procedure is the same: do not make a big fuss. Eventually, they will tire of the game if there is little fuel to keep the conflict going.

3. Occasionally, an officer takes a personal disliking to an inmate that is beyond the inmate's control. But the procedure is the same: do not make a fuss. Eventually, they will tire of the game if there is little fuel to keep the conflict going.

4. A homemade alcoholic brew, usually concocted through the fermentation of sugar and fresh fruit.

5. Informer.

6. Population refers to the major living area where most of the inmates in the prison reside.

7. If volunteers are given the opportunity to increase their exposure to the rest of the inmate population, I encourage them to take it. By doing so, they will greatly enhance the ministry of the gospel by coming into contact with the many inmates who never attend a chapel service.

Chapter 8

1. Some Christians would probably disagree with me here, but I believe that a TV set goes a long way toward making an inmate's life a little less frustrating. Television helps keep them in touch with the society that most will someday reenter. It is also a pleasurable experience that helps to pass the time. By saying that, I am in no way endorsing most of the rubbish that makes up TV programming. I am simply saying that it does meet a need and that it does make their time a little easier to do.

2. The majority of riots that occur within prisons start in the dining areas.

3. It is estimated that the majority of in-prison murders are precipitated by homosexual altercations.

4. The practice of a stronger inmate using a physical threat to force a weaker inmate to provide favors.

5. The choice to seek protective custody. This decision usually succeeds in providing a modicum of protection but results in the inmate's reputation taking a nosedive. The PC inmate is usually in the lowest position on the society's totem-pole structure.

6. Be careful here. It may be against the rules for you to bring in any material that is not approved "religious material." Always ask

your chaplain before bringing *anything* in. In many prisons, printed material such as books and magazines can only be sent to the inmate directly from the publisher.

Chapter 9

1. One occupant to a cell.
2. In New Hampshire 287 inmates were housed at the state prison in 1980. By 1997 the population had reached 2,136. A growth rate of nearly 87 percent in 18 years! To bring this growth rate into perspective, consider the fact that the population of New Hampshire State Prison was 185 when I entered it in 1966. One hundred years before (1866), the population was 161, a difference of 24 inmates over the course of a century.
3. The story of a king who went around naked, thinking he had beautiful clothes upon his body. None of his officials dared tell him otherwise, so they flattered him and agreed that they were fine clothes indeed. It took a child watching the king go by in a parade to exclaim, "The king has no clothes!"
4. Correctional officers.
5. A large, open space that is used by the inmates for either recreation or for passage to and from other buildings. The prison yard today is designed less as an area for recreation than for security reasons. Open areas make it easier for officers on the walls or in towers to view what is going on while the inmates are out of their living areas. They are built with a minimum of nooks and crannies so inmates cannot hide from view. In some yards it is illegal to stop and congregate; they must keep moving to their next assignment. Even when this is allowed, most prisons have a limit on how many inmates can congregate together, perhaps only two or three.
6. Description of an arrest for an infraction of prison rules that results in inmates being escorted (lugged) to a more punitive holding area.
7. Informing on another.
8. An inmate who has proved his mettle; one in whom adherence to the prison code can be counted upon.
9. A cell or tier used for extreme cases of bad behavior. There are no amenities here and absolutely no privileges. Fifteen days can feel like fifteen months.
10. Special housing unit.
11. General population.

Chapter 11

1. MCI stands for Massachusetts Correctional Institution. Cedar Junction is the name of the particular prison.

2. This incident was also rare in that 90 percent of the inmates you meet in going cell-to-cell will dialogue with you. Even those who do not want to talk will respectfully say something like, "I'm all set." Never attempt to force a dialogue. If an inmate has made it clear he does not want to speak to you, respect those wishes and keep going.

Chapter 12

1. A sexual offender whose crime involved molesting young children; pedophile.

2. Receiving a written disciplinary report for an infraction of prison rules.

3. Getting close to one's release date.

4. Days taken off a sentence for good behavior. In many states now, however, good-time is calculated off one's maximum sentence, as opposed to coming off their minimum release date. For example, if a man or woman receives a one- to three-year sentence, good-time will be figured off the three years as opposed to the one year. This usually occurs in states that have implemented the "truth-in-sentencing" law, which means an inmate must actually serve every day of his minimum sentence.

5. The complete file of an inmate's criminal history.

6. "Do not revile the king even in your thoughts, or curse the rich in your bedroom, because a bird of the air may carry your words, and a bird on the wing may report what you say" (Eccles. 10:20).

7. There are many similarities between prison life and the military. This "paramilitary" organization contains a ranked hierarchy of uniformed officers who are charged with overseeing a large constituency of "privates." There are mess halls and predetermined times for rising and sleeping. There are work and living-quarter assignments. In many institutions, "yes sir" and "no sir" are required protocol. Even a predetermined discharge date is required before one may return to civilian life. In fact, many volunteers *have* been referred to by staff and inmates alike as "civilians," recognizing that they are on "the base" only by virtue of a special visitor's pass.

8. "The Spirit of the Sovereign LORD is on me, because the LORD has anointed me to preach good news to the poor. He has sent me to bind up the brokenhearted, to proclaim freedom for the captives and release from darkness for the prisoners" (Isa. 61:1).

9. This advice is usually best sought from someone in the legal profession, *outside* the prison.

10. "If you forgive anyone his sins, they are forgiven; if you do not forgive them, they are not forgiven."

11. A "shakedown" is when a group of officers surprise a tier with a sudden inspection. These shakedowns could be described as chaotic thoroughness. "Thorough" in that they usually tear the cells apart from top to bottom, "chaotic" in that everything from mattresses to private papers ais usually thrown out in a heap on the floor outside the cell. Although these shakedowns are disruptive and seemingly insensitive to an inmate's private belongings, most prisoners accept them as a routine part of prison life. They do help to deter inmates from hiding contraband in their cells.

Chapter 13

1. The Hole, administrative seg, maxim security, isolation, or various tiers set aside for punitive purposes. If an inmate *chooses* to act out, he can pretty much determine his transfer to these quarters.

2. Coalition of Prison Evangelists. For more information, call (800) 949-0063.

3. For more information, call (508) 872-6194, or write New England Aftercare Ministries, P. O. Box 136, Framingham, MA 01704.

4. An interesting parallel to note is that stints of service in the military often result in one's first application of a tattoo, for here, too, is a culture that requires strict uniformity.

Chapter 14

1. A term for serving time. Like being "out of circulation." It does not denote being "down" as in being depressed.

2. Of course, there is also a negative side to these old connections. Sometimes the individuals were enemies on the street. The source of many violent episodes in prison has been due to these previous associations or opposing loyalties.

Chapter 15

1. "Lifer" is a term that can apply to those prisoners who are serving, or have served, long prison terms. It does not have to apply exclusively to those who are serving natural life sentences.

Chapter 16

1. From the comic strip *Pogo,* by Walt Kelly.

2. Slang term for the "habitual offender act." A law in some states that can be enacted against repeat offenders. The courts may deem that they have seen this individual on one too many occasions and rule that he or she is incorrigible, thereby leveling a mandatory sentence that will keep them off the streets for an excessively long period of time. Some states have enacted legislation that requires this punishment as mandatory after being convicted of a specific number of crimes.

3. Coworker at Vision New England and parachaplain at New Hampshire State Prison in Concord.

4. Parole violation.

Chapter 17

1. Nevertheless, I always affirm this desire of theirs. It serves several purposes. First of all, it gives them a positive goal to shoot for. They want to do something good with their lives and contribute to society rather than torment it. Second, they *can* relate to those young people who have begun to admire the "bad boys" lifestyle. Who knows what lives they may be instrumental in helping? Third, I use it as an incentive for them to stay close to the Lord and to continue to strengthen their spiritual walks. I tell them that they can't give what they don't have. Merely to relate to those young people will not be sufficient in the long run.

2. Human services, or the "program department," as it is sometimes called, is the arm of the prison staff devoted to the social improvement of the residents, be it educationally, psychologically, vocationally, or otherwise.

3. That a small number of officers should not hold the jobs they are holding for psychological reasons will, I think, always be true. The fire reveals the impurities.

4. Most new policies will be generally unsatisfactory and ill received by the inmates. Many times a rule has to be implemented

that the population may or may not understand, but perception still carries a lot of weight in this volatile environment. The *reasons* for changes in policy should always be made clear whenever that is possible.

5. In a prison, clergy do not have the "right" to demand to see an inmate. While most institutions will permit them to have special visiting privileges, it is always wiser to call ahead and verify the information with the right person. Most prisons and county jails usually go out of their way to honor bonafide clergy visits.

Chapter 18

1. Matthew 5:21–22.

Chapter 19

1. Although most inmates curb this tendency around religious volunteers, the visitor must expect to hear it regularly enough, especially if he or she is ministering anywhere outside the designated chapel areas.

Chapter 20

1. Forbidden items. Things like cash, drugs, weapons, or less obvious things like hard-covered books, too many books, clear pens, chewing gum, tape recorders that can still record, and a host of other items. A common complaint among inmates is that what is permissible one day can become contraband the next, on seemingly arbitrary or spontaneous decision by the administration.

2. Special Weapons and Tactics. Or Quick Response Teams (QRTs). A group of officers in riot gear. Such tactical squads are used to quell major disturbances or subdue hostile inmates. They are usually dressed in protective vests, helmets with visors, and body-length Plexiglas shields. They may also be carrying nightsticks or mace. Inmates often refer to them as "goon squads." In some states an officer is required to follow any SWAT team activity with a video camera to help ensure against lawsuits.

3. "Rolled in" is a term inmates use when such a squad enters a man's cell for the purpose of subduing him.

4. Unfortunately, the current trend in many women's prisons today is a sort of "turn-the-other-way" policy by the correctional staff. In many institutions, women can be seen walking around the compound holding hands or walking as couples with their arms

around each other. Flagrant signs of homosexuality are given a great deal of latitude and general acceptance in many women's facilities.

5. For parents facing this kind of threat, it is important not to let fear take over. What usually happens upon release is that ex-offenders get so entangled in their own immediate problems and issues that they are soon consumed by them. This does not mean that there won't be an initial challenge or two immediately upon release, but they will soon be dealing with a lot of other restrictions that will be tying them up. For one, they do not want to return to prison, so they have reason to stay within the parameters of their parole or probation requirements. Also, some of the underlying pressures for the five expressions mentioned above have been now somewhat alleviated. So be patient, keep praying, and trust that God will guide the situation.

Chapter 21

1. Canteen supplies include extra items the administration allows inmates to possess, if they have enough money in their accounts to buy them. Such items include things like stationary items, candy, soft drinks, approved canned goods, and a variety of junk food. Razor blades and shaving cream and other toiletries are also available. No actual money is exchanged; the totals are recorded and subtracted from the inmate's account.

2. I am not personally advocating the habit; it is physically life-threatening. But my task is to describe a culture to you, and although I write from a strongly Christian point of view, my assignment is to describe that culture as accurately as I can. For those who smoke it is pleasurable; the culture has few pleasures.

3. It should be noted here that what we are discussing is generally illegal as far as the prison administration is concerned. They do not support the idea that inmates can be buying or selling one another *anything*, whether the items be legal or contraband.

4. Some security officers will teach their staff that the whole scenario I just described here could also be a carefully staged situation in order to set someone up. The staff member (or volunteer) now views their "rescuer" as a friend who can be depended upon and may lower his guard around him, thus being open to manipulation. While I admit this is possible, it was not the case here. I had known this man as a good friend for over fifteen years.

5. One of the primary rules an institution sets for volunteers is that you are not to bring anything unauthorized into the institution, and you are not to take anything out. And they mean *anything*. If you are tempted to ask, "But what about such-and-such an item?" The answer will be, "What part of 'bring nothing in' did you not understand?" Authorized items for Christian volunteers are usually only paperback Bibles and pre-approved Christian literature. Little else.

Chapter 24

1. I know there exists a mind-set, on the outside, that most inmates claim to be innocent, but that is simply not true. Less than 1 percent of the inmates I have spoken to over the years make such a claim for themselves. I have met a few who claim they are not guilty of what they are being *charged* with, but even most of these will philosophically add, "That's OK. I figure this makes up for all the times I didn't get caught."

2. Usually, if Christian volunteers take too long getting around to the subject of God, the *inmate* will bring it up because they know it's your function. That is what you are there for!

3. State hospital, forensic unit.

Chapter 25

1. From *Faith Is the Victory*, John Yates and Ira Sankey.

Chapter 27

1. Chewing gum can be used to jam locks. The types of ballpoint pens that are illegal in most prisons are the types that are encased in clear plastic. Such pens can be modified to serve as syringes. Some institutions view any type of pen as a potential weapon.

2. I visited a church in Maine some years ago where this very thing had happened.

3. Homemade alcoholic brew, usually made from fermenting fresh fruit and sugar.

4. A "runner" is an inmate on the tier who is allowed out of his cell during regular lockdown times for cleaning the tier or "running" approved items back and forth between inmates.

Chapter 28

1. A large multipurpose room where inmates can hang out for recreation or chitchat.

Chapter 29

1. See information on resource providers in pages 286–87.

Chapter 30

1. Most prisons and jails do not allow ex-prisoners to return for at least a year anyway.

Chapter 31

1. From "O Little Town of Bethlehem" by Phillips Brooks.

Glossary

administrator. In some correctional facilities, the title given to the top official. (More common in smaller institutions such as county jails or city lockups.)

AV group. Alternatives to violence program.

AWOL. Absent without leave.

been down. A term for serving time. Like being "out of circulation." As in, "I've been down for seventeen years."

bid. The sentence an inmate has received, usually tied to its length. Such as in, "I got a three-year bid."

bit. Same as "bid."

Bitch, the. Slang term for a sentence leveled under the Habitual Offender Act.

blue shirt. Correctional officer. (Or "white shirt," depending on the specific color of the officer's uniform.)

camp. Designation given to some federal institutions.

canteen. Generally refers to the prison store where snacks and toiletries may be purchased through the inmate's account. But the term is more commonly used in referring to the entire purchase. As in, "I got my canteen today."

CO. Correctional officer.

commuted. An original sentence that has been changed by the courts (usually upon appeal) to a less severe status. *Commutate* means the same thing.

con. Convict. Acceptable title among the inmates themselves.

concurrent. A sentence that is running at the same time as another sentence.

conjugal visit. The practice of allowing married inmates to spend an evening or a weekend with their spouses in specially designated quarters on the prison grounds.

contraband. Forbidden items.

crime jacket. (Or just "jacket.") The complete file of an inmate's criminal history.

D board. Disciplinary board. An in-house "court" where infractions within the prison are handled and possible punishments are meted out.

D report. A citation given for an infraction of the rules while in the prison. The officer writes a written report, and the case is assigned to the "D board" for a hearing.

dirty urine. Term given for the results of a drug test that comes back positive. As in, "He got caught with a dirty urine."

DOC. Department of Corrections.

DSO. Designation given in some states for a dangerous sexual offender.

DSS. Department of social services (youth being troubled by others).

DYS. Department of youth services (youth getting *into* trouble).

FBP. Federal Bureau of Prisons.

forensic unit. Designation given to the area that houses criminals with psychological problems.

getting a ticket. Being written up for an infraction of the rules; receiving a disciplinary report.

getting short. Coming near to one's release date. As in, "Joe's getting short."

good time. Time taken off a sentence for good behavior.

goon squad. Derogatory term for the in-prison SWAT team.

GP. General population.

halfway house. Usually a minimum security residence where inmates can be sent just before their full release. Although still under the jurisdiction of the DOC, the residents can work in the community and make a more normal transition into society.

Hole, the. A cell or tier used for extreme cases of bad behavior. Often the same as "punitive degregation" or "isolation."

house of correction. Designation given to a county facility or other short-term facility.

human services. The department responsible for social programs, education, and counseling.

jail. A correctional institution smaller than state or federal prison. People sentenced to a jail are more than likely serving less than two and one-half years.

kite. A letter.

lifer. A term given to inmates who have served (or received) long sentences.

lockdown. A security state of alert within the prison during which all inmates are locked in their cells. Applied during times of security unrest or for punitive measures.

lockup. A jail or small facility with only a few cells.

lugged. The act of being escorted to a more punitive area of the prison for an infraction of the rules. "Al got lugged to SHU today."

mando. Slang for a mandatory sentence.

mash. A homemade alcoholic brew, usually concocted through mixing fresh fruit and sugar.

max out. To serve the entire, maximum time of a prison sentence.

maximum. The highest designation of three security levels for prisons. Can also refer to a section within a prison that is reserved for highest security.

medium. The middle range of security designation assigned to correctional facilities.

minimum. The lowest level of security designation. Such facilities usually do not have walls around them, and inmates are often permitted to be outside.

movement. Those times of the day when the prison schedule allows for inmates to travel from one area to another.

on and after. The term used to describe a second sentence which does not begin to be served until another sentence has been completed.

PC. Protective custody.

penitentiary. Older name for state prisons. Still used to describe some federal prisons.

pop or population. The area where the majority of the inmates live. General population.

predator. The designation used by some prisons to assist in the classification of certain inmates. These people are classified as a threat to others.

prey. Another classification for certain inmates. These individuals are particularly endangered by those classified as predators.

prison. The general term for a state or federal correctional facility.

programs. An alternative name given to the human services department.

punitive. A segregation tier for disciplinary cases. Also referred to as "seg" or "punitive seg." In many prisons, also refers to "the Hole."

PV. A parole violation.

R and R hearing. Revise and revoke. A hearing whereby the original sentence may be altered in the inmate's favor.

rat. Or "snitch." Negative term for one who informs on another.

ratting. What a rat does.

rehab. A drug rehabilitation facility, clinic, or group. Can also refer to being in the process. As in, "She's in rehab."

rolled in on. The term used for the situation when the SWAT team enters an inmate's cell for the purpose of subduing or, in some cases, punishing the inmate.

runner. An inmate who is allowed out of his cell during regular lockdown times for cleaning the tier or "running" errands for the officers.

security. The department responsible for maintaining security at all levels within the prison. Can also be used in a personified way, as in, "Security's been watching me lately."

seg. Segregation unit. A place in the prison used for punitive discipline.

shakedown. Usually a surprise and thorough inspection of an inmate's cell or of the entire cell block. Inmates can also be searched or "shaken down" at any time.

shank. Homemade knife.

shock program. Or shock incarceration. Usually reserved as an alternative, shorter sentence for first-time convictions of youthful offenders.

SHU. Special housing unit.

single-celled. One inmate to a cell.

skinner. Derogatory name given to a sexual offender whose crime involved molesting young children.

stand-up con. An inmate who is esteemed by his fellow prisoners. One who has proven his mettle.

strong-arm. The practice of a stronger inmate using the threat of physical harm to force a weaker inmate to provide favors. Usually used as a verb, as in, "He strong-armed him into giving up his canteen."

strip search. A body search for contraband that requires the inmate or visitor to be undressed.

super-max. The area of highest security in the prison.

superintendent. Title given to the highest official of the prison. Same as "warden."

suspended. A legal form of sentence that puts the actual serving time "on hold" pending good behavior.

take a PC. Phrase used to describe an inmate's choice to seek the sanctuary of protective custody.

wake-up. The actual day of release. As in, "Joe's got three days and a wake-up left."

warden. The traditional title for the highest official of a prison.

write-up. The written citation filed against an inmate for an infraction of the rules. "You're going to get a write-up if you don't get back in your cell right now." Or, "Keep mouthing off, and I'll write you up."

yard, the. The courtyard or large common area inside the prison.

Prison Ministries and Resources

Bridges of Canada (formerly Cons for Christ)
Box 3414 – Station B
Fredericton, New Brunswick, Canada E3A-5H2
(506) 443–9960
Provides oversight to Canadian prison ministries.

Chaplain Ray Books
Acclaimed Books
P. O. Box 180399
Dallas, TX 75218–0399
(800) 527–1212

Christian Prison Ministries
P. O. Box 1587 (or 2100 Brengle Ave.)
Orlando, FL 32801
(407) 291–1500
CPM is a national prison ministry.

Christian Aftercare Ministries
50 Lowell St.
Manchester, NH 03101
(603) 669–5090
Aftercare ministry for New Hampshire.

Coalition of Prison Evangelists
2400 Ludelle St. #10
Fort Worth, TX 76105
(888) 256-2673
www.copeministries.org
International prison ministry networking hundreds of grass-roots ministries.

Institute for Prison Ministries
Wheaton College
Wheaton, IL 60187
(630) 752-5727
www.wheaton.edu/bgc/prisonministries

Kairos Prison Ministry
140 N. Orlando Ave. Suite 180
Winter Park FL 32789
(800) 298-2730

LifeWay Christian Resources
1 LifeWay Plaza
Nashville, TN 37234
(800) 458-2772
www.lifeway.com

New England Aftercare Ministries
P. O. Box 136
Framingham, MA 01746
(508) 872-6194
Residential aftercare ministry for the New England area.

Prison Fellowship
P. O. Box 17500
Washington, DC 20041-0500
(800) 645-5298
Chuck Colson, executive director—International prison ministry organization, www.pfm.org

Radio Bible Class
P. O. Box 2222
Grand Rapids, MI 49555–0001
(Materials, *Daily Bread*)
www.rbc.net

Straight Ahead Ministries
9 Charles St.
Westborough, MA 01581
(508) 616–9286
http://straightahead.org National ministry focusing on troubled
youth. Has materials and resources.

Vision New England
34 Franklin St. #B–5
Nashua, NH 03064–2699
(603) 881–7704
www.nepm.org